LESSONS FROM

ELIJAH AND ELISHA

BY ALAN TOMS

Copyright © Hayes Press 2016

All rights reserved. No part of this book may be reproduced, stored in a retrieval system, or transmitted in any form, without the written permission of Hayes Press.

Published by:

HAYES PRESS Publisher, Resources & Media,

The Barn, Flaxlands

Royal Wootton Bassett

Swindon, SN4 8DY

United Kingdom

www.hayespress.org

Unless otherwise indicated, all Scripture quotations are from the Revised Version, 1885 (Public Domain).

Scriptures marked NKJV are from the HOLY BIBLE, the New King James Version® (NKJV®). Copyright © 1982 Thomas Nelson, Inc. Used by permission.

All rights reserved. Scriptures marked NIV are from New International Version®, NIV® Copyright © 1973, 1978, 1984, 2011 by Biblica, Inc.™ Used by permission. All rights reserved worldwide.

Scriptures marked NASB are from the New American Standard Bible®, Copyright © 1960, 1962, 1963, 1968, 1971, 1972, 1973, 1975, 1977, 1995 by The Lockman Foundation. Used by permission. (www.Lockman.org)

CHAPTER ONE: AN INTRODUCTION TO ELIJAH

The story of Elijah's public ministry begins in 1 Kings 17, but the Holy Spirit complements the Old Testament through the pen of James - showing that his spiritual experience had a private beginning long before. "He prayed". Men of God must learn to pray privately before they may stand before kings. The man of God whom we see standing before king Ahab had first of all stood before the Lord, the God of Israel (1 Kings 17:1). There he had learnt God's Word and had prayed according to the will of God. Elijah had prayed according to the Word of God, knowing the scripture, "Thou ... shalt not turn aside ... to go after other gods to serve them ... The Lord shall send upon thee cursing, discomfiture and rebuke ... because of the evil of thy doings, whereby thou hast forsaken Me ... And thy heaven that is over thy head shall be brass, and the earth that is under thee shall be iron. The LORD shall make the rain of thy land powder and dust" (Deuteronomy 28:14-24). Thus his prayer was answered with a great famine, as the Lord Jesus Himself described it in Luke 4:25.

We know very little concerning the background of Elijah. Rather, we are caused to consider "the Spirit and power" (Luke 1:17) which were manifested in his life. He came from Gilead, possibly from a place called Thesbon (Septuagint), a Tishbite. His tribe presumably would have been Reuben or the eastern half of Manasseh or (I suggest) Gad. Elijah comes to mind when we read Genesis 49:19 and Deuteronomy 33:20-21. His name means "Jah is God" and would seem to indicate that God-fearing parents had named him. It was with the truth embodied in his own name that he challenged the people on Mount Carmel: "If the LORD be God, follow Him" (1 Kings 18:21).

He was a hairy man and wore a leather girdle (2 Kings 1:8) and a mantle (1 Kings 19:19). He was undoubtedly a physically fit man who could put his face between his knees in prayer (1 Kings 18:42), could run ahead while Ahab rode a distance of some 15 to 20 miles (v.46) after the slaying that day of 850 false prophets (v.40); and on the last day of his earthly life walked perhaps in excess of forty miles from Gilgal to Bethel to Jericho to the Jordan, and beyond perhaps toward the mountains of Moab.

Elijah was raised up by God with a ministry towards the ten northern tribes of Israel. King Ahab was on the throne, a wicked man with perhaps an even more wicked wife, Jezebel. "There was none like unto Ahab, which did set himself to do that which was evil in the sight of the LORD, whom Jezebel his wife stirred up. And he did very abominably in following idols" (1 Kings 21:25-26). This woman of Zidon had brought the worship of Baal into common practice and turned the hearts of the people to her idols. Perhaps Elijah would keep the injunction that "three times in the year all thy males shall appear before the LORD God" (Exodus 23:17), but we have no record of any of his dealings with Judah or Jerusalem except for one notable exception.

In character Elijah was fearless, although at times he knew what it was to be afraid. During the severe drought he had gone from the brook Cherith which is 'before' (east of?) Jordan through to Zarephath "which belongeth to Zidon". Truly a man of God under divine protection, he passed through the breadth of hostile and unbelieving Israel to the very region of Jezebel's origin. He reverenced God, covering his face in his mantle (19:13) and bowing himself down upon the earth (18:42). He was very jealous for the Lord (19:10,14) and consequently knew the loneliness, isolation, discomfort and suffering of the godly. Himself a man of decision, he called for decisive action by others, saying "How long halt ye between two opinions?" (18:21). He poured contempt upon the vain hope of the people who had forsaken the knowledge of the true God (18:27). And yet the man who had stood before the king, before the people, before 850 false prophets carrying knives and lances while he taunted them, "went for his life" before the threat of a woman (19:2-3), and gave up hope, longing to die (v.4). Possibly later also he feared when the captains and their companies of fifty men were sent to take him (2 Kings 1:15), and he brought the fire of God down upon them.

Of interest is how this man of God appeared to others. To the widow of Zarephath and to the third captain, Elijah was "thou man of God". To Obadiah who feared the Lord greatly, but apparently secretly, Elijah was "thou, my lord Elijah". To wicked Ahab, he was "thou troubler of Israel" and "O mine enemy". Well might any Christian long for a like spiritual stature through the Word of God and through prayer that it should provoke such responses from such diverse persons.

The recorded instances of Elijah's praying are to be found in James 5:17: "that it might not rain"; 1 Kings 17:20-21: "let this child's soul come into him again"; 1 Kings 18:36: "that Thou art God in Israel"; 1 Kings 18:42 with James 5:18: "he bowed himself down, and he prayed again"; 1 Kings 19:4: "that he might die"; 1 Kings 19:10,14 with Romans 11:2: "he pleaded with God against Israel". And there on a sad note the record of his prayer life is ended.

There are many lessons to be learnt by sinner and saint from the stories concerning Elijah, but from the man himself there is a vital lesson to be learnt in 1 Kings 18 and 19. Elijah's great desire, expressed in prayer (18:37), was to turn the people's hearts back again. And to this end he worked by fire (v.38) and by sword (v.40). But the messenger with Jezebel's threat showed that the longed-for national conversion had not occurred and he fled to Beersheba far south of Jerusalem, putting as much distance as possible between him and Jezebel, and cried concerning his mission that "I am not better than my fathers".

We cannot doubt his deep agony of disappointment and in consequence of it he pleaded against Israel. God fed him and then sent him to Horeb, where Moses had met God at the burning bush (Exodus 3:1) and where God had spoken to His people "out of the midst of the fire" (Deuteronomy 4:10,15). But now God will not speak in fire. First, He sent a great and strong wind which split the mountain and broke the rocks in pieces, and then an earthquake, and then a fire, but the Lord was not in these. He was in "a sound of gentle stillness" (19:12 RV margin). This is a lesson not easily learnt. Even the Lord's disciples asked, "Lord, wilt Thou that we bid fire to come down from heaven and consume them?" - possibly having in mind the action of Elijah in regard to the companies of fifty (2 Kings 1) but the Lord turned and rebuked them (Luke 9:54-55 RV margin).

And so it was that from that time on the Word of the Lord did not come singularly by Elijah; others were used, not by fire nor by sword but by the faithful speaking of God's Word. "Is not My word like as fire? saith the LORD; and like a hammer that breaketh the rock in pieces?" (Jeremiah 23:29). God said to Elijah, "The journey is too great for thee" and gave him Elisha for a companion and minister, while others would also speak for God. Among these were an unnamed prophet (1 Kings 20:13), and another (20:35) and Micaiah (22:8). And by the time that Elijah was to be taken up by a whirlwind there were companies of prophets in Bethel and in Jericho and in Gilgal (2 Kings 2:3,5; 4:38) and probably even in the city of Samaria itself where Micaiah lived.

Elijah was used by God to confront Ahab in the matter of Naboth (1 Kings 21) and to rebuke Ahaziah (2 Kings 1), but over long periods (for example, three years according to 1 Kings 22:1, and then two years according to 1 Kings 22:51) there is no word of Elijah's public ministry. However, it could be that Elijah engaged in the teaching and preparation of these "sons of the prophets". Dear Elijah! God has not forgotten his heart's desire to turn the people's heart back again and Elijah will perhaps in a coming day labour in Jerusalem itself in preparation for the coming of the Son of Man to "turn the heart of the fathers to the children, and the heart of the children to their fathers" (Malachi 4:6).

I am disposed to think that Elijah will be one of the two witnesses mentioned in Revelation 11:3-13. Their testimony will be for three and a half years during which they will "shut up the heaven that it rain not; and in the hour of their ascension in the cloud there will be a great earthquake, causing the deaths of seven thousand". But in 1 Kings 19 God would not plead by an earthquake with His erring people.

In 2 Chronicles 21:12-15, Elijah bears his last prophetic word and it would seem that this was done by a letter prepared before the prophet's departure. Jehoram was a king of Judah, not of Israel, but he had the daughter of Ahab to wife, and the word of Elijah seems thus to have pursued the house of Ahab, to which he refers in his letter. The written word ought to have had a strong impact upon the king's mind.

Finally, we think of Elijah who had gone up by a chariot of fire and by horses of fire by a whirlwind into heaven (possibly from near Mount Nebo as we consider the places he visited on that day), coming again in glory with Moses to the mount of transfiguration, that holy mount (2 Peter 1:18) where they spoke of the more wonderful departure that Jesus was about to accomplish at Jerusalem (Luke 9:30-31).

There is very much more in the story of Elijah which will be enlarged upon in future chapters, but here are two points to note - firstly, the twice repeated question of the Lord to His servant - "What doest thou here, Elijah?" (1 Kings 19:9,13); a searching question at any time for a servant of God. And secondly, I love the faith of the godly prophet who could hear the sound of the abundance of rain when there was as yet no cloud, not even as small as a man's hand (1 Kings 18:41,44). Elijah, a man of like passions with us, could hear by faith when sight showed nothing, and so "he prayed again".

CHAPTER TWO: AT CHERITH'S BROOK (1 KINGS 17)

"Now I know that thou art a man of God, and that the word of the LORD in thy mouth is truth" (1 Kings 17:24). So said the widow woman to Elijah when he brought her dead son to life. He had lived with this woman and her son, so they had had plenty of opportunity to observe his way of life, and this was her conclusion: Elijah was a man of God. What makes a man a man of God? What was there about Elijah that made him answer to this title? When he went to speak to king Ahab he described himself as a man who stood before the Lord. The angel who spoke to Zacharias said, "I am Gabriel, that stand in the presence of God" (Luke 1:19), and Elijah did the same, waiting the divine command, ready to speak what God said and ready to go wherever God sent. That is what makes a man a man of God. Timothy was another young man who had the distinction of being called a man of God, and he was urged to flee from such things as the love of money and to follow after righteousness, godliness, faith, love, patience and meekness.

Away in the hills of Gilead, Elijah heard of the fearful sin of God's people the other side of Jordan and his spirit was burdened about it. God's name was being dishonoured and Elijah decided the time had come when something must be done about it. God had plainly said: "Take heed to yourselves, lest your heart be deceived, and ye turn aside, and serve other gods, and worship them; and the anger of the LORD be kindled against you, and He shut up the heaven, that there be no rain, and that the land yield not her fruit" (Deuteronomy 11:16,17). The days in which he lived answered exactly to that description and Elijah knew that

God must be true to His Word, that the rain must be withheld until His people turned to Him in repentance. So he began to pray. James tells us that. We would not know, apart from the word in James chapter 5, that Elijah prayed fervently that it might not rain, and it did not rain on the earth for three years and six months.

Having received the assurance that God had heard his prayer, he then went boldly to king Ahab with his message, "there shall not be dew nor rain these years, but according to my word". He knew only too well that Jezebel had put some of the prophets of the Lord to death but at this time he was fearless. "As the LORD, the God of Israel liveth" (v.1) was his word, and therein lay his strength. God was still alive despite the fact that all but seven thousand of Israel's people worshipped Baal, and He was still their God.

When he had delivered his solemn message at Ahab's court, Elijah went out, and then God had a message for him. He told him to hide himself by the brook Cherith. Away in that lonely place God was going to provide for him during the famine, and at the same time teach him many lessons that could only be learned in a place of seclusion. God has done the same thing with many of His servants. Joseph's years in the prison, Moses' time in the far side of the desert, Paul's three years in Arabia were all used as training periods. And there is no doubt Elijah's time by Cherith's brook was put to good use.

"I have commanded the ravens to feed thee there". Ravens, Lord? You can almost hear the query that must have risen in his mind. Would they not devour the food long before it reached him? But he did not argue with God. The record distinctly says, "he went and did according unto the word of the LORD". Simple words but what a lesson they contain. It was the obedience of faith. By Cherith's brook he learned that with God all things are possible. As long as he was there, never a morning or evening passed without the ravens delivering his supply of bread and meat. He was better fed than the prophets Obadiah hid in the cave. And he had quietness to learn the lessons God had to teach him. So, like the Thessalonians, his faith grew exceedingly. And so will ours, in the very same way, by taking the promises of God at their face value and acting upon them. As we do so, God will be glorified in our lives.

God loves to be taken at His Word. We honour Him when we take His promises and claim them by faith. "The LORD is good," said Nahum, "a stronghold in the day of trouble; and He knoweth them that put their trust in Him" (Nahum 1:7). And not only does God know and love such men and women of faith, but David speaks of those who put their trust in God before men. In other words, he is reminding us that the world is looking on, and people around us take note if we are trusting in the Lord. Our lives affect others, so let us encourage one another to trust in the Lord at all times and to claim the sure promises of His Word. "Trust ye in the LORD for ever: for in the LORD JEHOVAH is an everlasting rock" (Isaiah 26:4).

"Walk in love, even as Christ also loved you, and gave Himself up for us, an offering and a sacrifice to God for an odour of a sweet smell" (Ephesians 5:2).

CHAPTER THREE: IN THE WIDOW'S HOME (1 KINGS 17)

In loneliness by Cherith's brook, Elijah communed with God and no doubt he learned many a lesson which prepared him for the experiences which lay ahead. He was dwelling in the secret place of the Most High and learning the sweetness of abiding under the shadow of the Almighty. But Cherith's brook began to dry up. He watched the level of water getting lower and lower and he must have wondered what God was going to do. Every morning and evening when the ravens arrived with his ration of food he was reminded of God's unfailing care, so he would learn not to be anxious. And when the brook finally dried up, and not before, God spoke again. How important that we each learn that lesson - not to move until God speaks. Sometimes we are apt to get impatient and make our own plans in life, when if we waited God would show us His way.

All in good time God spoke again to Elijah. "Arise, get thee to Zarephath, which belongeth to Zidon, and dwell there: behold, I have commanded a widow woman there to sustain thee". God's instructions were clear and they left no room for argument. Zidon was the very place where Jezebel's father was king and it looked as though he would be putting his head in the lion's mouth! However, faith learns to trust when God leads the way and the scripture distinctly says "he arose and went to Zarephath". That is the obedience of faith, and it points to a most important lesson for us - to trust and obey when God speaks to us, even though we cannot see the way ahead.

Elijah set off on his long journey, some eighty to a hundred miles; when he reached the gate of the city, there was the widow gathering sticks for a fire to bake the very last cake for herself and her son - not a likely sort of person to care for God's prophet. But that was just the point. God was leading His servant to the most unlikely places and the most unlikely people to teach him that his trust must be in God and in Him alone. There was a measure of humbling in the experience, too. God could have provided for His servant in the home of some wealthy person had He chosen to do so, but He didn't. Elijah had to learn to be content in the home of a very poor widow, for "godliness with contentment is great gain."

Elijah was learning his lessons in God's school and so also was the widow. When she explained she had only a little meat left and a drop of oil and that she was baking the last cake for herself and her son, the word from God's prophet was "make me ... a little cake first". God first - that was the lesson. "Seek ye first His kingdom, and His righteousness; and all these things shall be added unto you" (Matthew 6:33). The things the Master referred to were the daily necessities of life. Never a command without an accompanying promise, both for ourselves and the widow, for Elijah added "thus saith the LORD, the God of Israel. The barrel of meal shall not waste, neither shall the cruse of oil fail, until the day that the LORD sendeth rain upon the earth".

And to the woman's credit it is recorded that "she went and did according to the saying of Elijah". They are simple words, but we cannot emphasize too strongly the important lesson they contain. God loves that sort of obedience that starts immediately to do what He says, without any protest or argument. The woman's faith was abundantly rewarded, for it says that "the barrel of meal wasted not, neither did the cruse of oil fail, according to the Word of the Lord, which He spake by Elijah". Of course they didn't. How could they, for God had spoken and His word can never fail.

But we notice God did not fill the barrel with flour, nor the cruse with oil. She did not receive a supply for the next week or two. No, it was a day by day supply. Each morning she found sufficient for another day. "Give us this day our daily bread", and in answer to that prayer God's supply never failed. Surely the woman and her son would never forget that lesson.

Nor Elijah, for in that humble home God taught him more about the life of faith. Zarephath means "place of refining" and it was a refining experience for him, such as the apostle Peter speaks of when he says that manifold trials are for "the proof of your faith, being more precious than gold that perisheth, though it is proved by fire" (1 Peter 1:7). Through life's experiences God leads us, sometimes allowing trials to come so that our faith may be strengthened, "for the proof of your faith worketh patience. And let patience have its perfect work, that ye may be perfect and entire, lacking in nothing" (James 1:3,4). So let us take courage, if sometimes the way seems hard. It may well be our heavenly Father is allowing it for our good and for His praise and glory and honour at the revelation of Jesus Christ.

CHAPTER FOUR: RAISING THE DEAD (1 KINGS 17)

It was in a widow's home that God provided for His prophet when the rain was withheld for three and a half years, but while he was staying there the widow's son fell sick and died. Elijah could not understand why God had allowed this great sadness in the life of the woman whom He had commanded to care for him. However, he took the dead body of the lad to his own room and laid it on his own bed, and he stretched himself upon it three times and prayed. "O LORD my God, I pray thee, let this child's soul come into him again". The Bible record says "the LORD hearkened unto the voice of Elijah; and the soul of the child came into him again, and he revived" (vv. 21,22).

This is the first instance in Scripture of resurrection from the dead, and Elijah was the instrument God used. It contains important lessons, for we live in a world where many around us are spiritually dead, described as dead through their trespasses and sins, and therefore completely insensitive to God and to His claims upon them. Elijah did not give the lad life. Only God can give life. But Elijah was used in the process, as we long to be used as men and women are brought to the experience of the new birth and to receive eternal life through faith in Christ.

What lessons can we learn from this incident that will help us in our deep desire to be used in this way? Two points stand out clearly. Firstly, Elijah was a man in contact with God, and secondly, he was willing to make contact with the dead boy, unpleasant though that must have been. In regard to the first point, Elijah was a righteous man and James says "the supplication of a righteous man availeth much in its working" (James 5:16). He prayed the prayer of faith. Hebrews 11:33,35 distinctly says that "through faith women received their dead by a resurrection".

We are reminded of the words of the Lord Jesus: "all things whatsoever ye pray and ask for, believe that ye have received them", and of course it's true, but how can we believe and pray this prayer of faith unless we are assured of the will of God? So we must link the Master's promise with the further word in 1 John 5:14 that "this is the boldness that we have toward Him, that, if we ask anything according to His will, he heareth us". Mustn't we ask therefore that the Lord the Spirit, our great prayer-helper, will guide us into the will of God, putting a burden of prayer into our hearts, and then we can present that prayer in the assurance that God will answer it to His glory?

Further, we notice that Elijah prayed persistently. Three times he stretched himself on the lad and prayed his earnest prayer. God could have given life the first time, but he chose to do so on the third occasion so that Elijah might prove his earnestness. Men ought always to pray and not to faint the Master said, and he went on to teach us about the importunity of prayer (see Luke 18:1-8). From Elijah we learn these lessons, that prayer is to be simple, specific, earnest and in faith. And then we read, "the LORD hearkened unto the voice of Elijah". Wonderful words! God in heaven answering a man's prayer. How we long that that might be true of us.

However, it was not by prayer alone that new life was brought to the lad. Elijah had to make contact with him, and that is our second point, and he did so in his own room and on his own bed. It touched Elijah personally. It cost him something. He had to put aside any feelings of revulsion he may have had. Paul said that "I am become all things to all men, that I may by all means save some" (1 Corinthians 9:22) and that will cost something.

We remember the Lord Jesus said "Come ye after Me, and I will make you to become fishers of men". What is involved in coming after Him? "If any man would come after Me, let him deny himself, and take up his cross daily, and follow Me" (Luke 9:23). Saying "No" to ourselves is perhaps one of the hardest things we have to learn. How shall we learn it? A careful study of the master Soul-winner, working with individuals, as for instance, in the early chapters of John's gospel, will introduce us to some of the things involved.

He was not upset about being disturbed at night by the Jewish ruler. He was glad to rise and talk with him, to meet the need of his burdened heart. He was prepared, too, for the long and weary walk to Sychar in the heat of the day, for that was the only time He could meet the Samaritan woman at the well. And the pool at Bethesda did not repulse Him, for He knew the man who had been there for thirty-eight years desperately needed His help.

How deeply He cared. He was making contact with souls who needed Him urgently and He Himself was the great Life-giver.

From heaven He had come, vacating its throne for a little while so that sinners dead through their sins might be brought to new life through Him. It cost Him everything. He was on His way to Calvary where He was "cut off, having nothing". "The Son of God ... loved me, and gave Himself up for me". And one way we shall show our love to Him is by reaching out to those whom He died to save. May God help us to maintain that vital contact with Him through faith and prayer and to make contact with as many as possible whom we can introduce to our Saviour and Lord. It will cost us something, but through eternal ages we shall be glad we did.

CHAPTER FIVE: AT CARMEL (1 KINGS 18)

"How long halt ye between two opinions?" was the question with which Elijah challenged the people of Israel when he gathered them on Mount Carmel. They were all there, the king and his people, 450 prophets of Baal and 400 prophets of Asherah, all gathered at the word of Elijah. The angel Gabriel spoke to Zacharias about the spirit and power of Elijah, and it was remarkably demonstrated at Carmel, for they obeyed his word without dispute.

Maybe the people expected he would give them rain, but before the rain could come sin had to be judged. For years they had yielded lip service to God, but in their hearts they were idol worshippers and the long years of drought had not changed them. So the call rang out "How long halt ye between two opinions?" The word "halt" could be translated "to totter", like a drunken man whose feet go first one way and then another. That is how His people had been behaving, like the double-minded man whom James speaks about, unstable in all his ways. But God cannot be satisfied with that. He is a jealous God and He claims, and deserves, the undivided loyalty of our hearts. The people had no answer to Elijah's challenge, so he proposed they build two altars and offer two bullocks, and let them call on their gods, and he would call on the living God, and the God who answered by fire, let him be God.

Elijah knew his God. He knew what Hebrews 12 tells us that our God is a consuming fire. He appeared to Moses in a flame of fire when the bush burned and was not consumed. When He met Israel at Sinai He descended to the mountain in fire and when He led them through the wilderness it was by a pillar of fire by night. Elijah was confident that in response to his prayer, God would answer by fire. The prophets of Baal went first for they were many, and although they called on the name of Baal from morning to noon there was no answer. Elijah mocked them, but it made no difference when they slashed themselves with knives until the blood flowed. Of course not! For the gods they served had ears which could not hear.

Then it was Elijah's turn. The people watched intently as he took twelve stones, one for each tribe, and with them he built an altar in the Name of the Lord. Around it he dug a trench which was filled with water and the bullock cut in pieces on the altar was drenched with water also. It was the time of evening sacrifice as Elijah stepped forward to pray, the time when the burnt offering was being consumed on the altar at God's house in Jerusalem.

And Elijah began to pray, "O LORD, the God of Abraham, of Isaac, and of Israel" -reminding them of God's promises to their forefathers and to them as a nation. God was a covenant-keeping God. He never failed to keep His promises and on that ground Elijah now called upon Him. His Name had been greatly dishonoured in Israel, a fact which he deeply lamented, and he now called on God to clear His Name of all dishonour. "Let it be known this day that Thou art God in Israel, and that I am Thy servant, and that I have done all these things at Thy word". That was the great burden of his heart, that God's Name would be glorified. "Father, glorify Thy Name" the Lord Jesus prayed, and that must ever be the burden of our hearts as we pray forward the work of God. "Not for us, O Lord, not unto us, but unto Thy Name give glory".

And there was a second burden on Elijah's heart as he made his impassioned plea to God. "Hear me, O LORD, hear me, that this people may know that Thou, LORD, art God, and that Thou hast turned their heart back again". It was all so completely in tune with God's deepest desires, and God in heaven answered by fire. The fire of the Lord fell and burned up the sacrifice, the wood, the stones and the dust, and even licked up the water in the trench. And when all the people saw it, they fell on their faces and cried, "The LORD, He is God: the LORD, He is God".

Sin was judged that day, the false prophets were slain in the Kishon valley, and then they were ready to receive the rain. "Get thee up, eat and drink," said Elijah to the king, "for there is the sound of abundance of rain". Ahab could not hear it, but Elijah could, for he was in touch with God. He knew so well that God was going to be true to His promise and that the rain was already on its way. The apostle Peter spoke about seasons of refreshing from the presence of the Lord. How our hearts long for them. Then let us learn the lesson of Carmel's mount and be quick to judge sin in our lives. The next step will be to claim the promise of Malachi chapter 3 and bring the whole tithe into God's storehouse, to give Him the first place in our lives that belongs to Him, and then He will fulfil His Word and open the windows of heaven and pour us out a blessing such as we have not room enough to contain it.

CHAPTER SIX: PRAYING FOR RAIN (1 KINGS 18)

On Mount Carmel Elijah stood boldly before the people as he urged God's claims upon them. But later when he climbed to the top of the mountain he was no longer pleading with men, but with God, and he bowed himself to the ground with his face between his knees. That praying man has much to teach us about the important subject of prayer, and the first lesson is the basic one that we have to ask to receive. James comments on this experience in Elijah's life, and reveals that it was because of Elijah's prayer that God withheld the rain in the first place. And then he adds, "he prayed again, and the heaven gave rain, and the earth brought forth her fruit" (James 5:18).

But God had already promised the rain. That was the message he sent to Ahab: "I will send rain upon the earth". Why then did Elijah need to pray for it? The answer is that it is a principle with God that He gives in answer to our prayers. "Ask, and it shall be given you" the Lord Jesus taught, "for everyone that asketh receiveth" (Matthew 7:7,8). Conversely James says: "ye have not, because ye ask not" (James 4:2). That's a heart-searching word and we might well ask ourselves if it is true in our lives. Is God's blessing being withheld simply because we have not learned the importance of asking in prayer? The precious and exceeding great promises of God which fill our Bibles are to be claimed by faith and prayer. God is honoured when we reverently remind Him of them and claim them through the prayer of faith. Then we notice that Elijah sought the solitude of the mountain top to be alone with God, reminding us the Lord Jesus said that "when thou prayest, enter into thine inner chamber, and having shut thy door, pray to thy Father which is in secret, and thy Father which seeth in secret shall recompense thee" (Matthew 6:6). How important that we make time in our busy days for the secret place if we are going to be strong to serve the Lord.

Thirdly, Elijah prayed specifically. He asked that it might not rain and then just as definitely, three and a half years later, he asked God to send the rain. There is no doubt that God wants us to come to Him with our specific requests, and sometimes He lays burdens upon our hearts so that we shall come to Him, pouring out our hearts for those very things. Then we find that Elijah prayed fervently. He 'prayed with prayer', the margin of the Revised Version says. He was deeply in earnest about it. There are degrees of earnestness, for it says about our Lord Jesus in Gethsemane's garden that being in an agony He prayed more earnestly. Prayer was made earnestly by the Church in Jerusalem when Peter was in prison: the word means "to stretch out" like a piece of elastic. It's wonderful when we are so burdened about what we are asking for that our hearts reach out to God in deep earnestness.

Point number five is that Elijah prayed in faith. That is clear because each time he prayed he sent his servant to look for the coming clouds. "Watch and pray" the Lord Jesus said (Matthew 26:41), and when the apostle Paul urged the Ephesians to be praying at all seasons in the Spirit, he added, "and watching thereunto in all perseverance" (6:18). The Lord Jesus gave us a remarkable promise when He said "all things, whatsoever ye shall ask in prayer, believing, ye shall receive" (Matthew 21:22). How can we pray that sort of believing prayer? Surely it requires that the Holy Spirit guide us into the mind of God on that particular matter. Elijah knew that it was God's will to send the rain, so he prayed in faith, looking confidently for the answer.

Linked with that is the sixth point of Elijah's persistence in prayer. He did not give up until the answer was received. Six times he prayed and each time the servant reported there was nothing. But he kept on praying. We "ought always to pray, and not to faint" the Master said. The seventh time, the servant came back to say there was a cloud the size of a man's hand. Surely it teaches us that if we have a burden upon our hearts we should keep on praying until God gives an answer.

Point number seven is that Elijah prayed as guided by the Holy Spirit. One version of the verse in James 5 says "the inworking supplication of a righteous man availeth much", and the One who works in us for our guidance and help in prayer is the Holy Spirit. "In like manner the Spirit also helpeth our infirmity: for we know not how to pray as we ought: but the Spirit Himself maketh intercession for us with groanings which cannot be uttered" (Romans 8:26). What a wonderful contemplation: the Holy Spirit so burdened within us that He groans as He directs us into prayer according to the will of God. Praying at all seasons in the Spirit is an aspect of prayer we maybe need to learn more about.

Finally, "the supplication of a righteous man availeth much" (James 5:16). Elijah's strong praying was backed up by a righteous life. He was a man in touch with God. "If I regard iniquity in my heart, the Lord will not hear" (Psalm 66:18). "Beloved, if our heart condemn us not, we have boldness toward God" (1 John 3:21), and that is the boldness we need so much.

CHAPTER SEVEN: DISCOURAGED (1 KINGS 19)

"Elijah was a man of like passions with us" (James 5:17). "A man just like us" is the NIV translation and this chapter shows us how true that was. The one who was so strong and fearless is now seen in the depths of despair and running for his life. And the reason? Because Jezebel the queen had threatened to kill him. He was a very tired man, of course, and he had been under great stress, and then he heard the queen was after him. Faith gave way to fear and he ran as fast as he could go! If only he had stopped a moment to consider what Jezebel had said. "So let the gods do to me, and more also, if I make not thy life as the life of one of them ..." She was referring to her heathen gods and they had proved themselves very ineffective. They could not produce rain during the drought, or call down fire from heaven, even though their priests leapt about and called on them from morning to evening. They were indeed "things of nought" as God described them.

If Jezebel was trusting in those then her threat did not amount to very much! But Elijah was in no state to reason the matter out; he put as great a distance between the queen and himself as he could and sat down under a juniper tree, a very discouraged man, so much so that he requested for himself that he might die. Dear Elijah, if only he had known what God had in store for him! He was not going to die; at least not for thousands of years. Some consider that during the tribulation period he will die, for he will be one of God's two witnesses at the time of the antichrist, and they are going to be killed and their dead bodies will lie on the streets of Jerusalem for three and a half days (Revelation 11:3-12).

But, as far as his present service was concerned, he was going to have an abundant entrance into the eternal kingdom. A whirlwind was going to sweep him to glory. Little did Elijah know about that as he sat under his juniper tree.

"Why art thou cast down, O my soul? And why art thou disquieted within me?" (Psalm 42:5). The sons of Korah had obviously felt the same way, as many of us do at times. Periods of discouragement can lead to deep depression, and we need to remind ourselves that Korah's sons went on to say, "Hope thou in God: for I shall yet praise Him, who is the health of my countenance, and my God". And how shall we hope in Him? Jeremiah supplies the answer when he says, "His compassions fail not. They are new every morning; great is Thy faithfulness. The LORD is my portion, saith my soul; therefore will I hope in Him" (Lamentations 3:22-24). When faith lays hold of the promises of God we once again begin to praise Him, and the Lord brings us safely through as He did His servant Elijah.

We notice how gently God dealt with him. He sent His angel to prepare a meal for His weary prophet, and when it was ready, baked over hot coals, he touched him and said, "Arise and eat". Then he slept again, for "He giveth to His beloved in sleep" (Psalm 127:2 RV margin). And the angel touched him a second time and there was another meal ready. There was no rebuke (not at this time, at any rate), but just what God knew he needed so much, sound sleep and nourishing food. It reminds us so much of that morning by the sea of Galilee when seven of the apostles came back from their fishing trip and the Lord Jesus had prepared a cooked breakfast for them on the beach. And as He invited those tired men to eat, He served them. What wondrous grace: the Son of God Himself, raised and glorified and visiting them from heaven, and providing for them despite their waywardness. That was a demonstration of the love that "beareth all things, believeth all things, hopeth all things, endureth all things". "Agape" love never fails. It didn't in this case, and it never will.

For our strong encouragement we remind ourselves that "Jesus Christ is the same yesterday and today, yea and for ever" (Hebrews 13:8). The same gentle, tender Master sits today on heaven's throne and He cares for us as deeply as He did for those fishermen. The writer to the Hebrews highlights His present work upon the throne when he says: "we have not a high priest that cannot be touched with the feeling of our infirmities; but one that hath been in all points tempted like as we are, yet without sin" (Hebrews 4:15).

How thankful we are that He is there at His Father's side, understanding us so completely in all our frailty, and because "He Himself hath suffered being tempted, He is able to succour them that are tempted" (Hebrews 2:18). "Able to succour" and "able to save". Putting those two great promises together faith has strong encouragement to draw near to God through Him. For the promise is that "He is able to save to the uttermost them that draw near unto God through Him, seeing He ever liveth to make intercession for them" (Hebrews 7:25). There is no experience in life in which He cannot help; no depths to which we sink from which He cannot deliver us, if we come to God through Him. So when Satan tempts us to despair let us send up our urgent prayer to the throne of grace, and at the right time we shall receive the help we so much need. We shall, for Elijah did, and Elijah's God is ours.

CHAPTER EIGHT: IN THE CAVE AT HOREB (1 KINGS 19)

When Elijah was sitting under the juniper tree, God sent His angel to serve him with the nourishing food he so much needed, and he "went in the strength of that meat forty days and forty nights unto Horeb the mount of God". When he got there he dwelt in a cave. What memories would come flooding into his mind, for it was at Horeb that Moses first met God in the burning bush, and on this very mountain when He gave His law He revealed Himself in fire to His people and the mountain burned and shook. It was here Moses asked God to show him His glory and God hid him in a cleft of a rock and covered him with His hand, and then He passed by and declared the Name of the Lord.

Some have wondered if it may have been the very spot where Moses had that great experience with God. Certainly the language used is similar, for it says "the LORD passed by". Doubtless it was an experience Elijah would never forget. First there came a mighty wind which tore at the mountains and broke the rocks in pieces and that was followed by an earthquake and then a fire, great demonstrations of the mighty power of God to remind His discouraged servant that the God who controlled the whirlwind and the earthquake could very well take care of the threats of a wicked queen. But more than that, for it says God was not in the wind, the earthquake and the fire. He sent them, it's true, and they contained a message for Elijah, but there was something more important, for after the fire there came a still, small voice, the sound of gentle stillness. When Elijah heard it he stood at the entrance of the cave and wrapped his face in his cloak. God was speaking to him. The same question was repeated.

"What doest thou here, Elijah?" Was God giving him an opportunity of confessing his failure and asking for forgiveness? It would have been well for Elijah if he had grasped it, but he didn't. He poured out the same complaint: "I have been very jealous for the LORD, the God of hosts; for the children of Israel have forsaken Thy covenant, thrown down Thine altars, and slain Thy prophets with the sword; and I, even I only, am left; and they seek my life, to take it away." He was feeling very sorry for himself and that may well have been at the root of his trouble, thinking too much about himself. When we get our eyes off the Lord there is always that danger. "Looking unto Jesus the Author and Perfecter of our faith" (Hebrews 12:2) is an exhortation we must never forget.

In Romans 11, the apostle Paul comments on this incident in Elijah's life; he quotes what he said to God, and the divine comment is "he pleaded with God against Israel". That word gives us an insight into the prophet's mistake. It is one thing to confess the sin of one's people; many men of God have done that, but always with a view to their forgiveness and restoration. But in his deep discouragement Elijah prayed against them and that was a serious mistake.

But let's get back to the cave and consider Elijah standing at its entrance as he quietened his heart and heard God speaking to him in that sound of gentle stillness. "I have stilled and quieted my soul; like a weaned child with his mother" David said, and we need to do that, too. Only as we quieten our hearts shall we hear His voice. If we are full of anxieties and distractions it will be hard to hear God speaking to us. And He wants to speak. "It is the voice of my beloved that knocketh" said the woman in the Song. "Behold, I stand at the door and knock; if any man hear My voice and open the door, I will come in to him, and will sup with him, and he with Me", says our Beloved. It is His call to our hearts for fellowship with Him. He wants to share with us the rich spiritual blessings He has for us.

But we shall need to quieten our hearts first to hear His voice and to obey what He says. "Mary hath chosen the good part" said the Lord Jesus as she sat at His feet, and we shall need to choose, too. God's word to Elijah was "Go, return". He had to go back the way he had come, for there were men to be anointed for service and one of them was young Elisha who was to be prophet in Elijah's place. It is very touching how he threw his cloak over the young man's shoulders. Elisha hearing the call rose up and followed. We notice God's final word to Elijah that day was that there were seven thousand in Israel who had not bowed the knee to Baal. So Elijah was wrong when he said that "I, even I only, am left". There were seven thousand whose hearts were true to God, although maybe some of them were too timid to make it known. And is it not most likely that Elijah, so bold for God through most of the years of his service, had been a great encouragement to those seven thousand? If only he had realized that he may not have been so discouraged. We also might well take note of that, for as we press on with God, obeying His Word and living to please Him, others will be encouraged by our example. We do not live to ourselves. We are "known and read of all men". Let us make sure that they will read in our lives something that will encourage them on the heavenward way.

CHAPTER NINE: ANOINTING ELISHA (1 KINGS 19)

Go, return on thy way" was God's word to Elijah when he met him at the entrance of the cave. Elijah had made a mistake. He had run away without any instruction from God and he had to retrace his steps and go back the way he had come, as we have to do sometimes when we make mistakes. One of his immediate tasks was to anoint young Elisha to be prophet in his place. God had another man ready, as He always has, and Elijah found him ploughing in the fields and himself guiding one of the yoke of oxen. This young man was not afraid of a day's hard work. God had been speaking to Elisha's heart. He was calling him to His service and now the old prophet arrived with confirmation of the call he had been feeling so strongly. He understood the significance of Elijah throwing his cloak over his shoulders, and when Elijah turned as though to walk away, the young man ran after him. "Let me, I pray thee, kiss my father and my mother, and then I will follow thee", he said. "Go back again", Elijah replied, "for what have I done to thee". But that was said to prove him surely, to give him the opportunity of counting the cost.

Elisha was equal to it. His mind was made up, his heart was set. Slaying his oxen and burning the ploughing equipment to make a fire to cook the meat, he gave it to the people with him and they ate together in a parting meal, and then he was on his way, following Elijah. He had made the break with family ties. There was nothing whatever to hold him back. It says "he arose and went after Elijah, and ministered unto him". It was humble work to start with, but Elisha was content. "Whosoever would become great among you, shall be your minister", the Lord Jesus said (Mark 10:43), and the younger man would count it an honour to wait upon God's prophet.

Elijah had been a unique man, one who had towered above his fellows. He had withstood onslaughts of evil as a rock shakes off the waves that beat upon it. He was one of the most dramatic figures in Israel's history. His name means "My God is Jah" and his service for God had been characterized by fearless judgement. But his service was nearly over and the younger man stepping into his place was called to a gentler ministry. Elisha's name means "My God is salvation" and in many ways his life reminds us of the Lord Jesus in His service. The mighty works Elisha did were mostly for healing and blessing, in contrast to Elijah who was so often called to acts of judgement on account of the people's sin.

The end of his life-work was now in sight, although God graciously gave him a few more years of service. One of his main tasks during his sunset years was the ongoing training of Elisha in the prophetic ministry and also the sons of the prophets to whom we are first introduced about this time. They appear to have been gathered in groups of fifties and there were groups at Bethel, Jericho and Jordan and maybe in other places too. We are left to imagine how they were brought together, but possibly it was the result of Elijah's far-seeing vision.

He would understand the need for men to lead God's people and teach them His ways, and so the sons of the prophets, as they were called, were trained for service. They may well have been among the seven thousand who had not bowed the knee to Baal. We are not told very much about them, although there are frequent references to them at the close of Elijah's life and throughout the ministry of Elisha. There is no doubt Elijah was used to help them; so much he would be able to pass on to them of the ways and will of God, out of his long experience.

It takes us in thought to Paul's word to Timothy, "the things which thou hast heard from me among many witnesses, the same commit thou to faithful men, who shall be able to teach others also" (2 Timothy 2:2). God's truth must be passed on as each new generation rises. It was not just a question of the things Timothy heard Paul saying when he was in his company. It was definite systematic instruction, the older man passing on to the younger a precious deposit of divine truth which he was to treasure and guard and in turn pass on to others. Four generations are envisaged in this one verse, faithful men passing on divine truth as younger men rose to responsibility. And we notice the careful instruction, "the things which thou hast heard from me ... the same commit thou to faithful men". That is important. God's truth must be preserved and passed on in all its purity, nothing added to it and certainly nothing taken away.

We are living in days when we need to be especially watchful about this, for Satan is doing his utmost to undermine the confidence of believers in the Word of God. We must stand boldly for the truth of the inerrancy of Scripture, that every word of our Bible in the original languages was the inspired Word of God. We believe that "every scripture is inspired of God, and profitable for teaching, for reproof, for correction, for instruction which is in righteousness; that the man of God may be complete, furnished completely unto every good work" (2 Timothy 3:16,17 RV margin). So let us treasure every part of it and grasp every opportunity of teaching it to others as diligently as we can.

CHAPTER TEN: NABOTH'S VINEYARD (1 KINGS 21)

Elijah may well have wondered whether because of his failure he had forfeited the right to be used by God. But it was not so. Whatever regrets may have filled his heart in regard to his despondency when he sat under the juniper tree and asked to die, God was taking up His servant once again. It says "the word of the LORD came to Elijah the Tishbite". It was just like the old days when the Word of God came to him and he had to speak it out faithfully and fearlessly. Once again he was being sent with a message to king Ahab. "Arise, go down to meet Ahab king of Israel, which dwelleth in Samaria: behold, he is in the vineyard of Naboth, whither he is gone down to take possession of it".

Ahab had not changed despite the remarkable demonstration of God's power on Mount Carmel and despite the fact that the prophets of Baal had been slain. He was still the same Ahab and his wicked queen was still scheming behind the scenes. in this case it had to do with Naboth's vineyard which adjoined the king's palace. Ahab wanted it badly and offered to do business with Nahoth. He was prepared to give him a better vineyard or the value of it in money. But Naboth would not agree. It was his God-given inheritance handed down from his fathers, and he would not let it go. God had said it was to be passed down the family line, so as far as Naboth was concerned it was God's word versus the king's, and he was such a man that neither the king's reward nor the king's wrath would persuade him to go against the word of the Lord. Fearlessly he stood his ground. He explained it was the inheritance of his fathers and he could not, and must not, give it up. All honour to him!

His courage and faithfulness stand on the page of Scripture as a great example to us, for we have an inheritance which God has given us and we are required to guard it with similar diligence. It is not the inheritance of which the apostle Peter writes which is incorruptible and undefiled and reserved in heaven for us. We cannot lose that inheritance. It belongs to all who have been born again. There is another inheritance of which the apostle Paul spoke to the elders of Ephesus, when he said, "I commend you to God, and to the Word of His grace, which is able to build you up, and to give you the inheritance among all them that are sanctified" (Acts 20:32). Obedience to the Word of God brought them into an inheritance in God's house which was something very precious, and was to be guarded by faith. It is referred to in Ephesians 5:25 "this ye know of a surety, that no fornicator, nor unclean person, nor covetous man, which is an idolator, hath any inheritance in the kingdom of Christ and God". That is the kingdom of God over which Christ has been placed in absolute authority, and obedience to His Word and resulting conformity in holy living is required if we would continue to hold our inheritance in it. We can see then the need for diligence on our part.

When Jude set out to write about our common salvation the Holy Spirit directed him to write instead about contending earnestly for the faith once for all delivered to the saints. The difference between the two subjects is important to notice. Our common salvation has to do with the inheritance which is reserved for us in heaven. There is no need to contend for that. But the faith which has been entrusted to us has to be contended for, because our Adversary is doing his utmost to undermine it. Certainly it is worth contending for, and as we do so we come into our inheritance of divine service within God's house and kingdom.

Guarding his inheritance cost Naboth his life, for Queen Jezebel conspired to have him slain and then Ahab walked into the vineyard to take possession of it; or so he thought. But God in heaven had other thoughts. And that is the point where Elijah comes into the story again. It is the old Elijah we are so familiar with. No trace of fear now, not even of queen Jezebel. "God gave us not a spirit of fearfulness; but of power and love and discipline", and in that spirit Elijah approached the king with his solemn message of God's judgement. Young Elisha, never far from his side, would take note of how fearlessly and faithfully God's servant delivered the message. It is required in stewards that a man be found faithful and Elisha was learning this sort of faithfulness from a man who had been true to it nearly all his life. May God help us also to similar faithfulness for it is something which God rates very highly indeed.

CHAPTER ELEVEN: GILGAL TO JORDAN (2 KINGS 2)

"And it came to pass, when the LORD would take up Elijah by a whirlwind into heaven, that Elijah went with Elisha from Gilgal". It is clear that Elijah knew his last day on earth had come, and the sons of the prophets knew it too, and so did Elisha. But it made no difference to their programme for the day. There were certain places God wanted them to visit, from Gilgal to Jordan, and the chapter is an instructive one for those who are followers of Christ. We see how closely Elisha kept by the side of Elijah and how blessed he was because of it.

At Gilgal their journey started and that was the starting place for the people of God when they first entered the land under Joshua's leadership. Gilgal means "rolling" and there the men were circumcised and the reproach of Egypt was rolled away. It speaks to us about cutting away from our lives all that appeals to the flesh, for the lust of the flesh and the lust of the eyes and the vainglory of life are not of the Father but of the world. The world has so much to offer that is attractive to the flesh, but the follower of the Lord Jesus must say "No" to the world.

> Nay world, I turn away;
>
> Though thou seem fair and good,
>
> That friendly, outstretched hand of thine,
>
> Is stained with Jesus' blood;
>
> If in thy least device I stoop to take apart,

All unaware thine influence

Steals God's presence from my heart.

Elisha could have stayed at Gilgal if he had so wished. But his mind was made up. He was determined to follow. "As the LORD liveth, and as my soul liveth, I will not leave thee", he said. So on they went to Bethel, which means "the house of God". However, God's house was not there any longer. It was now in Jerusalem, and at Bethel Jeroboam had introduced a spurious worship, setting up a golden calf and encouraging his people to worship there. It was all so contrary to God's desires and repeatedly He spoke about the sin with which Jeroboam made Israel to sin. We need to guard against any form of worship which is opposed to God's Word. His pattern for worship and service is set out so plainly in the New Testament scriptures and followers of Christ should adhere to it.

From Bethel they moved on to Jericho, the city of high walls, so challenging to faith. Hebrews 11 says "By faith the walls of Jericho fell down". Following Christ will bring us into situations where faith is strongly challenged. Once again Elisha had opportunity to opt out, but nothing was further from his thoughts. "I will not leave thee", he said and the scripture records "they two went on". Jordan was the final place to which God sent Elijah and Elisha went with him. Elijah took his cloak and with it struck the waters of Jordan and they parted to allow the two prophets to go over on dry ground. Then the older man said, "Ask what I shall do for thee, before I be taken from thee", and it drew from Elisha that remarkable request, "I pray thee, let a double portion of thy spirit be upon me". Obviously he was very conscious of the great responsibility resting upon him and he knew he could only go forward by the enabling of the divine Spirit who had been so much in evidence in Elijah's life. But Elijah said it was a hard thing that he had asked, for the fulness and power of the Holy Spirit is not something which God grants lightly. It calls for a holy life, devoted to God.

There are conditions to be fulfilled and for Elisha the condition was "if thou see me when I am taken from thee, it shall be so unto thee". And he did! He allowed nothing to come between himself and Elijah, nothing that would obscure his vision of him. What a lesson for those of us who follow the Lord Jesus. The scripture says "they two went on", "they two stood by Jordan", "they two went over" referring to Jordan, and then "as they still went on, and talked, that, behold, there appeared a chariot of fire, and horses of fire, which parted them both asunder; and Elijah went up by a whirlwind into heaven". So God's great servant was away home to glory, truly an abundant entrance into the eternal kingdom.

Elisha picked up Elijah's cloak which fell from him as he went. He knew it well. Had it not rested on his shoulders when God confirmed His call to him, when the old prophet anointed him with oil? Taking it up he stood by the Jordan river. "Where is the LORD, the God of Elijah?" he cried. Where is He indeed? He is with His young servant and He proved it by parting the waters of Jordan to allow him to pass over. And the sons of the prophets saw it happen and they said, "the spirit of Elijah doth rest on Elisha".

"Verily, verily, I say unto you, He that believeth on Me, the works that I do shall he do also; and greater works than these shall he do; because I go unto the Father" (John 14:12). So said our Lord Jesus and He went on to tell them about the coming of the Comforter, the Holy Spirit, through whom this wonderful promise would be made possible. We might well ask ourselves, all of us who serve the Lord in any way, Are the sons of the prophets, our young men and young women, waiting to see a demonstration of God's power in us?

CHAPTER TWELVE: ON THE MOUNT OF TRANSFIGURATION

The apostle Peter never forgot the experience he had, along with James and John, on the holy mount when the Lord Jesus was transfigured before them. "We were eyewitnesses of His majesty", he said, "for He received from God the Father honour and glory" (2 Peter 1:16,17). It was His inward glory, the glory of God, shining out from His human body. They had never seen Him like this before. His face shone like the sun and His garments became white as the light. God is light and He covers Himself with light like a garment, so when the Lord Jesus was revealed in power and glory He was enveloped by light that was brighter than the noon-day sun.

Moses and Elijah appeared, talking with the Lord Jesus, and they also were seen in glorious splendour: Moses the great law-giver and Elijah representing all the prophets. They spoke with Him about His departure which was soon to take place at Jerusalem. It was a subject they were both familiar with, for the law and the prophets had foretold that the Christ must suffer and die. As they spoke together the three disciples would be listening. What an experience for them. Peter said, "Lord, it is good for us to be here" and so it was. Any fresh revelation of their Master was good for them, as it is also for us. It will affect our lives as it did theirs.

Then a cloud came and overshadowed them and they were afraid as they entered into it. They need not have been, for they were about to have one of the greatest experiences of their lives. God's presence was in the cloud, as it had been in the past. When

He descended on mount Sinai and gave Moses the law for His people, the mountain was covered with a thick, dark cloud. But this was a bright cloud, for we are "not come unto a mount ... that burned with fire, and unto blackness, and darkness, and tempest" (Hebrews 12:18). No, that belonged to the old covenant and to the giving of the law. We are no longer under that law; we are under grace and the voice out of the cloud brought the supreme message for our day of grace. "This is My beloved Son, in whom I am well pleased; hear ye Him" (v.5). God had spoken the same commendation of His Son once before, at the river Jordan when the Lord Jesus was baptized by John, and now once again, the same important, timeless message, with these words added, "hear ye Him". And when they looked up, they saw no one but Jesus only. Yes, that is the message of this mountain. Whatever other lessons we may learn, and there are plenty, this one stands supreme. It is a timeless message never to be repealed. In Christ the shadows of the law are all fulfilled and now withdraw. Moses and Elijah have gone and Christ alone is seen, transcending all others.

"God, having of old time spoken unto the fathers in the prophets ... hath at the end of these days spoken unto us in His Son" (Hebrews 1:1). That is the message. They saw no one, but Jesus only. Christ alone is to fill our vision, to capture our hearts' affections, to command our obedience. To Him all authority has been given, in heaven and on earth, and the Father says, "This is My beloved Son ... hear ye Him". We cannot over-emphasize the importance of that word. If all authority has been given to Him, then there is no question that His word must be obeyed at all times.

We live in days when the Word of God is being challenged, and when some are casting doubt upon the authority of the word of Christ. We need to hear again the divine command from the holy mount, for our acceptable service to God depends upon our obedience to it. And is it not interesting, and comforting, that the first words which fell from the lips of the Lord Jesus after the Father's stirring command were, "Arise, and be not afraid"? They had been afraid, but now the experience of His glory has passed, and they see Him again as they have always known Him, the same gentle, caring Master, and He spoke peace to their hearts.

With their fears calmed they wended their way down the mountainside. How they would love to have stayed longer. Maybe that is why Peter proposed building three tabernacles. Did he think the Lord Jesus was going to introduce His glorious kingdom and take up His power and reign? Maybe, but that is not yet. The way to the throne was via the Cross, and down below human hearts were breaking and crying out for the help which He alone could give. So from the mountain they descended, but not alone. Moses and Elijah have gone, but the One whom they had glimpsed in His glory and power was with them still, in lowly form, still going about and "doing good, and healing all that were oppressed of the devil; for God was with Him" (Acts 10:38). As they listened to Him and gave Him the allegiance of their hearts, they had a part with Him in His ministry to those who were suffering because of sin. And so shall we. One day we are going to see Him in His glory, and not just a passing glimpse, but lasting for ever. Until that glorious day it is our privilege to serve the One whom the Father has delighted to honour.

CHAPTER THIRTEEN: AN INTRODUCTION TO ELISHA

Elisha was called to his prophetic ministry about 900 B.C. and succeeded Elijah at a time when Israel was steeped in idolatry. Truth and error existed in the same country and both were talked about in the same domestic circles. The prophet laboured in the northern kingdom of Israel which, seventy-five years before, had rebelled against the house of David under Jeroboam who was crowned king by the rebel faction in the nation (1 Kings 12). To discourage the people from going to Jerusalem to worship, he set up two golden calves, one in Bethel (south), and the other in Dan (north). These became the objects of national worship.

Evil in any dimension, whether spiritual or moral, often commences imperceptibly, and rationalizes in such terms as, "there is no harm". The playful kitten of permissiveness grows into a killer. Error is so skilful at imitating the truth. A watchful eye, and a mind taught by the Spirit of truth are very necessary. One evil made way for another in Israel, and the days of Elisha saw another system of idolatry entrenched in the nation, that of Baal-worship. An unequal yoke in the marriage of Ahab to Jezebel of Phoenicia had brought this idol into the country (1 Kings 16:29-33). King Ahab was a weak, despicable individual, unable to make a right decision: "There was none like Ahab who did sell himself to do that which was evil in the sight of the LORD, whom Jezebel his wife stirred up" (1 Kings 21:25). Baal was the male consort of Ashtoreth, the female goddess of fertility, and together they were worshipped with lewd rites and human sacrifices.

The prophets were familiar with the political and religious currents of their times. They knew and loved the law of God, and their manner of life, often involving obscurity, made them sensitive to the mind of God. Their lives were a rebuke to the godlessness around them, and their predictions of judgement were fulfilled with amazing accuracy. Their messages were black and white, and struck terror into the hearts of all who were named in their prophecies. The man of faith walks at ease with God, and in the quiet confidence that he is right because he is on God's side, and knows God is on his. Such a man was Elisha, upon whom the mantle of Elijah fell.

His Call

Elisha, whose name means "God is Salvation", was the man God had ready to succeed Elijah in prophetic ministry to Israel. According to Bible chronology, Elisha's ministry lasted about seventy years, compared to Elijah's twenty years, approximately. The sovereignty of God seems the only answer to this apparent imbalance. The emotional breakdown of Elijah after the Carmel victory, and his flight from Jezebel are given by some as the reasons for his removal from the prophetic office.

If God did this in every spiritual lapse of His people, not many of us would be in the service of God. His period of human weakness, an inexplicable let-down after victory such as we have all known at some time, did not take God by surprise. God did not say, "Because you have been a failure at the end of your life, you are being replaced". There is no word of censure or condemnation throughout the entire transition of prophetic office from Elijah to Elisha. There are never any emergency situations in the purposes of God; divine sovereignty always governs what He plans. Elijah's ministry of judgement and Elisha's ministry of blessing and healing typify the dual ministries of the promised Messiah and Prophet. One man is never a complete type of Christ.

It is evident from 2 Kings chapter 2 that there were schools of the prophets. Probably Elisha came from one of these, and was well-known to Elijah. Elisha's occupation of ploughing and sowing on the family homestead provided valuable days for preparation and meditation. He saw the value of the yoke as he turned each gleaming furrow. He knew the disciplines of sowing and harvest as part of the daily task. There is a restlessness in our generation which is affecting the disciplines so necessary to spiritual growth. Neglect of the out-of-sight roots that can only flourish through the ministry of the Spirit may be the reason that the ranks of anointed men are getting thin. Faith, prayer, reading, meditation and the pursuit of holiness are all marks of men who are taught of the Spirit. There are no short cuts or easy courses to divine anointing for the service of God. Only a renewed hunger for God and holy living can produce a revival ministry in our hearts and assemblies.

Elijah's crossing the field to meet Elisha, and casting his mantle over him was an unforgettable moment for the young prophet. His excitement to follow Elijah overlooked other higher priorities by his request that he might run and kiss his father and mother goodbye. What about the plough in the half-turned field? Should there not be some tangible evidence of renouncing the old life? Renunciation comes before consecration. Elisha understood Elijah's advice to "go back again", and on sober reflection took a yoke of his own oxen, and the ploughing instruments, tokens of his livelihood, and through fire and sacrifice provided food for the people.

These alphabet blocks of his first lesson taught him the truth of renunciation. As a priority he must be prepared, as we all must be, for a drastic shift from enjoying creature comforts to helping meet the need of others. Do not most of us have this problem in our Christian experience? The prophet's mantle was only a sign of his appointment. It was his total commitment as a bondslave of the

Lord that would mark him out as God's man for the times. True discipleship is not wearing a badge, but rather carrying a cross. To be a disciple in name is one thing, but to be a disciple indeed involves following hard after Christ.

> Who answers Christ's insistent call,
>
> Must give himself, his life, his all
>
> Without one backward look.
>
> Who sets his hand upon the plough,
>
> And glances back with anxious brow,
>
> His calling hath mistook;
>
> Christ claims him wholly for His own,
>
> He must be Christ's, and Christ's alone.

The call of God has no options, and leaves no room for human opinion. A bondslave turns everything over to the will of another, and has no secret compartments in his life. The Lord Jesus knew this in the will of His Father. Paul knew it as a bondslave of Jesus Christ, and so on down the long line of anointed witnesses for God.

Elisha's simple act of slaying and burning for the blessing of others is an eloquent lesson of the place of self-sacrifice in the service of God. Here he must learn the truth of death to self and the world. It is at the cross we all must learn the truth that kills, before we learn the truth that makes alive, in resurrection. This was Elisha's Calvary. Dead to self and alive to God, he arose and followed. To renounce all that is sinful in our lives, and put it to death, is a requirement, the neglect of which, in our theology and practical Christian lines, lies at the root of barrenness (Colossians 3:5).

His Commission

Before the mantle fell on Elisha, The Lord sent Elijah to Bethel, Jericho, and Jordan, no doubt scenes of his earlier prophetic labours. His request for the young prophet to wait until he returned was a test of what he had said at the plough, "I will follow thee". Three times he asked him to wait, and as many times the answer came back, "As the LORD liveth, and as thy soul liveth, I will not leave thee".

The first stop at Bethel would stir many memories of Jacob's night on the stony pillow, and the vision of the house of God. How unlike the house of God the place of that early revelation had become, for Jeroboam's golden calf was there. The idol was a visual lesson for Elisha that one of his tasks was to restore the people to the worship of the true God of Israel. Jericho would recall the conquest for God of that city by Joshua. The destruction of the city which represented the idols of the Canaanites was another sign that God wanted all those nations destroyed. The visit to Jordan reminded the two prophets of the crossing by the nation more than 500 years before, and what it meant in terms of the reproach of Egypt being tolled away and the new life in the land.

Standing on the hallowed ground of these experiences would give Elisha a deep sense of the reality of his ministry as he prepared to call the nation back to God. Finally, his request for a double portion of Elijah's spirit was granted by God, for he saw his spiritual father swept up by a whirlwind into heaven. The rich endowment of the Spirit of God was like Elisha's Pentecost, and during sixty years of his ministry God worked at least eleven signs of various kinds, so that none could deny that the source of his power was the God of Israel. The areas of power were, four times over water, once over oil, twice over death, once over food, twice over disease, and once over eyesight. These are found in 2 Kings 2 through to 2 Kings 13.

Miracles in any age were never given by God to be sensational, or to satisfy man's craving for signs and wonders. Elisha's miracles were acts of divine sovereignty by which God spoke to His wayward people, to bring them back to Himself. Over Elisha's ministry could be written the words of a later prophet, "Not by might, nor by power, but by My Spirit, saith the LORD of Hosts" (Zechariah 4:6). The fulness of the Holy Spirit is clearly taught in the New Testament for disciples of the Lord. It is not optional. It is a command of the Lord in Ephesians 5:18, and is not related to either miracles or tongues, but to praise, thanksgiving and submission to one another. The indwelling of the Spirit is historical and permanent, and His infilling is His complete control of those He indwells. It is not that we should seek more of the Holy Spirit, but that we should yield ourselves to Him. It is right that we should obey the Lord in seeking a sound Bible-based spiritual experience of the fulness of the Spirit in our lives for His glory.

Elisha's Message

The prophet's message to Israel was backed by one of the few brief periods in its long history when God intervened with miraculous signs. The fragmented worship of the nation no longer held any consistent pattern. Polytheism had completely broken down separation from the nations around. Except for a few godly amongst them the people were insensitive to the frightful apostasy into which they had plunged. "Thou shalt have no other gods before (literally, in front of, or above) Me" (Exodus 20:3) had long since lost its place in the hearts of an apostate nation. Children grew up to know nothing but idol worship.

Some of the choice words of Elisha that brought blessing to many are selected. To the widow of a prophet he said, "Go borrow thee vessels ... not a few", The sequel, her debt was paid. When he cast meal into the poisonous pot of stew, and assured, "Pour out ... there was no harm in the pot". The beloved story of Naaman the Syrian general, with its powerful gospel base, "Go and wash in Jordan seven times". To his fearful servant who, in the day of battle did not see the surrounding host of the Lord, "LORD, I pray Thee, open his eyes". In profile, Elisha was a man of no compromise with evil or wicked men, sought no honour for himself, dispensed much blessing, and had this rare testimony from king Jehoshaphat of Judah, "The word of the LORD is with him" (2 Kings 3:12).

CHAPTER FOURTEEN: HEALING THE WATER (2 KINGS 2)

Elijah's name means 'God is my salvation' or 'God my Saviour', which is significant as it indicates the sort of ministry to which he was called. His was a gentler ministry than Elijah's, one of correcting and healing, bringing salvation to those who would humble themselves to receive it.

His first miracle was performed in Jericho. He was on his way back after Elijah had been caught up by God in a whirlwind into heaven, and he was revisiting the places they had visited together on that last memorable journey. Jericho, the city of palm trees, was excellently situated but the land was barren and unproductive. Blossom would appear on their fruit trees, but the fruit fell before it ripened and the men of the city brought their problem to Elisha. "Bring me a new bowl and put salt in it", he said, and he threw the salt into spring water, crying as he did so, "Thus says the LORD: I have healed this water; from it there shall be no more death or barrenness" (2 Kings 2:20,21). So it was God who brought the healing, not Elisha. He was but God's servant, with no resources of his own except a living faith in the God whom he served and a great willingness to be used by Him. And God did use him, repeatedly and remarkably, as we shall see.

This first miracle on Jericho's unproductive land is a reminder of the state of the whole nation, for in their departure from God they were forfeiting the blessing God longed to give them. Their problem was in relation to the water and in the Scriptures water is often illustrative of the word of God. The apostle Paul writes of "the washing of water by the word" (Ephesians 5:26). The people had rejected the living word of God and filled their hearts instead with the word of false prophets. That was where their trouble lay. Elisha called for salt in a new bowl and salt is a preservative. We recall Paul's word to the Colossians: "Let your speech always be with grace, seasoned with salt" (Colossians 4:6). Salt was always included in the meal offerings which came to God's altar and tell us about Christ's perfect life.

The salt reminds us of the words of grace and truth which poured from His lips. The people hung on His words when He spoke gracious words, but some turned away when the strong, correcting words of truth reproved their sin. That did not stop the Lord Jesus speaking to them, of course, for He knew so well that the blessing He had come to bring could only be received by hearts that were broken in repentance. We also need the searching, correcting word of God to go deep into our hearts, do we not? Could it be that the cause of so little fruitfulness in some of our lives is because we are not submitting to the cleansing, healing word of the Lord? God wants to heal and to bless and to make us fruitful for Him. About that there is no doubt. It is the lesson from Elisha's first miracle.

CHAPTER FIFTEEN: JUDGEMENT AT BETHEL (2 KINGS 2)

At the close of 2 Kings chapter 2, we read about two bears coming out of the woods and mauling to death forty-two youths. It happened as Elisha entered the city of Bethel. The youths mocked him and he pronounced a curse upon them in the name of the Lord. At first sight it seems out of character with Elisha's gentle ministry of healing and blessing, but when we examine the circumstances we understand the reason for it. Bethel means 'house of God'. It was where God met Jacob as he fled from his brother Esau, and He revealed Himself to him in a new way.

But Bethel was no longer the house of God, for when Jeroboam became king over the ten tribes of Israel he set up golden calves in Bethel and Dan and encouraged his people to worship there rather than in God's house in Jerusalem. It was spurious worship, of course, and God hated it. He never allowed His people to forget the sin by which Jeroboam caused Israel to sin. Jeroboam substituted idol worship for the true worship of Jehovah and it led the ten tribes further and further away from God. So it was into this atmosphere of rebellion against God that Elisha the prophet came. It is true there was a school of the prophets there but they would be very much in the minority and the bulk of the people had no regard for God's word or for His servant.

So the youths were only speaking what they had learned from their fathers and when they mocked God's prophet it was not just youthful playfulness, but something far more serious. It was what 2 Chronicles 36 speaks about, which eventually led Israel and Judah into captivity; they mocked the messengers of God, despised His words, and scoffed at His prophets, until the wrath of the LORD arose against His people, till there was no remedy (verse 16). That was what happened that day at Bethel and brought such swift judgement from the Lord. "Go up, you baldhead! Go up, you baldhead!" they cried (2 Kings 2:23). Maybe they had heard what had happened to Elijah and were saying 'you go up, too, you baldhead'.

But in mocking God's prophet they were also reproaching the God whom he served. In their hearts they had rejected Him and His word and there was only one answer for that, the solemn judgement of God. It certainly is solemn and it should speak loudly to our hearts. Does it not teach us the importance of valuing and reverencing the Word of God? Then those who speak it to us will be respected, counted worthy of double honour as Paul wrote to Timothy, especially those who labour in the word and doctrine (1 Timothy 5:17). We cannot impress too strongly upon one another the importance of God's Word and the supreme place it should be given in our lives. But on this one will I look", God says, "on him who is poor and of a contrite spirit, and who trembles at My word" (Isaiah 66:2). That is a trembling we all need to learn!

CHAPTER SIXTEEN: DIGGING DITCHES (2 KINGS 3)

Jehoshaphat king of Judah was a good man and he feared the Lord, but when he joined Jehoram king of Israel to fight against the Moabites he was a good man in a wrong place. When they reached the wilderness of Edom there no water to drink and Jehoram feared they would all perish. The story is recorded in 2 Kings 3:4-20. It is interesting to notice the differing reactions of men in times of crisis. Jehoram was a man out of touch with God and he feared the worst. But Jehoshaphat's faith rose to the occasion and he asked if there was no prophet through whom they might enquire of the Lord. And there was. Elisha the prophet was at hand. The kings did not know he was there, but one of the servants did. Maybe the Lord had arranged for him to follow the armies as they went to battle, so He could pass His message through him.

A solemn message it was for king Jehoram, and a very stern rebuke. God was only willing to speak to them because He regarded the presence of godly king Jehoshaphat. The instruction was that they were to dig the valley full of ditches and God would fill them with water. In the morning, at the time when the burnt offering was being offered on the altar in Jerusalem, God gave a bountiful supply of water for themselves and their cattle, and He did it in His own miraculous way without sending wind or rain. That God's provision for them was linked with the offering on the altar would not mean anything to Jehoram, for he worshipped false gods, and the service of God's house would be far from his thoughts.

But it would be very significant to Jehoshaphat, for that is where he worshipped, in God's house in Jerusalem. It means a lot to us as we learn our lessons from these incidents in Elisha's life. It reminds us that God wants to satisfy the spiritual thirst of our hearts, to give us the living water of His Word. Refreshment flows to us because of Christ's work upon the Cross and God intends that it should result in service in His house today. All our spiritual blessings flow from Calvary, do they not? When we come into times of spiritual drought we need to dig our ditches, in earnest supplication, ditches of repentance and humbling and brokenness of heart, for the sacrifices of God are a broken spirit.

Let us also with remind one another that the One who dwells in the high and holy place dwells also with him who "has a contrite and humble spirit, to revive the spirit of the humble, and to revive the heart of the contrite ones" (Isaiah 57:15). And is that not what we so much long after, reviving deep in our hearts? "Will You not revive us again?" the psalmist cried (Psalm 85:6), and as we humble ourselves and call upon Him, God will revive us and the living waters will flow. "If anyone thirsts, let him come to Me and drink", the Lord Jesus cried. "He who believes in Me, as the Scripture has said, out of his heart will flow rivers of living water" (John 7:37,38). Let us claim the promise and drink deeply day by day.

CHAPTER SEVENTEEN: THE JAR OF OIL (2 KINGS 4)

The story of the widow with her jar of oil is one that holds a very pertinent lesson for us. When her husband died she was left in deep poverty, so deep that the creditor threatened to take her two sons as slaves in lieu of her debt. In her dilemma she came to Elisha and he asked her, '"What do you have in the house?" "Your maidservant has nothing in the house but a jar of oil," she replied' (2 Kings 4:2). It was all she had, but as we shall see, it was all she needed.

Elisha told her to borrow from her neighbours as many empty jars as possible, and then, behind closed doors, to pour her oil into the jars and to set them aside as they were filled. She and her boys got busy filling jar after jar and still the oil flowed. As long as they had empty vessels, there was no limit to the supply. "Bring me another vessel," she called, but there wasn't one. She had filled the last. And then the oil stopped flowing. The lesson to our hearts is clear when we remember what God said about the two sons of oil in Zechariah 4, "Not by might nor by power, but by My Spirit,' says the LORD of hosts" (v.6). And with that word we link the Master's parting words to His apostles, "You shall receive power when the Holy Spirit has come upon you; and you shall be witnesses to Me" (Acts 1:8).

In all our witness and service for the Lord we are completely dependent upon the enabling of the Holy Spirit of God. There is a sense in which, like the widow's jar of oil, He is all we have, but it is also true that He is all we need. The gracious Holy Spirit, sharing with the Father and the Son the almighty power of Deity, has come to indwell each of our hearts when we believe on the Lord Jesus. "Do you not know that your body is the temple of the Holy Spirit who is in you, whom you have from God?" (1 Corinthians 6:19). Maybe we are sometimes apt to forget the implication of this tremendous truth and, like the Corinthians, we need to be reminded. The Holy Spirit, one of the Persons of the eternal Godhead, is living in each of our hearts and one of the reasons is to enable us to witness to our Lord Jesus and His power to save.

"This will turn out for my deliverance through your prayer and the supply of the Spirit of Jesus Christ," wrote the apostle Paul to the Philippians (Philippians 1:19). Notice the two things linked together - your prayer and the supply of the Spirit of Jesus Christ. The one depends on the other. Behind closed doors the widow worked away with her sons, where no eyes of friends or neighbours could see. "'When you pray, go into your room, and when you have shut your door, pray to your Father who is in the secret place; and your Father who sees in secret will reward you openly" (Matthew 6:6). In the secret place, alone with God, we shall be strengthened with might through His Spirit in the inner man, that Christ may dwell in our hearts through faith. It is through faith, as we claim the rich promises of His Word. Such a promise as John 7:38,39, "'He who believes in Me, as the Scripture has said, out of his heart will flow rivers of living water.' But this He spoke concerning the Spirit, whom those believing in Him would receive."

Let us learn well the lesson of the widow's jar of oil. There was an unlimited supply as long as there were pots to receive it. God is "able to do exceedingly abundantly above all that we ask or think, according to the power that works in us" (Ephesians 3:20). Who is able to do? God is able to do. And how? According to the power that works in us, and that is the power of the Holy Spirit. Oh, let us learn the lesson of God's unlimited supply and remember His word, "According to your faith let it be to you" (Matthew 9:29).

CHAPTER EIGHTEEN: THE GREAT WOMAN OF SHUNEM (2 KINGS 4)

The narrative suggests she was great in rank. But she was great in many other ways, too. Her hospitality was outstanding, for every time Elisha passed her way he stopped at her home for food. Equally outstanding was her discernment, for it did not take her long to perceive that he was a holy man of God. And then in fellowship with her husband her generosity provided the room on the wall with every need supplied, for which Elisha was so grateful. "He that receiveth a prophet in the name of a prophet shall receive a prophet's reward," and Elisha was concerned that the prophet's reward should come to his friends in Shunem.

And once again the greatness of the woman shone out. "Godliness with contentment is great gain." She was not wanting to be spoken for to the king or to the captain of the host. She was well content with what God had given. Into such hearts and homes God loves to pour His overweights of joy, and as with Sarah her great predecessor, when the time came round, she embraced a son, although her husband, like Sarah's, was old. The divine narrative passes over the months and years of their joy without comment, but it requires little imagination to picture it, as a little child's laughter brightened their home. "Oh how great is Thy goodness, which Thou has laid up for them that fear thee."

But the fear of God deep in their hearts did not make them immune from sorrow. The day came when the child died on his mother's lap, and like so many before and since, she was left to wrestle with the great "Why?" of human suffering. An elderly sister in Burma whose pathway has been strewn with many a sorrow has the text above her dining room table, "Before I was afflicted I went astray; but now I observe Thy word," and sometimes she shares with her friends the deep experiences through which God had led her and the spiritual enrichment that has resulted.

Maybe for some such wise reason God allowed this sorrow to enter the Shunem home. Certainly had it not come we would have missed a gem which shines so brightly on the sacred page. To the puzzled query of her husband as to why she was hastening to the prophet at such a time she sent the one word "Shalom," peace, or "it shall be well." And when Gehazi met her with his master's query about the well-being of herself, her husband and her child her reply was the same. It was a remarkable word of faith.

How could it be well when her only child lay dead on the prophet's bed? Only as she aligned herself with those women of whom the Hebrews epistle later speaks, who by faith received their dead by a resurrection (Hebrews 11:35). She had heard of Elijah raising the widow's son and she had every confidence that if the word of God through Elisha was powerful to the providing of a son in her husband's old age, it would be equally powerful in restoring that son to life. As she fell at the feet of the man of God and refused to leave him, she was expressing her confidence in the God he served, that He would show Himself strong on her behalf. And "the scripture saith, whosoever believeth on Him shall not be put to shame" (Romans 10:11). It was a wonderful demonstration of faith. She believed that the God who had given life in the first place was well able to give it again and therein lay her peace. And her faith was rewarded. In her case God, eventually, gave her back her son.

It does not always happen that way, but as Mr Spafford reminds us in his lovely hymn, written not long after he lost his four girls in a tragedy at sea, God is able to give peace even in adversity; even when everything seems to be against us. And He does it by faith. Let us learn from the great woman of Shunem!

When peace, like a river, attendeth my way,

When sorrows, like sea-billows, roll;

Whatever my lot, Thou hast taught me to say,

"It is well, it is well with my soul."

There was no power in the prophet's staff. Elisha sent his servant to lay his staff upon the child's face. But there was neither voice nor hearing. And he returned saying, "The child is not awaked." Elijah had not brought the widow's son to life by the use of his staff. Why then should Elisha think to do so? That must remain an unanswered question, unless it be to teach us the lesson that in bringing dead souls to life human effort is unavailing. It required something much more serious than that, and maybe that fact was impressed upon Elisha's own heart as he travelled the remainder of the journey to the Shunem home. For when he arrived he went in and shut the door upon himself and the dead child and prayed to the Lord.

As we watch this servant bowed in the presence of the Lord and then see him stretching himself upon the child, mouth to his mouth, eyes to his eyes and hands to his hands, we learn something of the seriousness of helping dead souls to new life in Christ. The flesh of the child grew warm as though to encourage Elisha to continue in prayer, and when he stretched himself again upon the child he sneezed seven times and opened his eyes. Do we not learn that the two things combined, earnest prayer in the secret place and a willingness on our part to become all things to all men, is the way by which we shall by all means save some? And that surely is the deep desire of all who love our Lord Jesus.

CHAPTER NINETEEN: MULTIPLYING BREAD (2 KINGS 4)

There was a famine in the land when Elisha came to Gilgal to meet the sons of the prophets. But there was a man from Baal Shalisha who had done some reaping despite the famine and he brought to Elisha the firstfruits of his harvest, twenty barley loaves and some newly ripened grain. Normally he would have taken it to God's house, but the ten tribes were not encouraged to go to Jerusalem, so he did the next best thing and brought it to God's prophet. Elisha told his servant to use it to feed the people. There were a hundred men in the place and the servant protested at the impossibility of feeding so many with so little. But he had not reckoned on the power of God, of course. Elisha simply repeated the instruction, "'Give it to the people, that they may eat,'" and then he added, "'for thus says the LORD: 'They shall eat and have some left over.'" It was a word from God and no word of His is void of power (2 Kings 4:42-44).

God multiplied the loaves according to His promise, they were all fed and there was some left over. And so there was on the day the Lord Jesus fed five thousand men with five loaves and two fishes; and also when four thousand were fed with seven loaves and a few fishes. In both cases, it was a question of hungry multitudes and unbelieving disciples. "Send the multitudes away," the disciples said. "They do not need to go away," the Master replied. "You give them something to eat." And when they brought their few loaves and fishes and placed them in the Master's hands, He multiplied them to satisfy the need of every hungry person there. Not one of them went away unsatisfied. And He did it through the disciples. That precious and important point we must notice carefully (see Matthew 14:15-21).

It has been said so often before, but we must say it again, as long as there are spiritually hungry multitudes around us, as long as men and women, boys and girls who touch our lives are dying without having eaten of the bread of life. The food passed from His hands to the disciples' hands, so it actually came true, they did give them to eat. They gathered up baskets full of broken pieces when the meal was over. There was enough and to spare. There always is in our heavenly Father's bountiful supply, but how shall His rich supply reach the hungry hearts of those around us unless we learn this vital lesson and are willing to put our little into His almighty hands? Put it another way. "For there is no distinction between Jew and Greek, for the same Lord over all is rich to all who call upon Him ... How then shall they call on Him in whom they have not believed? And how shall they believe in Him of whom they have not heard? And how shall they hear without a preacher?" (Romans 10:12-14). How indeed! How shall they hear unless we are willing for it to be through our lips? Shall we not have a burden to carry to them the glorious message of the One who satisfies the longing soul and fills the hungry soul with good? "He blessed and broke and gave." That is what the gospel record says. With His blessing, there is no limit to what the Lord can do with the little we are willing to put into His hands.

CHAPTER TWENTY: THE AXE-HEAD RAISED (2 KINGS 6)

Above the mantelpiece in a tiny home where an old missionary lady was spending her closing days, there was a wooden text with the words 'the iron did swim'. "Did you ever see iron swimming?" she asked, with a twinkle in her eye. It was obvious she reckoned she had, and she went on to recount some of her experiences when the Lord had stepped in and done things which seemed to be impossible. The quotation comes from the story of Elisha, when at the request of the sons of the prophets he had accompanied them to Jordan to build a larger place for them to live in. As one of them worked away at cutting the wood his axe-head fell into the water, and he cried out in his distress, "Alas, master! For it was borrowed." Elisha's response was to ask exactly where it fell and, cutting a stick, he threw it into the water at that spot, and the Bible record says, "he made the iron float", or as the KJV says, "the iron did swim" (2 Kings 6:6).

Only God could make that happen, of course. Humanly speaking, it was impossible. But isn't it true that sometimes God intervenes in our lives doing seemingly impossible things in order to demonstrate His power and encourage our faith? God loves to stimulate our faith. "Is anything too hard for the LORD?" was the question He put to Abraham when He promised him and Sarah a son in their old age (Genesis 18:14). It was left to Jeremiah to provide the plain answer to that question when he said, "there is nothing too hard for You" (Jeremiah 32:17). Through deep experiences in life Jeremiah had watched the Lord doing wonderful things, delivering him in times of great danger and his faith had been strengthened as a result. And ours will be also. God may put our faith to the test at times and, as we learn to trust Him, we shall be strengthened for the next experience (1 Peter 1:7).

CHAPTER TWENTY-ONE: THE UNSEEN HOSTS (2 KINGS 6)

There is a spiritual world around us of which some are more conscious than others. The Bible says the things which are seen are temporary, but the things which are not seen are eternal. However, the unseen, eternal things are every bit as real as the things we can see and handle. And they are infinitely more valuable, by as much as eternity is longer than time! We need to often remind ourselves of this fact and to be particularly mindful of the exhortation to "seek those things which are above, where Christ is, sitting at the right hand of God. Set your mind on things above, not on things on the earth" (Colossians 3:1,2).

We are reminded of this by an incident in Elisha's life in 2 Kings 6:8-23. He had been advising the king of Israel where the opposing king of Syria was planning to strike. When the king of Syria found out how the secret information was reaching Israel's king he sent his horsemen and chariots to take Elisha captive. One morning when Elisha's servant looked out he found the city surrounded by the Syrian hosts. "Alas, my master! What shall we do?" he cried. Elisha's reply deserves our careful thought. "Do not fear, for those who are with us are more than those who are with them," he said. But the young man could not see anyone with them. They seemed to be all alone and that was why he was so alarmed. Elisha could see what he couldn't see, for the spiritual world around him was real to God's servant.

He had seen the angels escorting Elijah to heaven as in a whirlwind and he had never forgotten it. He was conscious of the presence of those same angels right now when his life was in danger, and he simply asked the Lord to open the young man's eyes. And God did just that. He caused the servant to see what Elisha had been aware of all the time, a host of horses and chariots of fire, doubtless angelic beings, for Habakkuk wrote of the LORD riding upon His horses and His chariots of salvation (see Habbakuk 3:8). They formed a wall of protection around God's prophet and his servant.

The spiritual world is real. We know that. There are spiritual hosts of wickedness under the control of Satan, which are against us. But thank God there are also spiritual hosts under His control which are for us, and Elisha's word remains for ever true: "those who are with us are more than those who are with them" (2 Kings 6:16). So, with the apostle Paul we say with confidence "If God is for us, who can be against us?" We need the eyes of our hearts enlightened, do we not, so that we shall be more aware of our angel guardians, for "are they not all ministering spirits sent forth to minister for those who will inherit salvation?" (Hebrews 1:14).

Elisha could see more than his servant could see, and doubtless his greater enlightenment was due to his deeper knowledge of the Lord and of His ways. The apostle Paul prayed for the Ephesians "a spirit of wisdom and revelation in the knowledge of Him; having the eyes of your heart enlightened, that ye may know ..." and he goes on to cite three particular spheres in which he desired their knowledge to grow. Knowledge in that case is 'epignosis', a full and developing knowledge, with which comes a growing spiritual enlightenment. Let us pray for ourselves and for one another as Paul did for the Ephesians, that the eyes of our understanding may be enlightened that we may know:

1. "the hope of His calling";

2. "the riches of the glory of His inheritance in the saints"; and

3. "the exceeding greatness of His power toward us who believe" (Ephesians 1:18,19).

CHAPTER TWENTY-TWO: BOW AND ARROWS (2 KINGS 13)

Joash, king of Israel, reigned for sixteen years, but they were not good years, for he followed the evil ways of his predecessors. Toward the end of his life an interesting incident happened, for he came to bid farewell to Elisha who was terminally ill (see 2 Kings 13:14-20). He had probably ignored him during his lifetime, but now that the old prophet was about to depart, the king acknowledged the influence of his godly life. He used the same expression as Elisha used of Elijah when he was departing. He said, "O my father, my father, the chariots of Israel and their horsemen!" How true that a nation's strength lies in its men of God, the men who speak God's word. Elijah's faith and prayers and messages from God had done more for Israel than the horsemen and chariots of her army. And so had Elisha's. Joash the king appeared to recognize that fact, despite all his failings.

Then the old prophet asked him to do an unusual thing. "Take a bow and some arrows," he said, and then, "Put your hand on the bow." As he did so, Elisha put his hands over the king's hands. Do you get the picture? The old prophet standing beside the king as he opened the window toward the East, and together they directed the arrow and sent it toward its mark. "The arrow of the LORD's deliverance," declared Elisha, to remind the king that any victory gained over the enemy would be by the Lord's help and strength and not his own. As with Joseph before him, his hands would be "made strong by the hands of the Mighty God of Jacob" (Genesis 49:24). That was the lesson Elisha wanted to convey to the king and it was his last message before he died.

What an important lesson it was, not only for the king, but for us, too, for it applies for all time. Any victory achieved in our lives of service for the Lord will be by the strength that He supplies. "I can do all things through Christ who strengthens me", was the apostle Paul's testimony (Philippians 4:13). And more than that, he found that his very weakness was the opportunity for the Lord to demonstrate His power. So he learned to take pleasure in anything which cast him in dependence upon the Lord, for "when I am weak, then am I strong", he said (2 Corinthians 12:10).

Finally, Elisha told the king to take the remaining arrows and smite the ground, and he struck three times and stopped. The prophet was angry with him. "You should have struck five or six times," he said, "then you would have struck Syria till you had destroyed it." He did what he was told, but without enthusiasm. His heart was not in it. It is true that it is the Lord's arrow of victory, and that every spiritual victory comes through His strength alone, but we must pursue the work with zeal and fervour, "not lagging in diligence, fervent in spirit, serving the Lord" (Romans 12:11). That was what king Joash lacked. It is a striking lesson, the last from Elisha's lips; and in a sense the story of the prophet's life, for all his service had been rendered in the strength which God supplied and whatsoever his hand had found to do he did it with all his might.

Did you love *Lessons From Elijah and Elisha*? Then you should read *Different Discipleship: Jesus' Sermon on the Mount* by Hayes Press!

A practical, challenging study (complete with questions and prayer prompts) of the "Sermon on the Mount" for followers and would-be followers of Jesus. What makes Jesus and his followers "different"? Find out why this revolutionary, life-changing sermon is why Jesus Christ is regarded as one of the world's most important teachers, even by those who don't follow him as their Lord and Saviour.

CHAPTER ONE: THE SETTING OF THE SERMON
CHAPTER TWO: HAPPY ARE THE POOR AND

MOURNING
CHAPTER THREE: HAPPY ARE THE MEEK, HUNGRY AND THIRSTY
CHAPTER FOUR: HAPPY ARE THE PERSECUTED
CHAPTER FIVE: LET YOUR LIGHT SHINE
CHAPTER SIX: IN DANGER OF THE HELL OF FIRE
CHAPTER SEVEN: TURN THE OTHER CHEEK
CHAPTER EIGHT: SEEK GOD'S APPROVAL, NOT MAN'S
CHAPTER NINE: YOUR HEART IS WHERE YOUR TREASURE IS
CHAPTER TEN: LOVE YOUR NEIGHBOUR
CHAPTER ELEVEN: CUT DOWN AND THROWN IN THE FIRE
CHAPTER TWELVE: FIRST THINGS FIRST
CHAPTER THIRTEEN: THE TEACHER WITH UNIQUE AUTHORITY

About the Publisher

Hayes Press (www.hayespress.org) is a registered charity in the United Kingdom, whose primary mission is to disseminate the Word of God, mainly through literature. It is one of the largest distributors of gospel tracts and leaflets in the United Kingdom, with over 100 titles and hundreds of thousands despatched annually.

Hayes Press also publishes Plus Eagles Wings, a fun and educational Bible magazine for children, six times a year and Golden Bells, a popular daily Bible reading calendar in wall or desk formats.

Also available are over 100 Bibles in many different versions, shapes and sizes, Christmas cards, Christian jewellery, Eikos Bible Art, Bible text posters and much more!

Made in the USA
Columbia, SC
08 February 2021

MW01405075

The Devil in the Back Pew

Dealing with Dark Spirits in the Church

Joe Kovalcik

Text © 2018 Joe Kovalcik

Light In The Back Pew, LLC

Email: lightinthebackpew@gmail.com

Website: lightinthebackpew.com

All Bible quotations are in italics and from the New King James Version (NKJV, 1982 Thomas Nelson), unless otherwise noted.

KJV – King James Version (1796 Public Domain)

NIV – New International Version (2008 Zondervan Publishing)

MSG – *The Message* (2002 NavPress Copyright Eugene H. Peterson)

The quotation on pages 162 to 165 is taken from Derek Prince, *Blessing or Curse: You Can Choose*, 10th Anniversary Edition, pages 114 to 116. Chosen, a division of Baker Publishing Group, Grand Rapids, MI, 2000. Used by permission.

All rights reserved.

First edition 2018

Text design by Kim Hough

Cover design by Heather Kimura

ISBN 9781980863526

I dedicate this book to Patti –
my best friend, my girlfriend, and my wife.
Surely the greatest earthly gift
the Lord has given me.

Contents

Author's Notes		6
Introduction		7

Part I: **Understanding the Spiritual Environment** 13
Chapter 1   Beginning the Discussion   14
Chapter 2   The Spirit Realm   31
Chapter 3   Warfare Basics and Recognizing the enemy   58

Part II: **Countering the enemy's Tactics** 89
Chapter 4   The enemy at Work   90
Chapter 5   The Need for Inner Healing   127
Chapter 6   The Need to Forgive   137
Chapter 7   Blessings and Curses   146
Chapter 8   Generational Sin and Curses
and Dark Attachments   175

Part III: **Freedom: The Deliverance Prayer Process** 183
Chapter 9   Practical Aspects of Deliverance Prayer   184
Chapter 10   Before Praying   207
Chapter 11   The Confrontation   217
Chapter 12   After Praying   249
Chapter 13   Additional Information   259
Chapter 14   Putting It All Together   265

Afterword   273
Appendix I: The Poverty Mind-set   275
Appendix II: Angelic Activity, Authority and Power   278
Bibliography   282

Author's Notes

It is my preference to ignore conventional rules of capitalization and use the lower case for satan, devil, lucifer, beelzebub, and related references to dark spirits, in both the body of the text as well as in headings. In quotations, I have bracketed [ ] the lower case first letter to continue the practice.

The designations "satan," "devil," "lucifer," "demon," "enemy," "enemy of your soul," "power of darkness," "unclean spirit," and "dark spirit" are used interchangeably to refer to those spirits which rebelled against God.

The examples and experiences described in the text are true occurrences, though nonrelevant details have sometimes been "blurred" to conceal an individual's identity.

The terms "pray-er" and "prayee" refer to the person praying and the person receiving prayer, respectively.

I would like to thank Bob Morton, Leslie Johns, and Patti Kovalcik for all their excellent feedback. Especially, I am grateful for the professional editing skills of Rhonda Crouse. Her assistance has been invaluable.

DISCLAIMER: Nothing in this book should be construed as a substitute or replacement for medical, legal, psychological, or psychiatric help provided by an accredited professional. Such expert counsel should be sought if there is possible need. Additionally, local or other laws may require the reporting of instances of violence, neglect, abuse, or other extreme behavior. The reader assumes full responsibility for compliance with applicable statutes.

Introduction

Dealing with Darkness

There is something distasteful about writing a book which gives so much attention to satan and the dark spiritual realm. The focus on the enemy, though, is 100% for the purposes of exposing his deceptive ways and bringing him under the lawful authority of the believer. I intend no regard, no respect, and certainly no admiration – whatsoever – for the one who wars against all that is good and Godly. My hope is that, by the Lord's grace, this writing may play a small part in shining the light of the Savior on those places darkened by the prince of evil.

If you are a Christian believer, and you feel uncomfortable or troubled reading this book, I suggest you take that as a clear sign that you *should* be reading it. Assuredly, the enemy of your soul does *not* want you learning how to expose his work – and to defeat him in your life.

For those who consider the topic strange, irrelevant, or even fantasy, this text offers much to refute that by way of Scripture, examples, and testimonies. However, at the onset, I raise a few questions for the doubter:

- Do you believe in Jesus Christ?
- Do you believe He died and bodily rose again?
- Do you believe what He said about the enemy of your soul?

As author C.S. Lewis stated, Jesus is either a liar and a lunatic, or He is Lord. There is no middle ground. Jesus claimed to be God; if

THE DEVIL IN THE BACK PEW

He is not, He is to be ignored – but if He *is* God, we deny Him at our peril! He told us about the ways of satan, and from His words and other Scriptures, we learn how to overcome this adversary and his cohorts.

Our worldly inclination about things of life might be: "Show me, then I'll believe." But the Kingdom[1] way is different. There is a Biblical principle about spiritual revelation which has to do with faith, obedience, and understanding. In the Old Testament account of the priests carrying the ark through the dry riverbed of the Jordan River, importantly, the river did not part *until they stepped into the water* (Joshua 3:13)! Likewise, in 2 Corinthians 3:14–16, Paul states that those who refuse to believe in Christ have a "veiled" understanding of the Old Testament, but *"when one turns to the Lord, the veil is taken away."* Significantly, the order is not "once I see, then I'll turn to Jesus." It's precisely the opposite. And the same with the priests at the Jordan: the river did not part before they stepped in, but afterward.

It may seem an absurdly simple truth, but we can only learn what we don't know. If there is a bias for or against a particular belief, we may limit our ability to learn and grow. Knowledge can be categorized in three ways: *intellectual knowledge, heart knowledge,* and *spiritual knowledge.* We are engaged in life, for the most part, on an intellectual level – that is, with what we grasp and perceive with our minds. We pass the majority of our existence functioning in this manner. Beyond this is heart knowledge, the full expression of which we call *love.* We can throw brain-sourced words toward a description of love, but none will adequately explain the experience of knowing love in our heart. It's beyond our words and thinking. But then there is an undeniable spiritual knowledge, different and deeper than that of the brain and the

---

[1]In this book, "Kingdom" is used to refer to God's chosen plan for mankind from creation to the time of the *"new heaven"* and *"new earth"* (Revelation 21:1) – as revealed through the life of Jesus and the message of the Bible.

8

Introduction

heart. It is not comprehended like intellectual or heart understanding, but it is real, and it is both foundational and powerful. It is, in many ways, our link to the spiritual realm. If this concept is foreign, I ask that you forge on and remain open to what the Holy Spirit may reveal to you.

My bottom-line suggestion for any believer who struggles with this topic is to accept what Jesus says – what the Bible says – about the works of the dark spiritual realm. And become equipped to drive this very real enemy out of your life, and those of others.

If you still question the reality of Christians being pestered by dark spirits, there's more on page 46 in the Chapter 2 section entitled "Can a Christian Really Have a demon?"

Why This Book?

A few years ago, I began to hear from attendees of our *Dealing with the demonic* class that I should write a book on the subject of deliverance. I did not, at that time, feel led by the Lord to pursue it, though it did stir inside of me.

As my wife, Patti, and I continued in the healing prayer ministry, with its frequent confrontations with demonic spirits, a frustration grew in me: there is too much work being left undone. Not enough people are equipped to help victims of spiritual attack, and there are far too few who even understand this aspect of spiritual warfare. And, most significantly, there are *so many* individuals being harassed by the enemy who have no clue as to the nature of the problem or that real peace is within their reach. Bottom line, the issue is *ignorance*. Folks are uninformed – they just don't know! And, in many cases, they have been tricked or deceived and led to believe untruths about dark spirits and their own distress. The reality is that those things caused by the enemy – or aggravated by him – can be resolved.

This book is written with simplicity and practicality in mind. There are many texts which delve deeper theologically and even scientifically (psychology and psychiatry). My approach is more

9

THE DEVIL IN THE BACK PEW

"hands-on" and "how-to" than an exhaustive scholastic study. The goal is that you will understand that confrontational spiritual warfare is a routine part of the Christian walk. I am motivated by the words of Hosea:

"My people are destroyed for lack of knowledge." (Hosea 4:6)

During the process of writing this book, I felt prompted to list – for private assessment – the names of those who sought to be relieved of demonic torment but, for one reason or another, remained victimized. It saddens me to admit the list was rather long. Reviewing the details of each situation, there were many perceived "explanations" for why persons were not freed. But, in virtually every case, the person refused to confront an issue of *forgiveness* or *submission.* The tormented man or woman believed the enemy's lie that it was too difficult, that they couldn't change, or that the "problem" lay with someone or something else. Significantly, the wounded person's focus was very often not on the forgiveness or submission issue itself; instead, they were sidetracked by a debilitating fear which seemed to mask the underlying problem. I believe God's Word gives hope where they believe there is none. This book attempts to build that case – and to show practically how victory can be attained.

Should you, while reading, desire help to deal with dark influences on your life (and we all have them – that's what this book is about!), or if you wish to know more about the guarantee of freedom through Christ, you may wish to read the Afterword before completing the rest of the book.

What Is Deliverance?

This book is about recognizing and dealing with the enemy's everyday attempts to disrupt our lives. Perhaps you're drawn to read because you wish to learn more about deliverance prayer (i.e., freeing those who are demonized or oppressed). And you will, but there is much more. From my experience, most believers consider

Introduction

only the extremes: either you are wild-eyed, irrational, and blaspheming (i.e., seriously demonized), or you have zero problems with dark spirits. A foundational premise of this book is that satan and his cohorts are very active in between. With *everybody!* And we wish to be delivered[2] from all this harassment. Though much of the focus of this book is on confronting dark spirits in more troublesome situations, the battle tactics you will learn are likewise applicable to the enemy's lesser intrusions, like temptation.

How can satan gain ground with people who sincerely follow the Lord? An easy initial response is: deception. We also need to acknowledge that, if satan tempted Jesus, the powers of darkness will go after anyone, and that our imperfect human nature sometimes succumbs. Or we can be victimized from indirect or external sources. Suffice it to say, the consequences run the gamut from temptation to oppression to demonization, each discussed at length in Chapter 4.

Further, there are degrees to the intensity of the enemy's involvement. Some spiritual attacks are rather lightweight and easily dismissed, as in the case of a minor temptation, a sinful thought, or a flash of resentment or anger. When we prayerfully eject these and the enemy who plants them, this is a "deliverance" of sorts, but on a very small scale. Similarly, when we pray for someone's healing from disease, for example, we might command a "spirit of infirmity" off the individual. This simple, authoritative prayer is also, in principle, a form of "deliverance."

In this writing, however, the term "deliverance" is used to mean the process of confronting and forcefully ejecting an unclean spirit from a victimized individual. Often that spirit has demonstrated a right or ability to remain. Generally, these spirits are more powerful, more stubborn, and more aggravating than the lighter examples of the previous paragraph. But the battle is the Lord's, not ours. And Jesus is stronger!

---

[2]As Jesus instructed in the Lord's prayer: *"deliver us from the evil one"* (Matthew 6:13).

11

PART I

Understanding the
Spiritual Environment

Chapter 1

Beginning the Discussion

In writing this book, the most challenging aspect is convincing the skeptic that this subject matter is real – and that it affects *all* of us! To be clear, the skeptics of whom I speak are those *in* the Christian church. That is, those who believe in God, Jesus, the Holy Spirit, and basic Bible teachings.

Do you have difficulty accepting that God might supernaturally deliver someone from spiritual torment or heal someone's physical or emotional hurts in this day and age? Looking at most churches, we get the impression that the prevailing expectation is against any hope of supernatural intervention. Or perhaps there's a belief something like, "We know God *can* heal, but He doesn't seem to do it these days." Why, when the Bible encourages us to pray for healing and cast out demons, does so much of the Christian church not embrace this with faith and vigor?

In an age of politicians, professors, and media types saying absolutely anything to get attention (not to mention the lies of con artists and hucksters), it is necessary and appropriate to question what we hear and read. The Bible tells us that we should *"test everything"* (1 Thessalonians 5:21 NIV). Surely this verse means, at least in part, that we should use our God-given intellects. It also means we should *test our beliefs* about God, and *our beliefs* about

Beginning the Discussion

the Bible or how we interpret it. Maybe we are biased; maybe there are multiple meanings; maybe we are wrong! We really must test what we believe. Have we faithlessly put God in a box where He is powerless?

Beyond wonderful truths and guides to live by, the Bible contains history, allegory, symbolism, metaphor, parables, and many mysteries. Frankly, I cannot claim to have a theologian's depth of understanding of any of it. Yet I have seen God do the miraculous in ways some say are not possible. I encourage you, do not allow yourself to say, "God doesn't do [...] anymore," just because you haven't seen Him do it. Instead, ask yourself, "Why not?" We will talk about removing barriers to the supernatural throughout this book.

Our Journey

I believe that the only spiritual understanding which anyone can internalize emanates from God's revelation through the Holy Spirit. As a writer, my responsibility, therefore, is to bear accurate witness. I will begin by sharing how my wife, Patti, and I became involved in this ministry, which is misunderstood by so many believers.

My introduction to extended, hands-on healing prayer for individuals came many years ago at a weekend conference led by Francis and Judith MacNutt of Christian Healing Ministries.[3] Francis, a former Catholic priest, and his wife, Judith, a professional counselor, told of their successes in protracted prayer for healing. Francis shared their experience in one of his sessions: in praying for ten people, typically they see one or two people completely healed, one or two who experience no healing at all, and the remainder gaining some level of improvement. This, frankly, was a better record of success than I had seen or heard of before.

---

[3] A world-reaching ministry based in Jacksonville, FL. For information on classes, books, audio and video teachings, etc., go to www.christian-healingmin.org.

15

THE DEVIL IN THE BACK PEW

This practice of spending time praying for someone, of *soaking* a person in prayer, was nothing I had observed in any church that I had attended. In many congregations, prayer was limited to brief pulpit-led blessings or "mentions" of prayer needs, while in other churches, individuals were directly prayed for by leaders, special ministry teams, or folks nearby, but for a few minutes at most. The MacNutts taught of praying for an hour or longer, and doing so repeatedly over a period of days, months, or even years. And they gave examples of actual healings, even of major diseases.

Like you, perhaps, I wonder about the scarcity of powerful healings today when I read about the healings and promises of the New Testament. I cannot help but ask:

- What are we doing wrong?
- How is it that some are healed, but many are not?
- What barriers exist which we are not dealing with?

And so on ...

Irrespective of my personal experience, the internet permits me to see that wonderful healings do occur regularly *now*. Additionally, it is well-documented that there have been numerous healing ministries[4] where large numbers were miraculously healed (at times many rising from wheelchairs). Yet, notwithstanding these powerful displays, documented even by secular newspapers, many left those services unhealed. Healing prayer remains a spiritual mystery; the best stories we have still fall short of Biblical accounts where "all"[5] who came were healed.

---

[4]See Roberts Liardon, *God's Generals* (Whitaker House, New Kensington, PA, 1996).

[5]Scriptural examples where Jesus and the apostles healed all who came: *"And great multitudes followed Him [Jesus], and **He healed them all.**"* (Matthew 12:15, emphasis mine)
*"And through the hands of the apostles many signs and wonders were done among the people. ... Also a multitude gathered from the surrounding cities to Jerusalem, bringing sick people and those who were tormented by unclean spirits, and **they were all healed.**"* (Acts 5:12, 16, emphasis mine)

Beginning the Discussion

Nevertheless, the Bible encourages us to *always pray and not give up*" (Luke 18:1 NIV). So we stir our faith as best we can, eliminate known barriers, and cry out from the depths of our hearts … and pray for our brothers and sisters for healing. Much more about this in the chapters that follow.

Healing Prayer Ministry

After the MacNutts' teaching weekend, a wonderful couple who were respected lay leaders in the church that hosted the conference, was given the go-ahead to begin a healing prayer ministry modeling the MacNutts' prayer approach. The ministry began to grow, and several teams of two or three people met with prayer recipients twice a month for 40 to 60 minutes each. A few years later, Patti and I were drawn to join this church, and eventually became part of this ministry of extended healing prayer.

Moving forward several years, the couple who had begun and led the prayer effort, now called Soaking Prayer for Healing, stepped down. Patti and I took over the lay leadership, and the ministry eventually grew to 28 prayer teams of two to three prayers praying for in excess of 70 people twice each month. There were consistently 50+ people in the queue waiting for prayer, and there were, additionally, four monthly "open prayer" sessions, where anyone seeking prayer could be prayed for on an unscheduled basis. Folks were welcomed with any prayer need: physical, emotional, relational, familial, financial, and other.

In our leadership of this ministry, we rarely participated on any of the regularly scheduled prayer teams. Rather, we selected and prayed for those:

- we felt the Lord specifically led us to;
- who seemed most "broken," usually due to severe emotional trauma; and
- who might be called the "hard" cases (yes, some church people can be challenging!).

17

THE DEVIL IN THE BACK PEW

As a result of our selection process, we were exposed to many, many situations of demonic oppression and outright demonization (discussed in-depth in Chapter 4). For a season, we were involved in full deliverance prayer two and three times a day, several days a week. But it was all good ... and glorious! And, I have to add, not stressful to us whatsoever.

So, without seeking it, Patti and I have found ourselves, for nearly twenty years now, thrust into an amazing world of spiritual warfare. Our involvement with different churches, and their ministries to individuals seeking healing, has given us ever-increasing evidence of, and interaction with, the very real world of the demonic.

Equipping Others

As mentioned in the Introduction, the motivation for writing this book is simple: more are needed who can both recognize the enemy's lies and tricks, and expose and remove him from themselves and others. I believe it is a lie of satan that special power or authority is required to gain the freedom Jesus bought for each of us on the cross. This battle is winnable, and it is not hard. Really! We *can* defeat the enemy of our soul – as we face him *today!*

Throughout our involvement in these "activities," we have done much research, absorbed many teachings, and read many books – all of which encourage an aggressive approach. We remain convinced that spiritual warfare is, in some measure, *every* Christian's business and calling. It is not for a special few.

How great is the need? In the small world of our own experience, we have encountered few churches which can respond effectively when a need for deliverance presents itself. Sadly, I have seen pastors offering cursory prayers or recommending counseling for folks clearly caught in a spiritual battle with the enemy. Also, there are leaders and believers who proclaim, "No Christian, who is a temple of the Holy Spirit, can have a demon," so the problem is not addressed. And the person is not helped. Or, perhaps too

commonly, a person displays behavior indicating some level of oppression or dark influence, and they are ostracized by friends or the believers they should be turning to for help first. Maybe the individual is one of those "challenging" church people I mentioned earlier.

Brothers and sisters in Christ, this should not be so! We *all* should know many other Christian believers, pastors, leaders, and pray-ers who can bring victory to those caught in a spiritual battle. Significantly, Patti and I are regularly approached by struggling individuals who have sought us out by local reputation, because there is no resource in their own church to deal with their need.

The reality of the enemy in our midst today must become better recognized, and God's promises of victory must be more readily embraced by the people of the church.

The devil in the Back Pew

Oh yes, the devil's in the back pew. And many other places as well. But the case will be made that the tools and resources to deal victoriously with the dark spirits in the church[6] are effective and free for the taking.

When I teach this material in a classroom format, I typically explain that studying the subject is rather like jumping on a moving merry-go-round. There is no precise beginning or simple place to start, and many points seem to need a bit of context and prior explanation. So, the approach here will be similar. I will lay down basics, which will be broadened and expanded on later.

Note: This is not fiction. It is presented as an informational tool for the Christian church. There are many great books on this subject (see the Bibliography), but I was prompted to write this text explaining the topic using a how-to approach.

Note also: This doesn't pretend to be an exhaustive review or research effort. Its focus is simplicity, acknowledging that no text

---

[6]The church: the *people of Christ*, not just the building.

THE DEVIL IN THE BACK PEW

on the subject could be complete. Certainly, the enemy is crafty and quite creative in his deceptions, schemes, and methods. He is, however, no match for the Holy Spirit or the power behind the name of Jesus, and therein is the foundation for this teaching, as well as for all spiritual warfare.

It is fitting, in a writing like this, to make a comment about conclusions drawn from experience. Though one should be wary of forming any experiential theology (i.e., defining God or His works solely by what we have personally seen), there is much we can learn from what we observe. Author and teacher Derek Prince says it this way:

> *"Personal experience by itself is never a sufficient basis for establishing Biblical doctrine. At times, however, it can have the effect of illuminating a doctrine that previously one did not know how to apply."*[7]

The enemy's Schemes

Over the last few decades, several books have been published titled or subtitled, "The World, the Flesh, and the [d]evil." Such a description is supported Biblically, where Paul spoke to the Ephesians about what they were like before receiving God's mercy:

> *"And you He made alive, who were dead in trespasses and sins, in which you once walked according to the course of this **world**, according to **the prince of the power of the air [satan], the spirit who now works in the sons of disobedience**, among whom also we all once conducted ourselves in the lusts of our **flesh**, fulfilling the desires of the **flesh** and of the mind, and were by nature children of wrath, just as the others."* (Ephesians 2:1–3, emphasis mine)

This phrase will be used several times in this book for its plain

---

[7]Derek Prince, *They Shall Expel Demons* (Chosen, a division of Baker Publishing Group, Grand Rapids, MI, 1998), 27.

Beginning the Discussion

meaning, but we should be aware that the enemy not only works (attacks) on his own, but also is quite adept at "piling on" to worldly and fleshly circumstances and temptations. John 10:10 reminds us that satan comes only *"to steal, and to kill, and to destroy."* It is unwise to drop our guard and assume that an unfavorable situation does not, to some degree, involve the enemy.

Though more evidence will be presented later, I offer a few comments at this point. Some of the enemy's oft-used tools are *confusion, obfuscation,* and *trickery.* He does not want his presence or involvement suspected, because then he might be confronted. But we have the *power and authority* to cast him out when he comes after us or those we've been asked to pray for.

Dr. Ed Murphy writes:

"... in general, our churches are filled with believers who are hurting through the activity of evil spirits. Many are Spirit-filled believers by anyone's definition of the term. Yet a war rages inside of them and around them. Often areas of their lives are in bondage to feelings, thoughts, and practices not compatible with their Christian faith. They know something is wrong, but few suspect the possibility of a direct demonic dimension to their problem."

"While the Bible contains a vast amount of material about [s]atan, his evil angels, demons, and evil spirits, we will often be left still questioning because of what the Scriptures do not reveal. For example, the Scriptures do not directly explain the origin of [s]atan and his demons. They do not explain the relationship between malfunctions natural to human personality and personality malfunctions caused supernaturally. We are left mostly on our own in these and many other areas. The Bible does not develop a doctrine of [s]atanology or demonology ... "[8]

---

[8]Edward F. Murphy, *The Handbook for Spiritual Warfare – Revised and Updated* (Thomas Nelson, Inc., Nashville, TN, 2003), Introduction xv.

THE DEVIL IN THE BACK PEW

> *"Some dimensions of spiritual warfare are controversial both theologically and in practice."*[9]

Ed Murphy's observations are right on the money and, unfortunately, so many remain in the struggle because they do not deal with the real problem. The pathway to freedom is not followed because the source of the problem is not acknowledged.

What the Scriptures Say About satan and his demons

The Bible is God's story, and it reveals His goodness, His nature, and His victorious plans for us. Many Scriptures are instructive in how we can obtain that promised victory and overcome the enemy in our lives. These will be emphasized throughout this book. For now, I list some verses referencing the enemy's activities and power in order to broaden our understanding of who we are dealing with:

satan Is Active and Purposeful

> *"Be sober, be vigilant; because your adversary the devil walks about like a roaring lion, seeking whom he may devour."*
> (1 Peter 5:8)

> *"And the Lord said, 'Simon, Simon! Indeed, [s]atan has asked for you, that he may sift you as wheat.'"* (Luke 22:31)
> "You" in this verse is plural; satan was not seeking only Peter.

> *"And He [Jesus] said to them, 'I saw [s]atan fall like lightning from heaven.'"* (Luke 10:18)

> *"And the LORD said to [s]atan, 'From where do you come?' So [s]atan answered the LORD and said, 'From going to and fro on the earth, and from walking back and forth on it.'"*
> (Job 1:7)

---

[9]Murphy, *The Handbook for Spiritual Warfare*, Preface viii.

Beginning the Discussion

satan Can Inflict Physical Harm

"So [s]atan went out from the presence of the LORD, and struck Job with painful boils from the sole of his foot to the crown of his head." (Job 2:7)

"So ought not this woman, being a daughter of Abraham, whom [s]atan has bound—think of it—for eighteen years, be loosed from this bond on the Sabbath?" (Luke 13:16)

satan Can Interfere in Our Lives

"Do not fear ... the devil is about to throw some of you into prison, that you may be tested ..." (Revelation 2:10)

"Therefore we wanted to come to you—even I, Paul, time and again—but [s]atan hindered us." (1 Thessalonians 2:18)

satan Can Influence Our Thoughts and Minds

"... then the devil comes and takes away the word [of God] out of their hearts, lest they should believe and be saved." (Luke 8:12)

"But Peter said, 'Ananias, why has [s]atan filled your heart to lie to the Holy Spirit ...?'" (Acts 5:3)

"Then [s]atan entered Judas, surnamed Iscariot, who was numbered among the twelve." (Luke 22:3)

satan Is a Deceiver

"He [the devil] was a murderer from the beginning, and does not stand in the truth, because there is no truth in him. When he speaks a lie, he speaks from his own resources, for he is a liar and the father of it." (John 8:44)

"For [s]atan himself transforms himself into an angel of light." (2 Corinthians 11:14)

"The coming of the lawless one is according to the working of

23

THE DEVIL IN THE BACK PEW

[s]atan, with all power, signs, and lying wonders ..."
(2 Thessalonians 2:9)

"... that they may come to their senses and escape the snare of the devil, having been taken captive by him to do his will."
(2 Timothy 2:26)

"... he must have a good testimony ... lest he fall into reproach and the snare of the devil." (1 Timothy 3:7)

satan's Strategies Vary, But he Tempts Everyone

"Then Jesus was led up by the Spirit into the wilderness to be tempted by the devil." (Matthew 4:1)

"Now when the devil had ended every temptation, he departed from Him [Jesus] until an opportune time." (Luke 4:13)

"But He [Jesus] turned and said to Peter, 'Get behind Me, [s]atan! You are an offense to Me, for you are not mindful of the things of God, but the things of men.'" (Matthew 16:23)

"... a thorn in the flesh was given to me, a messenger of [s]atan to buffet me, lest I be exalted above measure." (2 Corinthians 12:7)

"In this the children of God and the children of the devil are manifest: Whoever does not practice righteousness is not of God, nor is he who does not love his brother." (1 John 3:10)

"Do not deprive one another except with consent for a time, that you may give yourselves to fasting and prayer; and come together again so that [s]atan does not tempt you ..." (1 Corinthians 7:5)
Paul is speaking of marital intimacy.

We Have Defenses Available

"Put on the whole armor of God, that you may be able to stand against the wiles of the devil." (Ephesians 6:11)

24

Beginning the Discussion

The armor, paraphrased: The belt of truth, the breastplate of righteousness, feet shod with the readiness of the gospel of peace, the shield of faith, the helmet of salvation, and the sword of the Spirit (the Word of God) (Ephesians 6:14–17).

"Therefore submit to God. Resist the devil and he will flee from you." (James 4:7)

There Is No Place for Pride in Exercising Spiritual Authority

"[Jesus said,] 'Nevertheless do not rejoice in this, that the spirits [demons] are subject to you, but rather rejoice because your names are written in heaven.'" (Luke 10:20)

"Yet Michael the archangel, in contending with the devil ... dared not bring against him a reviling accusation, but said, 'The Lord rebuke you!'" (Jude 1:9)

satan's End Is Certain

"... the everlasting fire prepared for the devil and his angels ..." (Matthew 25:41)

"For this purpose the Son of God was manifested, that He might destroy the works of the devil." (1 John 3:8)

"The devil, who deceived them, was cast into the lake of fire and brimstone where the beast and the false prophet are. And they will be tormented day and night forever and ever." (Revelation 20:10)

The Need in the Church

I mentioned earlier that troubled believers who are unable to get help from their own churches regularly seek out Patti and me. While each situation seems to have its own explanation, generally, these fit into one of the following categories:

25

THE DEVIL IN THE BACK PEW

- Some denominations and individuals do not believe the spiritual gifts of 1 Corinthians 12 are available today. Accordingly, no effort is made, other than perhaps praying at a distance.
- Some churches profess that it is impossible for a Christian to "have" a demon, so the problem is given a medical or behavioral label.
- Other churches acknowledge such occurrences, but are at a loss as to what to do to help.
- Still others acknowledge the possibility of demonization and profess belief that spiritual gifts are for today, but do not deal directly with the victims.
- Yet others appear to flat out disbelieve that satan and his demons are at work today – such beliefs are perceived as old fashioned or just superstition.

I have even read of a church leader who confided he did not want to confront "the devil" because he feared the enemy's retribution – that doing so would disturb his peaceful situation. Unfortunately, in an environment rooted in any of the above, the hurting person's church provides no relief.

I cite in this book many specific cases of freeing people from demonic activity. Modest research will reveal that many other sources testify likewise. Though we have never kept count of instances of our personal involvement in deliverance prayer, we certainly have encountered many hundreds of manifesting dark spirits in hundreds of people. And, significantly, many have been wonderfully freed. But, some have not! Why are particular folks not freed? In short, when referring to individuals,[10] the answer is

---

[10] This book addresses dark spiritual forces attacking individuals and does not purport to comment on dark forces of broader scope (over nations, for example). These are mentioned in the Bible, and we can reasonably conclude these spirits are of far greater power. It is also reasonable to conclude, therefore, that greater authority is required. Caution is therefore necessary.

26

Beginning the Discussion

simple: a dark spirit can remain as long as it has a "right" to be there. Break the "right," and it can be expelled; refuse to break the right (for example, decline to challenge[11] a sin stronghold[12]), and it can and will remain. Likely, forever. This is such a simple truth, but too much of the church appears to miss it.

When Jesus sent out his apostles, he said to them:

> *"And as you go, preach, saying, 'The kingdom of heaven is at hand.' Heal the sick, cleanse the lepers, raise the dead, **cast out demons**. Freely you have received, freely give."* (Matthew 10:7–8, emphasis mine)

Certainly, we do not see as much of the miraculous as we would like to, but it is absolutely untrue that we see none of it. I encourage you to refuse to back down when the enemy confronts you. Embrace the truths of Scripture and your God-given authority – and prevail.

Note: God will give you what you need, when you need it.

It is appropriate to mention two examples of misconceptions regarding deliverance-type prayers. Firstly, there are those who, in their zeal and with admirable words of faith, pronounce how easy it is to "cast the devil out" whenever he is encountered. They might speak words like, "You just tell the devil to leave, and he has to leave!" The problem with this mind-set is that you cannot override someone's free will. If the person wants to hang on to that which gives a dark spirit the right to remain, you can talk (pray,

---

[11]A dark spirit can uphold its right to stay put when there remains a willful, chosen sin. I believe that, when an individual is fighting against the sin or the sin propensity, this right can be broken. Scripture and experience support this.

[12]For purposes of discussion, the term "stronghold" is used to mean: a belief, sin, mind-set, vulnerability, or habit which opens the door to unscriptural behavior, fears, convictions, neuroses, etc. which the enemy can exploit. These range from simpler temptation to significant demonization.

THE DEVIL IN THE BACK PEW

shout, or command) till you are blue in the face, but *nothing will happen*. We will discuss later other common ways in which the enemy preserves his right to remain.

Secondly, there may be unreasonable expectations of the local church – that pastors, for example, should be able to easily rid anyone of an evil spirit. A real-life example might play out this way: the church secretary picks up the phone, and the caller requests, "My brother just got put into the local psychiatric ward. Can you have someone go there and cast the demon out of him?" Irrespective of the difficulties of entering the medical facility, and of having freedom to pray for the person, such situations have intricacies (and likely physical, mental, emotional, and perhaps pharmacological factors) which are not easily resolved by sending in the local pastor. We will talk about dealing with aspects of difficult situations but, all considered, we must follow the Holy Spirit's leading. And little about dealing with dark spirits is a one-step resolution.

Hopefully, a bit of the complexity of this topic is becoming apparent. The points I am emphasizing here are that:

- The enemy's tactics and activities need to be more broadly understood.
- We need more people who are comfortable with exercising their God-given authority.

Gaining this kind of experience and understanding not only equips us to help others get and stay free, but the improved insight helps us to be more victorious in our own life. We can all *get* free, and *stay* free.

How common are deliverance prayer sessions, or how common should they be? For a church of a few hundred, I believe this should be happening regularly. If there is an active prayer or counseling ministry, opportunities will arise. I cannot fathom any church, no matter how mature or stable, not having broken and hurting folks among the flock. These people need to be helped. It is unfortunate indeed that many houses of God rarely, or never,

Beginning the Discussion

cast demons out of hurting believers.[13]

Note:

- A large number of people sitting in churches carry painful hurts of the heart and need emotional, or inner, healing (see Chapter 5). Though many learn to manage their "stuff," inner healing prayer, when it confronts big hurts, can drive away the tormentors too. It is powerful, it works, and most victims do not realize a tormentor was active until it is gone.
- When someone is suffering physically, they very often have an emotional hurt as well, perhaps related to the suffering, but not necessarily. It is a mistake to assume a prayer need or a healing need is only for the physical body.
- Evidence of a deliverance prayer need can be easily dismissed or ignored – by the uninformed, the judgmental, and the fearful. Sadly, I have seen people with clear deliverance prayer needs either misunderstood or dismissed as being too difficult to deal with.
- When we were lay leaders of a prayer ministry at a church of several thousand, we were typically involved in many deliverance sessions *each week*.

Stand Your Ground

When you find yourself battling thoughts of doubt, despair, discouragement, or other negative emotion, it is a perfect time to employ a standard weapon of spiritual warfare. Proclaim this Biblical truth, aloud, if your situation permits, "Greater is He who is in me than he who is in the world."

---

[13]An underlying truth emphasized throughout this book is that dark spirits are actively involved in all types of persuasion and torment, not just the extreme cases. Importantly, the methodology and intensity of an effort to get rid of a demon is the same *whenever* the enemy is harassing, whether mildly and inconspicuously, as in a temptation, or demonstratively and brazenly, as in a demonization. Be equally intolerant of every type of incursion.

THE DEVIL IN THE BACK PEW

The first "He" is God (the Holy Spirit); the second "he" is satan. Or said another way, "Jesus, I know You are in me, and You are bigger than this lying devil who is trying to bring me down." This is from:

> *"You, dear children, are from God and have overcome them, because the one who is in you is greater than the one who is in the world."* (1 John 4:4)

The powers of darkness cannot withstand the truths of Scripture.

We will expand on these other Scripture-based, foundational truths later:

- Do not tolerate the enemy's lies, and do not permit him to plant seeds of fear in you. Jesus *does* love you. And He died for you!
- Your sins are *not* too big, nor have you fallen too often. Jesus' death on the cross is enough to cover it *all*.
- The devil is a liar. He cannot win in your life unless you give him permission.

Chapter 2

The Spirit Realm

Our Human Perception of the Spiritual

My personal prayer time always includes expressions of thanks for my many blessings. And nothing surpasses the gift of God choosing to reveal Himself to me. Bottom line, he invaded my heart and showed me that He is real. I have been fortunate in my Christian walk to have seen many miraculous events, but no miracle I have witnessed surpasses the one Jesus did inside of me three decades ago. As I write this, I don't have words to adequately express the elation and gratitude that I still feel today.

Jesus made this statement about conversion: *"No one can come to Me unless the Father who sent Me draws him ... "* (John 6:44). Though this truth can be studied from different perspectives, my emphasis here is that the Father's "drawing" emanates *from the spirit realm*, where God resides. For me, this "drawing" was a message which was initiated externally, but revealed *on the inside*. No clear English words came to mind, but I knew that my soul/spirit was being spoken to. And though I was unaccustomed to perceiving in this manner, I couldn't ignore it. You may have had a similar experience. Surely, when God reveals Himself to us, it is a life-changing, monumental event. And we celebrate that we fleshly

31

THE DEVIL IN THE BACK PEW

beings really do receive, and perceive, communication from the spiritual world!

But spiritual hearing has a dark side too. The enemy speaks to us (see Chapter 1, "What the Scriptures Say About satan and his demons," p. 22), and the world and the flesh also "draw" us. Sometimes it is unclear whether an impression comes from the world, the flesh, *or* the devil, or some combination of the three. For that reason, we must test our thoughts, hold onto the good, but reject the bad. I repeat the Bible's encouragement to *"test everything"* (1 Thessalonians 5:21 NIV). I will emphasize the following verse throughout this book:

"... we take captive every thought to make it obedient to Christ." (2 Corinthians 10:5 NIV)

This "testing" and "control" of thoughts is critical in spiritual warfare, and essential to live victoriously from day to day.

Is it difficult or uncomfortable for you to believe that you are being spoken to by spirits – both good and bad? Does this sound a bit far-fetched? Generally, in Western civilization, the spirit world is dismissed as fantasy, fairy-tale, or the like. In other parts of the globe, however, cultures freely accept the existence, and power, of the spirit realm.

I ask you now to consider your personal experience with *intersecting thoughts,* i.e., those which come to mind but are unrelated to anything you are doing, watching, reading, or otherwise thinking about. Consider the following. Do you occasionally have thoughts that seem to come "out of nowhere?"

- A person crosses your mind, and moments later the phone rings – and it is *that* person.
- You feel stressed or worried about someone, you call – and there is a problem.
- You have a hunch to call your spouse on the way home, and he/she needs you to pick up something.
- A piece of wisdom pops into your mind (do this; don't do

that) about a course of action you were not even thinking about – and it's a great idea.

Or, conversely:

- You have a suspicion that someone is taking advantage of you – and it proves totally false.
- You fear a person's (or people's) opinion of you or that they are angry with you – and it proves to be unfounded.
- You think inordinately of unfortunate events or topics of superstition, fearful that these may happen to you.
- You're trying to be disciplined in an area of your personal life, but tempting thoughts incessantly interrupt your thinking.

I suggest that some of these intersecting thoughts are planted by, or picked up from, the spirit realm (the Holy Spirit, angels, or demons), and are evidence that the spirit world is alive and active *in your life*. For now, all I suggest is that we be cautious and discerning. Often it is a challenge to identify the source.

Cultural Perspectives on satan

When our boys were young, as a family we regularly watched certain sci-fi TV reruns. These fantasies of explorers travelling to other galaxies were classic science fiction and, often, simple morality fables. The futuristic technology – food replicators, energy weapons, light-speed travel, "beaming" people here and there – was classic guy-stuff and good, clean fun. Only rarely was the subject matter of an episode objectionable enough to warrant turning it off.

On one occasion, I noticed in a preview that the upcoming episode was about the starship crew encountering the "devil." Thinking that watching this program with the family would not be a good idea, we skipped the show that night. A few days later, I questioned why I did not watch it to see how TV studios dealt with the topic, so I checked for the next showing, recorded it, and

THE DEVIL IN THE BACK PEW

watched it when the boys weren't around.

And what a surprise! I felt rather stupid for not having suspected the story line. Of course, as modern Western society would decree, *the devil is not real!* The details of the plot are not relevant, but the cultural positioning was as expected: the "devil" was merely a person masquerading as the enemy of God, scaring and manipulating folks for self-serving purposes. The starship crew exposed this fraud, and all those victimized lived happily ever after.

This example was one where the subject of the devil was dealt with in what is more or less mainline entertainment. Certainly, there have been, for decades, many explicitly dark offerings from the horror movie industry, and satanic organizations even list recommended films. For most people, even the satanic pictures are considered dark fantasy (merely "scary" movies), and viewers do not soberly consider the gravity of demonically related subject matter. To these moviegoers, it is simply not real.

But there also exists a segment of the population which embraces satan and the practices of the satanic "church." From the Christian's viewpoint, such involvement is grossly misguided and intrinsically evil. As I have many times witnessed the enemy's destructive work first-hand, I see no value whatsoever to expanding my knowledge of satanism or its methods. I trust completely that the Bible's revelations of the dark side are adequate for our ministry and life needs.

Church Perspectives on satan

In many Christian circles, dark spirits are not considered terribly relevant to daily life. If a person stays away from witchcraft and satanic cults, folks see themselves as essentially untouchable (and untouched) by satan and his demons. Other Christians flat-out disbelieve in dark spirits, or believe that, if they do exist, they have no impact on them. But, of course, the Bible tells a different story! And real-life experiences of many corroborate the Scriptural accounts. Indeed, the illustrations throughout this book bear wit-

34

The Spirit Realm

ness to demonic activity tangibly impacting God's people.

For a snapshot of present-day thinking on the demonic realm, a simple internet search reveals an abundance of content on satan, demonic possession, exorcism (the process of expelling an evil spirit), and the like. With many sources focusing on the Catholic Church's rite of exorcism, the topic is treated anywhere from an esoteric ecclesiastical concern to a subject deserving little serious attention. Some articles call satan "old school" or describe exorcists as the "crazy uncles" of the church, while others tell of a current increase in requests for help from people believed to be afflicted. Irrespective of public thought or the derision of secular journalists, the topic is getting attention.

Note also: The Catholic teaching on this subject suggests exorcism is only for the severely affected, and only to be administered by the specially appointed. The repeated references to a person being "possessed" (a frequently misapplied term) and admonishments about dangers related to the exorcism process paint a pretty grim picture of casting out demons.

Let me state here that I love the whole church of God, and all the various expressions of Christianity. I may wonder why a particular church "does what it does," but if it professes the roots of Biblical Christianity, I focus on our common love of Jesus, rather than the differences. Likewise, I love the Catholic Church in which I was raised, and which I attended for the first two decades of my life. Regarding the expulsion of dark spirits, however, the message of this book conflicts in a few major areas with the Catholic Church's proclaimed practice related to exorcism. I believe, and have experienced, for example, that neither is a specified ritual required, nor is any special church-sanctioned authority necessary. I feel strongly that this should be the business of everyday church leadership, and expelling a demon can be readily done by any solid Christian believer who knows what to do. Admittedly, there are tough, complicated situations which require experience and even professional help, but these are rare.

THE DEVIL IN THE BACK PEW

In our experience, we have often interacted with spirits which displayed the most unpleasant "temperaments," but these confrontations have *never* become ugly, uncomfortable, or unmanageable. And, *very importantly*, though the harassing spirit is admittedly unclean, the person victimized may not externally exhibit (or even be aware of!) the underlying cause for their torment or distress. In dealing with hurting people, it is wrong to assume a person is *not* demonized solely because they are able to behave or act "normally;" people can learn to manage the turmoil.

Although some who are demonized are able to control their internal discomfort, it is true that others are rather disagreeable or unlovable. From my observation, these people are also isolated socially. On several occasions, my heart has been stirred on behalf of a person who was not easy to be around. I have felt certain that, if I didn't reach out to them, no one else would. I confess my heart has not always been as soft as it is now in this regard. I have made the mistake of avoiding someone for whom I lacked patience. It is important to remember who the real enemy is; it is *not* the person who needs to be set free.

And what a wonderful blessing to see someone truly liberated from a life-stealing tormentor! Paul encourages us:

"We who are strong ought to bear with the failings of the weak and not to please ourselves. Each of us should please his neighbor for his good, to build him up." (Romans 15:1–2 NIV)

The ultimate question is: Is the devil real? Yes. Can he really get in and on people? Again, yes. But it is equally true that there can be much dark-spirit-caused, life-disrupting disturbance that falls far short of demonization. We will share many examples in the chapters that follow.

Biblical Perspectives on satan

The Christian church believes the angels were created prior to Adam. Protestant Christianity teaches that God created three

The Spirit Realm

archangels (chief angels), Michael, Gabriel, and lucifer, though other Christian traditions name more.[14] Isaiah tells how lucifer was seized with pride and attempted to gain power over other angels, and *"be like the Most High [God]:"*

> *"How you are fallen from heaven, O [l]ucifer, son of the morning! How you are cut down to the ground, You who weakened the nations! For you have said in your heart: 'I will ascend into heaven, I will exalt my throne above the stars [angels] of God; ... I will ascend above the heights of the clouds, **I will be like the Most High.**'"* (Isaiah 14:12–14, emphasis mine)

At some unknown point in time, lucifer fomented a rebellion against God, taking one third of the angels with him. In most places, the Bible refers to the post-rebellion lucifer as "satan" or "the devil." Significantly, it is absolutely incorrect to think of God and satan as similar adversaries, akin to opponents in a boxing ring. In truth, God is the *Creator*, satan is the *created*. This is illustrated below:

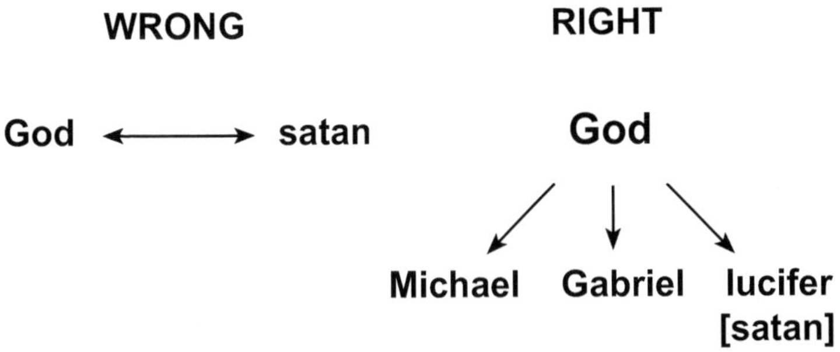

WRONG

RIGHT

God ⟷ satan

God

Michael Gabriel lucifer
[satan]

---

[14]The Catholic and Orthodox, as well as other churches which include the Apocrypha in the canon of Scripture, identify two additional archangels, Raphael and Jeremiel, named therein. Other noncanonical period books list as many as seven archangels.

THE DEVIL IN THE BACK PEW

How can the lesser possibly overcome the One who gave him every strength and ability he has?

In his epistles, Paul uses additional descriptors for spiritual and earthly forces, which some believe differ from satan and his demons. Referring to Jesus' position after the resurrection, Paul says He is now:

> *"... far above all **principality** and **power** and **might** and **dominion**, and every name that is named, not only in this age but also in that which is to come."* (Ephesians 1:21, emphasis mine)

And:

> *"For we do not wrestle against flesh and blood, but against **principalities**, against **powers**, against the **rulers** of the darkness of this age, against spiritual **hosts of wickedness** in the heavenly places."* (Ephesians 6:12, emphasis mine)

As Scripture does not explain the details of Paul's usage of these terms, we will continue to focus on the disposition of those dark powers which harass the individuals we encounter, and assume we have the authority we need at the time. The subject of authority over dark spirits is discussed more broadly in the section, "Understand Your Authority" (Chapter 9, p. 188).

demonic Power

In this section, we will probe aspects of the dark spiritual powers directed toward each of us. I address these in a Q/A format, responding to questions we are commonly asked.

Q. *How does satan get his power over us?*

A. Initially, satan obtained power over the earth[15] when Adam yielded it to him in the Garden of Eden, as told in Genesis 3.

---

[15]Jesus referred to satan as the *"ruler of this world"* (John 14:30), which authority he obtained when Adam fell.

The Spirit Realm

The power he gained was truly a legal right. Jesus won it back on Calvary, but satan will not be rendered wholly powerless until the events of the Book of Revelation take place. In the meantime, death remains certain here on earth, as do the other curses stemming from Adam's fall.

During Jesus' ministry, He gave His disciples power over the demons they encountered. This was not unlimited, open-ended authority over satan and his realm, but an ability to expel the dark spirits they met up with. This was necessary because individual people can be overcome by the influence and wiles of the enemy.

How do we become susceptible in this way? Most significantly, the enemy gains power over us individually when we are exposed to sin. Chosen sin is a "fall" of sorts, in some respects like Adam's, and gives the enemy the right to remain and do his dirty work. To the extent that sinful behavior is more extreme or entrenched or repeated, the strength of the enemy's attachment increases, and the greater the difficulty of severing the connection. In addition to willful sin, a person can become vulnerable to the enemy as a result of:

- unintentional or careless/reckless choices;
- unavoidable circumstances, such as a dysfunctional childhood home or inescapable destitution; or
- someone sinning against them, as in the case of sexual assault or an act of violence.

Regardless of the cause or source, a person might be traumatized so severely that he/she feels helpless and unable to break free of the emotional heaviness. Significantly, though, in my experience, the discomfort felt by the individual is only rarely discerned as being spiritual at the root. It is typically thought of as a bad memory or tough past experience. This is where Godly, informed people, walking in the power of Jesus, can bring help and freedom to those so afflicted.

The enemy gains his power over us when we sin or someone sins against us. The methods of dealing with that sin depend on

39

THE DEVIL IN THE BACK PEW

the details. Of course, if it's our own sin, it is simpler to identify and understand. We will talk about the complexities and the process of breaking the enemy's rights in coming chapters.

Q. *How is this connected to woundedness?*

A. Anyone experienced in dealing with dark spirits has observed the role of the demonic in emotional brokenness. The demons are quite skilled at exploiting and hanging on to heart wounds of all types.

As mentioned in the previous section, such woundedness can result from a person's own mistakes or poor choices. The most severe pain, however, typically stems from an individual being sinned against, and this occurs most often in childhood. These hurts may or may not have been inflicted intentionally, but commonly the perpetrator is someone who was similarly victimized.

Some of the most severe situations I have encountered concerned the *absence* of involvement (or provision or protection) rather than specific harmful actions. Quite often the hurts result from a parent or guardian appearing not to *want* the child, nor to be loving or dependable or even present. In these latter cases, a child may have to find ways to protect themselves or provide for their own basic needs.

Below is a simplified description of the process of extricating dark attachments related to emotional hurt:

- Tender, heartfelt prayers of healing, comfort, and blessing are spoken over the individual, encouraging the person to receive, now/today, Jesus' healing *back at the point and time of the offense,* especially if in childhood. This part of the process should not be rushed.
  Note: Jesus is not restricted by time in His ability to heal and bless.
- A dark spirit is exposed by the power of the Holy Spirit's presence.
- The dark spirit's rights are identified and broken; sin and

40

The Spirit Realm

unforgiveness issues are resolved.

- The spirit is confronted and expelled.
- The root or foothold of the hurt is removed.

We have witnessed this process unfold many times. It remains awesome and glorious. It also affirms to us how the enemy hangs on by trick, obfuscation, deception, and the like.

Q. *Should I have personal fear of the enemy?*

A. You need only fear the enemy if you are willingly serving him, because then you have made yourself vulnerable. Instead, let Jesus truly be Lord of your life. Confess your blunders, seek to serve Him, and rest in the fact that *"He who is in you is greater than he who is in the world"* (1 John 4:4). Should you fear the enemy? No! Again, he has no special power over you except what you give him or permit him to hang on to.

From my observation, the enemy's favorite tactic against those who profess Christ is to get us to believe lies. Stubbornly refuse to let down your guard! Corrie ten Boom wisely noted that the fear of demons is from the demons themselves.[16]

Q. *When praying against dark spirits, can they get on me?*

A. Assuming you are a sincere and committed practicing Christian, active interaction with the demonic brings no special concerns. It requires a level of care, rather like driving: pay attention to what you are doing and obey the laws (i.e., Bible teachings), but there is no reason to be fearful or uneasy. You can safely get where you want to go. Nevertheless, relevant New Testament warnings were made to Christians, not unbelievers. If you sense an unclean presence when praying for someone, get their permission and expel it! And follow up with a cleansing prayer after praying deliverance prayers over others. (See Chapter 11, "Always Pray a Cleansing Prayer after Praying for Anyone," p. 246.)

---

[16]Prince, *They Shall Expel Demons,* 10.

THE DEVIL IN THE BACK PEW

Q. *Are demons fallen angels?*

A. Biblical arguments can be made supporting the belief that demons are fallen angels, while a few verses seem to hint at other possibilities. Regardless, there appears no practical benefit to making a distinction; we just need to know how to deal with them. And that will be discussed. A few relevant verses:

We know fallen angels have been cast down:

> *"God did not spare the angels who sinned, but cast them down to hell and delivered them into chains of darkness, to be reserved for judgment." (2 Peter 2:4)*

> *"... into the everlasting fire prepared for the devil and his angels." (Matthew 25:41)*

We know demons do not want to be cast down into what appears to be the same place:

> *"They [the demons] begged Him [Jesus] that He would not command them to go out into the abyss." (Luke 8:31)*

Q. *How powerful are demons?*

A. The verses cited under "What the Scriptures Say About satan and his demons" (Chapter 1, p. 22), give examples of the abilities and activities of the dark realm. Revisiting a few points:

The account of Paul's thorn suggests an ability to torment:

> *"... a thorn in the flesh was given to me, a messenger of [s]atan to buffet me ..." (2 Corinthians 12:7)*

Note: The Greek word for "messenger" (*aggelos*) is translated "angel" 96% of the time.

Jesus' parable of the sower gives evidence of satan's ability to influence thoughts:

> *"... [s]atan comes immediately and takes away the word that was sown in their hearts." (Mark 4:15)*

Strong's Concordance defines "angel" variously as "messenger,"

42

The Spirit Realm

"envoy," "guardian," "executioner of God's purposes," one with "charge over earthly elements," etc. A search of the Book of Revelation alone yields 72 references to *angel*, the vast majority of which give evidence of special authority or enormous power. How effective, then, are demonic powers? It is obvious that there is much brokenness in the world: wars, hunger, persecution, disease, cruelty, broken homes, and the like. And death, perhaps the greatest "cost" of Adam's fall, remains inevitable for each of us. The prince of this world, satan, still has considerable influence, but not full and free reign. Scripture gives examples of satan seeking permission to have his way – *and being limited.*

The Lord restrained satan in his attack of Job:

> "... you [satan] incited Me [the Lord] against him [Job], to destroy him without cause. ... And the LORD said to [s]atan, '... spare his life.'" (Job 2:3, 6)

Jesus told of satan's request to persecute the disciples:

> "... [s]atan has asked for you, that he may sift you as wheat." (Luke 22:31)

Jesus was speaking to Peter, but the word "you" is plural, meaning satan was pursuing all of the disciples and, by extension, mankind.

And, most significantly, Jesus told us we could staunch satan's efforts when He instructed us to pray: *"[D]eliver us from the evil one"* (Matthew 6:13). This is important! Why would Jesus have recommended we pray specifically for protection from the evil one if it was not the Father's desire to grant such protection? Yes, demons have power, but there are limitations.

The Q/A above, along with other characteristics of the enemy mentioned earlier, form a foundation of understanding for confrontation with the demonic.

We will provide evidence of the superior Godly power available to us. And though we will discuss many revealed truths about exercising Godly authority, there is still much we do not know.

43

THE DEVIL IN THE BACK PEW

How, for example, this process actually works and where the "lines" are drawn (i.e., God's economy), is a mystery to the most learned. And a great deal appears paradoxical:

- Jesus paid the price of redemption for us all, but satan is still the prince of this world.
- Jesus was victorious on the cross, but committed believers still fall short of victorious lives.
- Death still reigns, yet resurrection and eternal life in Jesus are guaranteed.
- The enemy can still wreak much havoc, but we have an ability to overcome.
- Jesus has come as Redeemer, but He has not yet come in the fullness of His power.

Despite all this, we can still exercise the authority of God and expel demons that we encounter in God's people.

I have included additional Scriptures relevant to the activities, authority and power of angels in Appendix II.[17]

Healing Prayer Can Stir dark spirits

In the prior chapter, I mentioned how our participating in a soaking prayer ministry led to heavy involvement in deliverance prayer. A brief explanation of the soaking prayer process will help to show the connection between prayer and exposing enemy activity in people's lives. Later chapters will discuss dealing with strongholds, various types of enemy harassment, and "open doors" (enemy access points).

As described above, the soaking prayer process that we were part of involved teams of two to three people praying privately for individuals for 40 to 60 minutes, twice a month. Typically, at the initial meeting with a prayee, there would be a brief chat about the

---

[17]For an in-depth study of the angelic realm, see Bobby Conner, *Heaven's Host: The Assignments of Angels, Both Faithful and Fallen* (see Bibliography).

44

The Spirit Realm

specifics of the prayer need and about the person's connection to God, to the church, and to fellow believers. If there were indications of emotional hurts, the team would explore family history, interpersonal relationships, marital issues, history of trauma, fears, and so forth, as seemed appropriate.

On the subject of heart hurts, I believe it a fundamental truth that each one of us has some degree of "brokenness" in our lives. This fallen world leaves its scars. Such brokenness may stem from a particular physical or emotional hurt in our past, or it may result simply from a difficult life. Some folks are well aware of the emotional impact of these circumstances, and they have processed them, either in healthy ways or in not-so-healthy ways. Others have swept the memories away; they have hidden (or compartmentalized) the pain, and there has been no processing.

The prayer process is then begun, with the pray-ers physically surrounding the prayee, laying their hands on the person's shoulders, and calling on God. The pray-ers speak blessings of every sort: healing, comfort, freedom from pain, emotional peace, rest, abundance, prosperity, fruitfulness of life, good relationships, and so on, as the Spirit leads. When the sweetness of the Holy Spirit has been allowed to rest on the person receiving prayer, there is virtually always evidence of the spiritual transaction which has taken place. The person feels truly blessed, loved, bathed in grace, cherished by God, encouraged, and so forth. From my experience, it is rare indeed that a person, during and after receiving such prayer, does not "sense" the love of God in a very real way.

To the extent there is a demonic presence affecting the prayee, that dark spirit will be made *very* uncomfortable by this intimate, heartfelt, faith-based prayer. If the person is demonized to some extent (an actual demonic presence in, on, or about them), that presence will often become agitated, and there will be visible physical evidence or some sort of manifestation. It is appropriate then that the spirit be confronted.

Simply put, the deliverance prayer process can be described as

45

THE DEVIL IN THE BACK PEW

exposing dark spirits, nullifying their rights, and *commanding them out.* During the prayer process, it is generally necessary to review the prayee's past and assist him/her in making things right with the Lord (confessing, forgiving, renouncing). Strongholds must be identified and canceled, and all open doors acknowledged and closed. This warfare type of prayer explicitly welcomes the Holy Spirit, destroys the work of the enemy, and leaves the prayee in peace. With Patti and others, I have watched this work just wonderfully on seemingly countless occasions.

Jesus' ministry did not distinguish between deliverance prayer and praying for healing.

- When Jesus healed Peter's mother-in-law, Scripture states He *"rebuked"* the fever:

  "So He stood over her and rebuked the fever, and it left her. And immediately she arose and served them." (Luke 4:39)

- When Jesus healed the woman bent over for 18 years, He advised the ruler of the synagogue that satan had the woman *"bound:"*

  "So ought not this woman, being a daughter of Abraham, whom [s]atan has bound—think of it—for eighteen years, be loosed from this bond on the Sabbath?" (Luke 13:16)

Can a Christian Really Have a demon?

I begin with a personal experience, follow it with a corroborating example from author Derek Prince, and finally review the Acts 10 account of the apostle Peter's change of heart concerning one of his core beliefs.

The Spirit Realm

My Experience

For the first ten years or so of our Christian walk, Patti and I attended churches of a particular, well-known Protestant denomination. Those years were awesome experiences and gave us great foundational training and practice. In addition to the traditional Protestant tenets of the faith, we were taught – and it seemed totally reasonable, Biblical, and practical – that a Christian believer, a temple of the Holy Spirit, *could not* be demonized. This was impossible, a contradiction. How could a dark spirit inhabit anyone who was saved and whose *"body is the temple of the Holy Spirit"* (1 Corinthians 6:19)? This sounded totally logical, and we had no difficulty accepting this as truth.

Fast forward several years, and I am at an informal home prayer meeting, where a group of believers is seeking God, interceding for community and national needs, and praying for one another. As the prayer for individuals came around to one particular man, he became visibly agitated and started muttering, his face showing strong emotion and discomfort. It seemed obvious that some sort of dark spiritual presence was beginning to manifest. People in attendance immediately began commanding this *spirit* out. It was a rather chaotic scene, and it was the first time I had ever seen unquestionably demonic activity in (on/near) someone. Significantly, this individual was a recognized church leader, basically the assistant to his pastor. The prayers commanding the demon out continued for several minutes, whereupon a voice boldly spoke, proclaiming, "I will let him do works for God, but I'm not leaving!"[18]

To be clear, in Christian circles, we may sometimes hear a comment like, "I sensed the Spirit saying […] to me" when they per-

---

[18]To any reader who may be taken aback by this demon's attempt to assert itself, be advised it was singing a most familiar tune. Virtually any time a demon is cornered and must speak, it attempts to intimidate and make claims. The "I'm not leaving" comment is typical, as are "I have a right to be here," "You can't make me leave," "He/She wants me here," and so on. Subsequent chapters will show these are easily resolved.

47

THE DEVIL IN THE BACK PEW

ceived in their mind a holy insight, spiritual message, or word of wisdom/knowledge (see 1 Corinthians 12). That was not the case here: this person spoke audibly, with his own voice, and all heard. Regarding how, or if, the dark spirit was eventually overcome, I do not know. I can say pretty confidently, though, that no one present knew how to handle what happened.

This occurrence was tough to reconcile with any belief that a "saved" Christian cannot be demonized. The person was not delusional or psychotic, the only other possible explanations I could come up with. The thought of a demon in/on a Christian believer – and leader! – lay outside my frame of reference.

The Experience of Lydia Prince

In another example, Derek Prince tells the story of how his wife was delivered from a demon of fear (related to claustrophobia) which had tormented her for decades. Stemming from being accidentally closed in a small, dark closet during childhood, she would not take elevators, until the spirit was exposed and cast out. Curiously, she was only in the closet for a few moments (until an aunt responded to her screaming and pounding), but in that brief time, a spirit attached itself soundly enough to hang on for many years. I cite this case because of Lydia Prince's long-term, successful ministry in the city of Jerusalem. For twenty years prior to being delivered of this tormentor (again, she did not even recognize that it was a spirit), she led a Christian outreach facility for orphaned young girls. Her leadership and accomplishments for the Kingdom were significant and undeniable, yet she was victimized by a demonic presence![19]

These two examples give evidence of persons in Christian leadership who were being actively tormented by dark spirits. They clearly prove the dark connection, but are incompatible with the beliefs of those who maintain a real Christian cannot have a demon. For those, it seems, a *change of mind* is suggested.

---

[19]Prince, *They Shall Expel Demons*, 81–82.

The Spirit Realm

A Change of Mind

I turn to the Biblical account of Peter having his mind changed by circumstances and the revelation of God. Prior to his experience described in Acts 10, Peter had never associated with Gentiles; this was forbidden by Jewish law. But circumstances sovereignly orchestrated by God changed his heart. The account in Acts tells the story of how Peter became involved with a Roman centurion named Cornelius, and a ministry door opened to the Gentiles.

Cornelius, a devout Gentile, had a vision in which an angel told him to send to a nearby town for the apostle Peter. At nearly the same time, Peter was praying and had a vision in which he was advised to go with the men sent from Cornelius, even though doing so was in violation of Jewish law (which prohibited association with Gentiles, who were considered unclean). Since Peter's vision explicitly advised him: *"Do not call anything impure that God has made clean"* (Acts 10:15 NIV), he and a few disciples journeyed to the centurion's house. On arriving there, Cornelius explained to Peter the angel's instruction to send for him: *"Now therefore, we are all present before God, to hear all the things commanded you by God"* (v.33). Accordingly, Peter proceeded to tell the gathering about Jesus and, while he was speaking, the Holy Spirit fell on the Gentiles present, and they spoke in tongues and praised God.

For Peter, this was a colossal paradigm shift, completely outside his expectation and contrary to the Jewish belief about Gentiles having low standing with God. Prior to this, as with Jesus' ministry, the disciples' outreach was limited to the children of Israel (the Jews). Following the revelation by supernatural intervention, the Gentiles were baptized, and Peter continued to minister to them. Who could argue that the disciples should not abandon their former beliefs and share the story of Jesus with the Gentiles?

Likewise, how do we argue that casting a spirit out of a believer is somehow improper, when Jesus Himself describes a person who does so as one who *"works a miracle"* (Mark 9:39)? Plainly, this

THE DEVIL IN THE BACK PEW

supernatural act is something we do not (cannot!) do on our own; it only occurs with God's intervention and miraculous empowerment. And His approval and blessing.

We humans are comprised of body, soul, and spirit. Some writers state that a demon can only inhabit a Christian's body or soul, but never the spirit. Perhaps that argument is sound, but I choose not to join the debate. I put it in the category of a Kingdom truth about which I understand little, and involve myself in what I do know for sure: God has given us the ability to cast demons out of His people!

Lastly, of all the many demon-confronting deliverance sessions I have seen or participated in, as well as every one mentioned in this book, I know of none where the victim was *not* a Christian. In the section, "Should You Pray Deliverance Prayers for an Unbeliever?" (Chapter 10, p. 208), we will talk about the danger of expelling a demon from a person who is not a practicing Christian and actively in community with other believers.

The Gospel of John tells us that satan comes *"to steal, and to kill, and to destroy"* (John 10:10). No level of holiness or Godliness we might attain will cause the enemy to give up on us, thinking, as it were, "They're out of reach – too holy – I'll never be able to make them fall." Our enemy, satan, tempted Jesus and the apostles. He will not cease coming after each one of us. As mentioned in the opening paragraph of this book, this subject matter is real. My own personal best defense is to *never* drop my guard.

> *"[Y]our adversary the devil walks about like a roaring lion seeking whom he may devour."* (1 Peter 5:8)

Perspectives on Hell

Though it is beyond the scope of this book to study hell itself, I feel compelled to share a few relevant accounts. A quote from 17th century physicist and philosopher, Blaise Pascal, is enlightening:

The Spirit Realm

"Meditation on hell has filled paradise with saints."[20] Hell is certainly relevant to this discussion, considering that every demon is attempting to escort us there, and getting rid of demons is what this book is about.

An Encounter, in Detail

Some friends of Stanley had suggested he contact our ministry about getting prayer for healing of old emotional wounds. Questioning how the ministry works, he called and we spoke on the phone for a few minutes, agreeing to meet later for coffee.

Stanley, a man in his mid-fifties, seemed a bright, clear-minded thinker who carried some old pain. He wanted to understand if "soaking prayer" might be beneficial for him. We spoke of personal interests and experiences, then of our Christian beliefs and the specifics of the prayer process. Without going into great detail, Stanley explained that he came to pursue the Lord in his late twenties after experiencing a profound dream or vision of descending into hell. He did not share much more at the time, but emphasized with the utmost gravity and sincerity that hell was "100% hopelessness." Our conversation ended, but that description about the "hopelessness" really struck me. I had never heard anyone speak of hell or damnation with so great an emphasis on that word, but "hopelessness" seemed so accurate and all-encompassing and, indeed, terrifying!

I had already begun writing this book at the time of our first meeting, and Stanley's words and experiences were drawing me. I asked him if we could connect again so he could share more. He willingly obliged. Stanley said it had been many years since he shared the story; he had stopped doing so for it had not been well received. In his words:

---

[20]Fr Gabriele Amorth, *An Exorcist Explains the Demonic* (Sophia Institute Press, Manchester, NH, 2016), 141.

THE DEVIL IN THE BACK PEW

"No one really wanted to hear about hell. Nor could they understand what I saw. The truth is, there are no words to fully explain what I understood in that moment of eternity."

Stanley Pre-Christ

When we got together, Stanley began by stating, "I was as dark a man as you've ever seen; I thought evil night and day." He explained it was his habit to purposely stir evil thoughts in order to rid his mind of any semblance of conscience. Since he adamantly wanted to believe there was no God, he felt it was necessary that he have no conscience. He added that he would have been right at home and comfortable with the worst of people in prisons.

He described his mother as "pretty bad," and stated that violence was "in" his granddad. When he was very young (grade school and before), he actually wanted to be a professional killer, and he continued in his desire to kill people until he was twenty-eight years old. He also had recurring dreams of torturing and killing individuals that he didn't like.

When Stanley was nine years old, a seed was planted by his grandmother. She told him, "God is knocking at the door of your heart." He replied angrily, "You mean Jesus wants to come inside of me and know what I'm thinking?" When she said yes, he stated it felt like "someone reached inside of my chest and banged on the door of my heart within me. It shocked and jarred me so much I shook all over." But Stanley did not like this *intrusion*.

He continued, "In that moment I hardened my heart and became very angry, and said to her very hatefully, 'There is no one who will ever come into my heart and know what I'm thinking! Never!'" He did not want anyone to know that God had perhaps just left a mark on his heart, or to know about his hateful, murderous thoughts. It is noteworthy that, from this encounter onward, Stanley was plagued with thoughts of suicide. Additionally, he recalled, "From that time on, I wanted nothing to do with my grandmother."

The Spirit Realm

Throughout his life, Stanley "knew" that his destination was hell, and he likewise "knew" he couldn't bear it. He also had the insight ("knew") that all that existed in the world was temporary, even the sun, moon, stars, and things of this earth. And from the time he was young, he wanted an understanding of what was on the "other side" of death.

Darkness Revealed

Stanley had recurring dreams and visions of falling, and he wanted to know what was at the bottom. On one occasion, he arrogantly spoke out, demanding an answer, "I fear nothing! What's at the bottom?"

In response, Stanley sensed that an angel had hold of him and told him to reach out and "touch the wall" as he descended. He tried, but felt nothing, realizing there was a vast gulf and that he couldn't escape to the other side. A voice then told him to, "Look down," but not wanting to, he refused. Eventually Stanley cast his eyes below, and he saw a mysterious fire that didn't look like fire as he knew it. It burned as if to consume, yet it did not consume; it was fire, but it gave no light.

While descending, he began to hear a great noise beneath him, and as he drew closer, he recognized it "as horrible, wretched screams and the sound of gnashing teeth." Interestingly, at the time of this dream, Stanley had no knowledge of the Bible or any reference to teeth gnashing in torment. Stanley further explained, "The screams indicated absolute 100% hopelessness, and you can multiply that by a thousand times. When I recognized that these images were people (in an instant, I saw a thousand faces), I *had* to wake up! I knew my destiny!

"I didn't sleep the rest of that night. I was too scared to sleep, too scared to close my eyes, and too scared to go to work the next day. I turned to pot and drink for escape."

53

THE DEVIL IN THE BACK PEW

Eyes Opened

For the next year, Stanley continued to hide from his fear by numbing himself with marijuana and alcohol. At one point, he had not been drinking or doing drugs for "a day or two," and found himself as sober as he'd "been in a long, long time." He began to question who he was. He felt dead inside and wanted to die, but he knew his destiny. And he wanted rest.

Stanley asked himself how he could change his way of thinking, but he realized it was impossible. It would take a miracle. In the little he knew about Jesus, Stanley was aware that He was "a man of miracles."

As he sat alone thinking, he perceived a presence of both good and of evil in the room. A voice then spoke saying these exact words, "Stanley, you *know* there is God."[21] The voice profoundly scared Stanley and, shaking, he ran into the kitchen for a glass of water. He tried to deny the voice, but couldn't get it out of his mind. After a day or two, at his wife's suggestion, he invited to his house a high school friend who was studying to be a Christian missionary.

Stanley persisted in posing many questions to his old acquaintance, including, "Is it possible to know and talk with God? What on the earth is permanent? And what is there, on this earth, that I can possibly trust?" Stanley added that his queries were somewhat mixed with anger, and that he was even threatening to his friend as he demanded truth.

The friend replied with simple answers, and when he responded that you could trust the Bible, it "nearly knocked the breath out" of Stanley. The friend then answered his next question, "Who is this Jesus?" by showing what the Bible said about Him.

Finally, Stanley asked him about the door he could see in his heart, from his grandmother's prayer. The friend responded that it was a door only Stanley could open, and that he could use it

---

[21]Stanley was emphatic that these were the precise words spoken to him, emphasizing the "one-ness" and uniqueness of God.

54

The Spirit Realm

to invite Jesus in. Stanley sent his friend on his way and went to his room. He felt a "great springtime peace" and perceived a gentle light shining within him making him "all clean." For the first time, he felt like living, saying to himself, "I've got to find out who this Jesus is!" Stanley directed his life toward Jesus, and has not turned back.

Recapping the intensity and reality of his entire experience, Stanley concluded, "This was total desolation, with no way out. If you could give someone one millisecond of that experience, they would turn [to Christ]."

I restate here that Stanley is a clear-minded man, and there is no evidence whatsoever of confused thinking. In speaking with him on several occasions, I have no doubt about the accuracy of his account. He was serious and solemn as he told the story, and it was obviously a profound and life-changing encounter. I add that there is nothing in his description that is incompatible with what the Bible says about hell. Indeed, his words add human emotion and clarity to what most of us might only imagine an exposure to hell would likely reveal.

A Deathbed Experience

I share an additional account of the horrors of hell. As it was not possible for me to speak directly with the woman who told of this experience, I'll cover it briefly. To be clear, I do not disbelieve the story, but I was not able to question her or follow up in any way.

A good friend's mother had an acquaintance whose husband had recently died. The man was, without argument, a rebellious and ungodly soul. As he was nearing his final breath, he repeatedly mumbled complaining, "What's that smell? What's that smell?" There was no odor in the room. At the end, he cried in pain, "My feet are burning ..." Then he died.

THE DEVIL IN THE BACK PEW

St. Faustina

A 20th century saint, canonized by Pope John Paul II, Sister Maria Faustina detailed in her diary a spiritual experience of being led by an angel to the "chasms of hell." She describes seven general tortures experienced by all:

- Loss of God.
- Perpetual remorse of conscience.
- Unchanging conditions.
- Spiritual fire which penetrates the soul without destroying it.
- Continual darkness and a terrible suffocating smell, with yet an ability to see devils and souls of the damned, as well as each other and all evil.
- The constant company of satan.
- Horrible despair, hatred of God, vile words, curses, and blasphemies.

Additionally, she states: "There are special tortures destined for particular souls" ("in caverns and pits of torture where one form of agony differs from another"), and each of these souls "undergoes terrible and indescribable sufferings related to the manner in which it had sinned." She further notes "one common element: that most of the souls in hell are those who disbelieved there is a hell."[22]

Joseph Stalin's Final Moments

Whether a perspective on satan or on hell might be debatable, but Joseph Stalin's moment of death is certainly disturbing.

Some years ago, I heard Christian author and teacher, Ravi Zacharias, speak of Stalin's death, as related by his daughter, Svetlana. Stalin, the brutal Soviet dictator whose reign of terror directly resulted in the deaths of millions of his own citizens, was extremely agitated as the end neared. In his final moment, he

---

[22]Amorth, *An Exorcist Explains the Demonic,*138–139.

The Spirit Realm

half-raised himself off his bed and defiantly shook his fist toward heaven. He then threw his head back and died.

I cannot help but believe that our loving God made a last attempt to reach out to this hard-hearted man, irrespective of the evil he had perpetrated. For our God is good, and the power of the cross can cover the worst of sin – *if* we are willing to humble ourselves and submit to Him.

I find these accounts chilling ... But they remind me again of my gratitude for salvation.

Chapter 3

Warfare Basics and Recognizing the enemy

We saw in the previous chapter that spending time in direct prayer for an individual can disturb a dark presence. The demons get very uncomfortable when prayers are spoken which honor God, reject the demon's authority, expose the enemy's lies, are expressions of confession or forgiveness, and the like. Doing so is a most effective way for a Spirit-led Christian with minimal training to uncover and undermine the work of the enemy.

In this and succeeding chapters, we will give examples of the enemy holding ground where his presence was not suspected. After many years of encountering these well-hidden tormentors, I know they have a greater ability to conceal themselves than most believers have to recognize their presence – either in themselves or in others – without the Holy Spirit's guidance.

Praying Against the enemy

It has been shown that our comprehension of the spiritual realm is imperfect, but, importantly, our full understanding is not required. We pray in response to what has been *revealed*, and we trust in the *Scriptural promises* of the Lord.

Praying against dark forces should not follow a formula. It

would be a mistake to be inflexible when undertaking the process. However, there are basic principles and Scriptural truths which provide guidance.

When Patti and I initially meet with a person for prayer, I commonly say, "You know, we're nice people, but if God doesn't show up, not much is going to happen!" This is both an instructional truth for the prayee, as well as a reminder to us that the load is not ours to bear. I am not discounting the special skills that the Lord bestows on certain individuals for use in the Kingdom, e.g., the abilities to encourage, or to show love, compassion, understanding, and the like. But I am asserting that the "heavy lifting" is all the Lord's power and enablement. The people doing the praying miss the point if they think the benefits of prayer depend on their eloquence, spiritual superiority, or any other qualification. The fruit is from our wonderful God, and that fruit reveals both how He loves His children, and the authority He has given us to speak blessings. About the only responsibilities I feel comfortable assuming are those of conveying God's love and of getting out of the way when He is working.

In addition to Paul's list of spiritual gifts from 1 Corinthians 12 (see Chapter 9, "As Limited," p. 189), he discusses certain gifts more broadly in Romans:

> *"We have different gifts, according to the grace given us. If a man's gift is prophesying, let him use it in proportion to his faith. If it is serving, let him serve; if it is teaching, let him teach; if it is encouraging, let him encourage; if it is contributing to the needs of others, let him give generously; if it is leadership, let him govern diligently; if it is showing mercy, let him do it cheerfully."* (Romans 12:6–8 NIV)

Employing these and other giftings in a prayer setting seems to open the door to better results – for both healing and breaking the power of the enemy. Though the topics below are discussed in the context of warfare prayer, they are universally true and applicable to all prayer and intercession.

THE DEVIL IN THE BACK PEW

Pray According to the Lord's Prayer

Most Christian denominations place heavy emphasis on the Lord's prayer. After all, these were Jesus' own words when He taught His disciples how best to pray. Familiar to most Christians, the prayer begins: *"Our Father in heaven, Hallowed be your name"* (Matthew 6:9), a statement of praise and honor to God our Father. It is instructive that the prayer begins by honoring God.

Immediately following are the familiar words: *"Your Kingdom come. Your will be done, On earth as it is in heaven"* (v.10), phrasing which seems to affirm the establishment of God's Kingdom here, and that it might be as glorious here as it is in heaven.

Exploring this wording in depth is beyond the scope of this book, but one point is relevant: the verbs in Kingdom *"come"* and your will *"be done"* are, in the original Greek, in the imperative mood, which means they are commands, not requests or affirmations. Therefore, according to Jesus' instructions, we are to *command* the Kingdom of God to *come,* and to *command* the Father's will *be done* – proclaiming, if you will, *"Come,* Kingdom of God … *Be done,* will of God …"

The discussion below will emphasize the significance of our words, and our faith, for the situations into which we pray. Our words speak life, or they speak death: *"Death and life are in the power of the tongue"* (Proverbs 18:21).

The Lord's Presence

Kris Vallotton[23] is one of my favorite Christian teachers. He is an insightful author, pastor, and teacher, is prophetically very gifted, and has an untypically casual style. On a few occasions, I have heard him state, "Thanksgiving is our response to God's works; praise is our response to God's nature; worship is our response to God's presence."

---

[23]Kris Vallotton is Senior Associate Leader at Bethel Church in Redding, CA. He has authored many books and regularly speaks around the world.

To me, the importance of God's (the Holy Spirit's) presence cannot be overstated. It is at the core of what brought me into relationship with God, and it is what motivates me daily. I learned early in my Christian walk that you cannot be in the presence of the Lord and *not* be changed. And change is what we seek when we pray for people. It is especially, and often immediately, visible when we pray against demonic torment in someone's life.

My focus in this section is on the importance and significance of inviting and welcoming the Holy Spirit into the situation. It is about His power – which accompanies Him because of Who He is.

In the American King James Version of the Bible, Psalm 22:3 states that the Lord *"inhabits"* the praises of His people. Other translations render the Hebrew word with some variant of "enthroned." *Strong's Concordance* defines the root word as "dwells in," "inhabits," "abides," and the like. The meaning is clear: the Holy Spirit comes near when God is praised, worshiped, and welcomed. This is a spirit-realm transaction. I believe the presence of God is *indispensable* to effective prayer. As stated earlier, if God doesn't show up, not much is going to happen. It is *all* about God.

Dispelling Doubt

Most believers are familiar with Matthew's account of Jesus walking on water on the Sea of Galilee. The details reveal a very important lesson relevant to healing and warfare prayer.

After miraculously feeding five thousand people, Jesus ordered his disciples into a boat and directed them to the other side of the lake. In the middle of the night, the wind was against them, and they were struggling to make headway. The disciples reacted in fear when they saw what they thought was a ghost walking on the water, but Jesus identified Himself and they relaxed. Peter said to Jesus: *"Lord, if it is You, command me to come to You on the water"* (Matthew 14:28), and Jesus said, *"Come"* (v.29). Peter then stepped onto the water and began walking toward Jesus, but he soon became afraid and began to sink. Crying out to Jesus, Peter

61

THE DEVIL IN THE BACK PEW

exclaimed, *"Lord, save me!"* (v.30). Jesus stretched out His hand and caught him, asking, *"[W]hy did you doubt?"* (v.31).

For the record, let us not pass judgment on Peter for any character shortcoming in this whole event. But it is significant that, in the presence of Jesus – Son of God, indivisible member of the triune Godhead, and Creator of the universe – the *doubt* which Peter allowed to creep into the situation actually *killed a miracle while it was happening!* I do not pretend to know how this all works in God's economy. And I am not suggesting that God cannot do whatever He wants because of some overpowering "rule." Nevertheless, in this case, as well as others in Scripture, His blessing seems contingent upon, or at least to some extent subject to, our heart attitude.

Who among us has not struggled with doubt (i.e., faith) from time to time? This story shines a bright light on the damaging (power-stealing) effect of bringing doubt into a situation where we want God to move. Of course, not one of us is perfect. And, of course, we all battle doubtful thoughts. To the extent, though, that we can dispel doubt – purposefully and intentionally push doubtful thoughts out – we remove a barrier to seeing God move.

Spending Time

Our church involvement for the last three decades has been in congregations where direct, close-up prayer for individuals was common practice. Pastors, leaders, or other members prayed for any and all who had needs. With variation in style, the prayer was generally brief, typically a few minutes at most.

Though this is a great approach, and I have countless times participated as both a pray-er and prayee, it fits best as an end-of-service type prayer, openly offered to all comers. When one has a more severe problem, though, protracted prayer seems more fruitful.[24] Specifically, concerning the dark-spirit subject matter

---

[24]Methods and practices described in this book should not be construed as "the only way to do" any of what is suggested. Indeed, some minis-

62

of this book, brief prayers seldom "disturb" demonic elements which are harassing the prayee. From my experience, I have seen many, many occasions where a dark spiritual force has not become demonstrably apparent until it has been made uncomfortable by a longer exposure to prayer. It is as if a demon can tolerate a limited amount of Godly speech and activity, but then it can remain hidden no longer.

I have also observed a more rapid disclosure of enemy presence in faith-filled, special services or conference gatherings,[25] where dark spirits seem less able to contain themselves. Apparently the intense, God-seeking environment, like protracted prayer, is too much for them. A few of the demon encounters described in this book are from such events.

The enemy of Your Soul

> *"The thief [satan] does not come except to steal, and to kill, and to destroy. I [Jesus] have come that they may have life, and that they may have it more abundantly."* (John 10:10)

The powers of darkness work to steal lives, to destroy lives, to

---

tries experience miraculous healings with only brief prayers spoken. Bill Johnson, senior leader of Bethel Church in Redding, CA, sometimes proclaims, "Don't pray past the miracle." Further, many powerful healing ministries cited in *God's Generals* (see Bibliography), give examples of differing healing prayer approaches. There are also various testimonies that, when the miraculous healing touch of God is "present" in the room, people have been healed with no individually directed prayer.

[25]It is my belief that the faith component, along with the minimal presence of weak-faith people or non-believers, helps foster an environment where God will move more powerfully. Two Scriptural examples seem to support this: in the account of Jesus raising the synagogue ruler's daughter, He put those who did not believe *"all outside"* (Mark 5:40), and only Peter, James, John (v.38) and the parents (v.40) joined Jesus when He raised her from the dead. Likewise, when Peter raised Tabitha from the dead, he put the mourners *"all out"* (Acts 9:40) prior to praying over her. Removing unbelief and doubt was evidently important in these situations.

THE DEVIL IN THE BACK PEW

make you powerless, impotent, and ineffective, and to convince you to accept that kind of life. Jesus comes so that life may be abundant, full, fruitful, and joy-filled. Whose life do you choose? (See "The Poverty Mind-set" in Appendix I.)

The Bible tells us satan is the *"accuser"* (Revelation 12:10). His method of attacking individuals is commonly to allure and entice, then to shame and condemn. In the context of spiritual warfare, disconnectedness from the Father is also closely related to shame and condemnation. These can be profoundly debilitating if not dealt with.[26]

Very, very important: Each one of us faces a true choice when confronting strongholds, dark influences, and spiritual discomforts in our lives. Either we deal with and expel these with the strength and power of the Lord, *or we live with them forever!* Then our children live with them; then our children's children, until someone finally exercises their God-given authority and breaks the chain. Sadly, too many believers (out of ignorance, fear, or believing the enemy's lies) do not appropriate the freedom and victory that Christ offers.

Ultimately, the power of the enemy is defeated by love – the Lord's love for each of us, and that same love as we live it out with others. Love is about breaking chains, setting captives free, and spreading the Kingdom message. No part of freeing ourselves or freeing others should ever be a personal "power trip" (i.e., a sin of pride). It is *not* about us.

"For the weapons of our warfare are not carnal but mighty in

---

[26]A thorough discussion of the destructive power of shame or of disconnectedness from the Father is beyond the scope of this book, but these issues are of enormous significance to spiritual and emotional health. The Bibliography lists two excellent resources: an audio teaching entitled, *Shame-Fear-Control Stronghold* (Kylstra), and a book, *Healing an Orphan Heart* (Evans). When I teach the material of this book in a classroom setting, I always encourage everyone to get their own copy of each of these. I cannot recommend them too highly.

*God for pulling down strongholds, casting down arguments
and every high thing that exalts itself against the knowledge
of God ... "* (2 Corinthians 10:4–5)

The Mystery of Faith

The message that faith plays a role in the miraculous healings and
deliverance of the Bible is clear. The precise nature of that connection, however, is not as understandable, hence this section is titled
the "mystery" of faith.

The first definition of "mystery" in my Merriam-Webster Dictionary app is "a religious truth that one can only know by revelation and cannot fully understand." Though this source is obviously
secular, the definition fits our purpose here. The New Testament
usage of the word "faith," in the varying contexts of Jesus' miracles, confirms that the role faith plays is not easily defined. We will
discuss below selected references to "faith" in the New Testament:

Faith Is Compared to a Mustard Seed

Jesus stated this in three different contexts:

- In a partial response to the disciples' question as to why
  they could not cast a demon out of a tormented boy, Jesus
  said: *"Because of your unbelief; for assuredly, I say to you, if
  you have faith as a mustard seed ... nothing will be impossible
  for you"* (Matthew 17:20).
- In reply to the disciples' request to increase their faith, Jesus
  said: *"If you have faith as a mustard seed, you can say to this
  mulberry tree, 'Be pulled up by the roots and be planted in the
  sea,' and it would obey you"* (Luke 17:6).
- When teaching what the Kingdom of God (or Heaven) is
  like, Jesus said: *"It is like a mustard seed, which a man took
  and put in his garden; and it grew and became a large tree,
  and the birds of the air nested in its branches"* (Luke 13:19).

I offer no comment on the meaning of "faith as a mustard seed"

THE DEVIL IN THE BACK PEW

beyond what the plain text implies – that the seed starts small but grows to something much more, even serving purposes beyond what are initially evident. Jesus seems to say our faith should not be static, but growing.

Faith Is a Spiritual Gift

This implies that it is not earned *by* us, but is bestowed *upon* us. We are, additionally, encouraged to desire the best gifts, so it is totally proper for us to ask for more of it. *"[F]or to one is given the word of wisdom through the Spirit ... to another faith by the same Spirit ... But earnestly desire the best gifts ..."* (1 Corinthians 12:8–9, 31).

Faith Is a Fruit of the Spirit

This is from the Galatians 5 list of nine types of fruit.

Note: Some Bible translations use the word "faithfulness," while others use "faith." Irrespective, the Greek root word *pistis* (*Strong's* 4102) is most often rendered "faith," even in versions where "faithfulness" is the listed fruit of the Spirit. *"But the fruit of the Spirit is love, joy, peace ... faith ... "* (Galatians 5:22 KJV).

Faith Requires a Choice or a Response

Faith is even honored when it is imperfect. On five occasions (including Peter's doubt discussed in the prior section – see Matthew 14:31), Jesus remarked: *"You of little faith"* to individuals whose belief level was either lacking or needed some encouragement.

In another example, the story is told of a child tormented by a mute spirit, which the disciples were unable to cast out. The boy's father came to Jesus saying: *"[I]f You can do anything, have compassion on us and help us"* (Mark 9:22). Jesus replied: *"If you can believe, all things are possible to him who believes"* (v.23). The boy's father cried out: *"Lord, I believe; help my unbelief!"* (v.24). The father confessed to Jesus the imperfection of his faith, then Jesus healed the boy.

Warfare Basics and Recognizing the enemy

Related, in a testimony shared by Fr Gabriele Amorth, a prayee who was freed of demonic torment said of his struggle, "We must *want* faith."[27] That is a profound truth of the victorious Christian walk.

Faith and Divine Healing

In the following examples, the person with faith was the person seeking healing:

- In the case of the woman with the issue of blood for twelve years, Jesus said to her *"your faith has made you well"* (Matthew 9:22, emphasis mine) and she was healed.
- In the story of the two blind men following Jesus and crying out: *"Son of David, have mercy on us,"* Jesus asked them if they believed He was able to heal them. They replied: *"'Yes, Lord.' Then He touched their eyes, saying, 'According to your faith let it be to you.' And their eyes were opened"* (Matthew 9:27–30, emphasis mine).
- When the apostle Paul was speaking in Lystra, Scripture tells us he saw that a man crippled from birth *"had faith to be healed."* Paul said: *"'Stand up straight on your feet!' And he leaped and walked"* (Acts 14:9–10, emphasis mine).

In the following examples, the person with faith was *not* the person needing healing:

- In the account of the healing of the centurion's servant, the centurion stated: *"Lord, I am not worthy that You should come under my roof. But only speak a word, and my servant will be healed."* Jesus marveled at the centurion's words and said to His followers: *"Assuredly, I say to you, I have not found such **great faith**, not even in Israel! ... Then Jesus said to the centurion, 'Go your way; and **as you have believed, so let it be done for you.'** And his servant was healed that same*

---

[27]Fr Gabriele Amorth, *An Exorcist Tells His Story* (Ignatius Press, San Francisco, CA, 1999), 109.

THE DEVIL IN THE BACK PEW

hour" (Matthew 8:8, 10, 13, emphasis mine).

- In the account of the Canaanite woman whose daughter was demonized, Jesus initially responded to her request by denying her, because He was sent first to the people of Israel. When she responded *"... even the little dogs eat the crumbs which fall from their masters' table,"* Jesus stated: *"'O woman,* **great is your faith***! Let it be to you as you desire.' And her daughter was healed from that very hour"* (Matthew 15:27–28, emphasis mine).

That Jesus verbalized the importance of faith in each of these accounts is clear, but is there an implication that faith for healing is necessary on the part of the ill/injured, unless they are severely incapacitated? I think not. An example: in matters of all types and levels of demonic activity (simple temptation to severe demonization), as well as in many situations of physical healing needs, the prayee deals with the inevitable lies of the enemy. Often the person needing healing struggles with faith for no other reason than they are believing lies. As pray-ers, we help expose the lies and show how the truth of Scripture overcomes false beliefs.

Of course, there are many stories of healings, deliverances and miraculous events where the Bible makes no mention of faith or belief. Again, reading no more into these texts than what the plain words state, Jesus was obviously also revealing His authority, His power, His divine nature, His love, His compassion, the Kingdom of God, and more.

More About Faith

- Does faith follow our words, or do our words follow our faith? I offer no conclusive answer to this question, but Scripture tells us (as our experience does), that there is a definite connection between our words and faith. In this book, I mention in several discussions the significance of, and spiritual power behind, the words we speak. The Scriptural reference is: *"The tongue has the power of life and death"* (Proverbs 18:21

NIV). With our words, we can bless, curse, make vows, give the enemy rights over us, command the enemy away, stop the flow of good, and so on. Our words matter!

- Jesus did not do many miracles in His home town *"because of their lack of faith"* (Matthew 13:58 NIV).
- *"Now faith is the substance of things hoped for, the evidence of things not seen."* (Hebrews 11:1)
- *"So then faith comes by hearing, and hearing by the word of God."* (Romans 10:17)
- *"[T]his is the victory that has overcome the world—our faith."* (1 John 5:4)
- Testimonies of healings and deliverances encourage people to seek God's power, presence, and restoration. And testimonies increase faith, opening the door for more healings and deliverances.
- If a prayee is struggling with faith for healing, encourage them to lean on yours.

A word of caution: Some individuals take the position that, if you do not receive what you pray for, the problem is with you and your weak or insufficient faith. Often the emphasis is on riches or material prosperity, and the attitude may be one of "name it and claim it." The danger here is that the prayee, especially in situations of desperation, may feel rejected by God if they do not receive what they ask for. And this can be doubly painful when the need is great. I heard Francis MacNutt tell the story of a young man who entered a prayer gathering in a wheelchair, and departed devastated, "worse than when he came," because he was led to believe it was his insufficient faith that left him unhealed.

The Power in the Name of Jesus

Mainstream Christianity professes the Biblical doctrine that God is an indivisible triune Being – God the Father, Jesus the Son, and the Holy Spirit – and that He is the omniscient, omnipotent, omnipresent Creator, Who will sovereignly rule for eternity.

THE DEVIL IN THE BACK PEW

Jesus Christ the Son, fully God and fully man, by His voluntary death, paid for the sins of mankind and defeated the enemy, satan. Hence, He is our Lord and Savior. The power and authority of the name of Jesus, exhibited tangibly and irrefutably in encounters with the demonic, is remarkable indeed!

It is a foundational truth that we humans, on our own, have little to no authority in the spiritual realm. However, a committed Christian believer, in the power of the name of Jesus, can exercise truly miraculous authority over unclean spirits. This authority is not without limit, however, and the effective exercise of it is what this book is about.

Author Charles Kraft shares a thought about accessing that authority: "Our greatest weapon in fighting satanic influence – whether in ourselves or in others – is our intimacy with Jesus."[28] When declaring "in the name of Jesus," we are not uttering an "abracadabra"-like incantation; we are accessing the power which is behind our words, from Christ, Who lives in us.

The following Scriptures demonstrate the power behind the "name of Jesus:"

- Peter healed a man lame from birth:

    "... *In the name of Jesus Christ* of Nazareth, rise up and walk."* (Acts 3:6, emphasis mine)

- Paul commanded a demon out of a slave girl who predicted the future:

    "... *Paul ... said to the spirit, 'I command you in the name of Jesus Christ to come out of her.' And he came out ...* "* (Acts 16:18, emphasis mine)

- The seventy disciples celebrated the power of the name of Jesus:

    "*Then the seventy returned with joy, saying [to Jesus],*

---

[28]Charles H. Kraft, *Defeating Dark Angels* (Regal Books from Gospel Light, Ventura, CA, 1992), 97.

'Lord, even the demons are subject to us in Your name.'" (Luke 10:17, emphasis mine)

- Two other references testify to the power of Jesus' name:

Jesus said: "... whatever you ask in My name, that I will do, that the Father may be glorified in the Son" (John 14:13, emphasis mine).

"[A]t the name of Jesus every knee should bow, of those in heaven, and of those on earth, and of those under the earth ..." (Philippians 2:10, emphasis mine)

How Do You Know if a Situation Requires Deliverance Prayer?

For now, we'll define deliverance prayer as the prayerful confrontation of dark spirits which are troubling an individual. The mechanics and intensity of the prayer may vary according to the severity or type of the demonic harassment (see Chapter 4), but the activity is basically the same for all dark activity: break the spirit's rights and command it out/away.

The Spiritual Gift of Discernment of Spirits

One of the nine spiritual gifts listed by Paul in his first letter to the church in Corinth is *"discerning of spirits"* (1 Corinthians 12:10). This gift is an ability to see, sense, discern, or otherwise be aware of a spiritual presence or activity, either good and Godly in nature, or evil and dark. The revealed understanding or knowledge might concern a person, a physical location, or a situation.

When praying darkness off an individual, this gift is helpful in two principal ways. Discernment can reveal the *presence* of a dark spirit (the *source* of the problem), and discernment can reveal the *harm* the spirit is doing (the *nature* of the problem). With this knowledge, dealing with the spirit becomes less complicated and not as much of a fishing expedition. The pray-er knows he/she is

71

THE DEVIL IN THE BACK PEW

pursuing a demon and can more readily identify and undermine the demon's rights and authority. Significantly, as discerning spirits is a gift and not the pray-er's skill, it is available as the Spirit leads, which may be intermittently. Having been exposed to much demonic presence and activity, I have experienced occasions of this gift at work in me, but not with the consistency or sensitivity that I have seen in others.

Examples of Discernment

Here are several illustrations showing the gift at work in various ways:[29]

- Several years ago, I attended a special service at a church in a nearby town. James Maloney,[30] a gifted Bible school teacher and minister, was the guest speaker. James is extremely spiritually sensitive and prophetic, as much as anyone I have ever seen, and he tells how he often "sees" in the spiritual realm. To be clear, he *sees* angels and demons. For the example I give here, I offer proof which I can corroborate.

  James often conducts a personal ministry time after preaching a message. On this occasion, he had people line up and come near to him one at a time for him to pray or speak prophetically over them. At this particular service, a person I knew approached him. As the man neared him – before one word was uttered – James stopped him and very

---

[29]Certain of these examples arguably might indicate the spiritual gifts of *"word of wisdom"* or *"word of knowledge"* (1 Corinthians 12:8) as opposed to *"discerning of spirits"* (v.10). Considering the broader context of Paul's passage on spiritual gifts and the benefits thereof, I refrain from debating here which label is most accurate.

[30]Dr. James Maloney, an educated (three doctorates) and gifted minister and prophetic voice, is a Bible school teacher, author, world-wide minister, and president of Dove On The Rise International. See https://www.doveontherise.com/index.html.

72

Warfare Basics and Recognizing the enemy

diplomatically and gently advised him to first seek prayer from his pastor. The slightly veiled message, discreetly shared, was that James saw a demonic presence on this man and knew it had to be dealt with before other healing or blessing could take place. I had been involved in multiple sessions of demonic manifestation and prayer with this man, who I happened to know *very* well. Ground had been reclaimed from the enemy, but more deliverance was needed. James saw the demonic attachment immediately.

Note: It is common that several sessions are required for complete cleansing.

- Another example of someone who sees demons, and who also senses them by touch, is Kris Vallotton, cited earlier. Kris's stories of encounters are detailed in his books, as well as in messages preached at Bethel Church and at the Bethel School of Supernatural Ministries.[31] I have never heard accounts which match how he sees numerous demons in public places. Also, just as curious, I heard him comment recently that his "ability" to see demons en masse has diminished in recent times – that the high sensitivity was for a protracted period after a personal emotional struggle. Irrespective, his sensitivity was remarkable. He once commented that he had to very intentionally shut off the distraction of all the demons he would see, giving the example of going into a crowded restaurant and seeing the room also filled with demons hovering around the diners. Regarding the number of demons generally present among people, I heard him remark on one occasion, "No – there's not a demon behind every tree. But *almost* every tree."

- Friend A, a person I was connected with in ministry a few years back, could often see demonic presences in rooms or on people. That she truly saw them was, on many occasions, confirmed independently by others, who were simi-

---

[31] Many of these teachings are available online at www.bethel.tv.

larly gifted. There were also several instances where her discernment was not only of the presence itself, but also of the attributes (abilities, strengths) of the dark spirit. Her gift of discernment was very helpful in the deliverance prayer session. She exposed the vulnerability of the spirit, thereby making it easier to expel. I always encourage those who have this gift to get involved and assist those of us who do not possess it as strongly.

Curiously, on one occasion, though, this woman and I were praying for an individual with some deep spiritual scars, and I discerned a specific dark activity crucial to what was going on. While she typically was vastly more spiritually discerning than I was, in this circumstance she had no apparent spiritual sensitivity. And she even expressed surprise over what I discerned; it had escaped her completely. My discernment was proven to be accurate by what transpired in the session.

The important lesson: Spiritual gifting is available as the Holy Spirit wills, and we must be wary of preconceived dispositions or expectations. For each of us, it can be an error to assume that the discernment we experienced in the past is similarly available in the present circumstance.

- Friend B saw a dark spirit appearing like an unthreatening little girl in pigtails attempting to make a place in our house during my battle with cancer. She explained that the spirit became very angry when confronted. (See next example.)

- Friend C is a delightful mother of teenagers who has had experiences of seeing in the spiritual realm since she was a child. She has recounted several occasions of witnessing demonic activity on and around close acquaintances in times of high emotional stress. She observed a "large" angel standing guard in the corner of the room of a dying friend. She also confirmed the details of a dark spirit attempting to establish roots in my home during my cancer battle (see

Warfare Basics and Recognizing the enemy

Friend B above). Some weeks later, this lady saw the "little girl" spirit outside the house and quite upset at being forbidden entry. But outside!

One situation which merits mention concerns this friend's interaction with another Christian acquaintance. This second woman, an active, church-attending believer, had suffered a profoundly horrible personal loss several years before, and she adamantly refused to offer to God her forgiveness for the offending party. As this woman was recounting her hurt and anger, my friend could see a demon between them as they spoke; the spirit was physically in front of the grieving woman, a barrier of sorts between her and others.

- In one of his teaching videos, Francis MacNutt, who states he personally does not have a strong gift of discerning spirits, tells of relying on someone's gift of discernment while praying for a missionary suffering for years from ringing in the ears. As a team was praying physical healing for the missionary, one of the pray-ers said, "Francis, I think there is a spirit here ..." They immediately commenced praying against the spirit, believed to be from a tribal curse placed on the missionary while in Africa. The spirit left, and the ringing in his ears stopped! This is a wonderful example of the gift of discernment aiding the effort of healing prayer.

- Over the years, my wife and I, and others we have prayed with, have had many instances of discerning the nature or type of spirit which is tormenting a prayee. For example, we might be praying against a person's long-time battle with fearfulness, when one of the pray-ers is prompted to question if the fear is rooted in rejection – and the prayee tells of a profoundly humiliating grade school experience. Or perhaps communication between a prayee and the pray-ers is not clear or fruitful, and someone senses to pray against a spirit of confusion, and the obstruction lifts.

THE DEVIL IN THE BACK PEW

- Concerning discernment pertaining to a *physical location*, I once perceived a spiritual impediment of unknown nature. A few of us were in a small room of a church praying for a woman when I sensed a resistance while trying to speak blessings over her as we were beginning the prayer session. I stopped the prayer and invited all present to pray a prayer of cleansing over the room (see Chapter 8, "Retaking What's Yours," p. 182). I felt a "darkness," like a cloud of sorts, hovering on the high wall and ceiling area in one side of the room. Incidentally, this type of discernment is not typical for me. We all prayed a prayer of blessing and cleansing, for just a minute or two, and sensed the heaviness depart. In mentioning the experience to a church pastoral team member, I was advised that there had recently been immoral activity in the room by trespassing neighborhood teenagers. The darkness had been permitted entry by these kids' behavior, but in our authority, we commanded it out.

From these examples, we can see how the gift of discerning spirits can help identify the source of the problem, making resolution simpler. Importantly, though, full expression of the gift is not necessary to pray for deliverance. In truth, we have participated in countless successful deliverance prayer sessions where there was no evidence of this gift at work.

Important points about discernment of spirits:

- In deliverance prayer, as in doing other works for God, be confident that the Holy Spirit will give you what you need when you need it.
- If you are able to discern spirits ("see" or "sense" them) but are not experienced, *be careful about what you say about what you see!* Get help and advice from someone who is experienced.
- There is a "dark side" (demonic/occult) to discernment of spirits called "divination." Non-believers can have this discernment. When they become believers, they must firmly

Warfare Basics and Recognizing the enemy

and formally reject "dark" discernment and seek only that of the Holy Spirit.

There are other indicators that deliverance prayer may be called for:

The Person Will Tell You

Though not always reliable, an individual may suspect or sense a dark presence or influence related to "voices," thoughts, impressions, temptations, a perceived heaviness, a specific emotion, or other negativity. In severe cases, the victim may have involuntary physical manifestations or evidences come upon them, i.e., outside of a deliverance-type prayer session.

The Prayee's Behavior Suggests a dark presence

As mentioned, spending time in prayer can disrupt a demon's comfortable circumstance, while brief prayers do not generally force a demon out of hiding. When a demon is manifesting, it is common that the emotion expressed on the face of the prayee reflects the emotion, or even the nature of the spirit or the demon, like fear, anger, or arrogance.

Life Experiences Reveal a Vulnerability

Lives can be made horribly difficult because of circumstances beyond our control, or as the consequences of sin – on the part of the prayee, or against the prayee. Common entry points for demonic infestation include: trauma, abuse, abandonment, promiscuity, occult activity, pornography, substance abuse, habitual sin, and the like.

There is Discomfort with the Topic of dark spirits

Merely reading this book or attending a class on battling the enemy may disturb a dark spiritual presence. On a few occasions, we have had individuals nervously leave a class where this subject

THE DEVIL IN THE BACK PEW

matter was being taught, becoming angry or explaining the discussion made them very uneasy or fearful. The truth is basically this: dark spirits do not like anyone learning this material. Should you experience such anxiety, I would recommend you take it as hard evidence that you *need* to understand more about the dark realm. And that Jesus is bigger! The enemy is fearful he is about to be exposed, and it is *his* fear which is surfacing in the individual.

As I recall situations where a person in one of our classes felt compelled to leave because of personal discomfort, in every case a bit of probing revealed strong evidence of oppression or demonization.

Indications of Mental Disorders or Psychological Conditions[32]

There are a few in the Christian church who believe all mental disorders are the result of demonization. It seems clear, however, that the brain is susceptible to illness and malfunction just like any other part of the body. Perhaps demonization is at the root of a particular disturbance of the mind or brain, but perhaps it is not.

If there is evidence or suspicion of a mental disorder of any magnitude, I am comfortable only interacting with a prayee in a non-challenging or non-invasive way. If such a situation arises, we speak blessings and pray healing of emotional hurts and, if we sense it is appropriate, we command the darkness out with "if"-type prayers. A simple example would be, "If there is a spirit of abandonment here, I command you out and away in the name of Jesus Christ." Generally, I believe it best to avoid being confrontational, and referring the person to a Christian professional when possible. On occasion, it is helpful to work in tandem with a Christian professional, with each of us obtaining permission from the prayee to share information on the person's situation. The counselor/psychologist does their part, and we do the prayer

---

[32]Situations involving mentally or emotionally troubled individuals should be shared with the appropriate pastor or ministry overseer. For more on this subject, see Chapter 9, "Accountability," on p. 206.

78

Warfare Basics and Recognizing the enemy

and deliverance part. We have seen wonderful fruit from these joint efforts.

Many folks who come to us for prayer are taking medications to control bipolar tendencies, depression, and the like. Typically, these people are in counseling or receiving medical treatment of one sort or another, but there is most often no need for us to interact with their professional. The medications keep the person in control and settled, and we are able to go about the business of praying without any problem.

For those who may be uncomfortable ministering to people taking medication to settle the mind, I share a perspective given years ago by a Christian counselor friend. He stated that, with some individuals, a medication is needed to "turn down the volume" in the person's mind. There can be so much mental noise, confusion, jumbled thinking, and distraction that the person cannot manage it all and is unable to focus. The correct drug can take the edge off and allow the person to control their thoughts and decision-making processes.

His explanation was very helpful to me, and we have seen the benefits of the right medications wisely used. In one specific case, we prayed with a tormented young man and saw him delivered of dozens of dark spirits. He was freed to grow strong in his Christian walk, while the medications permitted a stabilization which was otherwise unattainable.

Note: Some psychological conditions present symptoms very similar to demonic manifestations. If this is a possibility, seek help from a Christian professional.

Serious Issues of the Mind and Emotions

In a prayer situation where there are indicators of difficult mental or emotional problems, we can still pray blessings, proclaim the truths of Scripture, speak Jesus' love and healing over the heart hurts, expose the enemy's lies, encourage the prayee to lean on the Scriptures (Psalms are great to build hope), and the like. Inner

THE DEVIL IN THE BACK PEW

healing prayer, appropriately administered, is uplifting, encouraging, loving, nonstressful, and always positive.

In the following, or any other situation deemed serious, be sure to exercise caution. An experienced Christian professional should also be involved:

- **Suicidal Thoughts**

  If a person has actual temptations to commit suicide (i.e., beyond a passing thought), or has devised a plan of how to carry it out, professional help should be sought immediately. If an individual is on the edge of proceeding, he/she should be strongly encouraged to contact a local Suicide Hotline, and to carry the hotline phone number on their person. If they are unwilling to cooperate, contact your church leadership, a loved one of the prayee, or other relevant party; even call the Suicide Hotline yourself. Don't leave an urgent situation unresolved.

- **Satanic Ritual Abuse (SRA)**

  In simple terms, SRA is the victimization, often including physical and sexual abuse, of a person, typically a child, and compelling their involvement in satanic or occult activities, ceremonies, sacrifices, or dedications. This can lead to deep emotional scarring and even Dissociative Identity Disorder (see below). Should you find yourself praying for someone who has been the victim of SRA, you will most likely need to seek help. In any but the mildest of exposures, protracted Christian-based therapy will be required. I know of one situation where the therapy necessarily continued for many years.

- **Dissociative Identity Disorder (DID)**

  DID, also known as Multiple Personality Disorder, is generally described as a mental disorder characterized by the existence, and appearance, of two or more distinct personal identities in one person. Controversial as to its diagnosis and origin, many believe it is a natural self-protective

response to circumstances where a person is in an inescapable, horrific situation.

We have had a few encounters where DID seemed evident, but our involvement in each case was minimal. In one case, we interacted with a young woman's "alter," an additional personal identity with a different name. We were able to lead the alter in a prayer of commitment to Christ.

Note: The "main" person was a professed Christian believer, but the alter was not. This is apparently common.

Circumstances were such that our prayer sessions did not continue, though she communicated to me about a year later, professing that she was doing well. Surely it would have been best for the young woman to seek help from a Christian professional. I do not know if that ever occurred.

In this particular case, we were quite sure we were dealing with the young woman's alter, not a demonic spirit. The professed desire to follow Jesus made that clear. I could easily see, however, the possibility of a demon representing itself as an alter in order to avoid detection.

Further Considerations

It is appropriate at this point to discuss a few topics relevant to personal warfare prayer. These are foundational to the process of confronting the enemy.

Dirt

Exposure to the enemy and his tactics is remarkably analogous to us getting dirt on ourselves. The concept of spiritual "dirt" or "dirtiness," referring to the accumulation of enemy contamination on a person, is very accurate. It builds up, it is unavoidable when we play in the mud, it is visible to others and to ourselves, if we are honest about it, and it must be removed if we want to be clean.

When we sin or encounter sinful stuff, we *cannot* avoid getting dirt on us, though the enemy will try to convince us otherwise.

THE DEVIL IN THE BACK PEW

But getting clean is easy, if we avail ourselves of the forgiveness God offers: *"If we confess our sins, He is faithful and just to forgive us our sins and to cleanse us from all unrighteousness"* (1 John 1:9).

But what if a person does not seek forgiveness? Or does not want to deal with the problem? Or is not a believer? Or just doesn't understand? He or she remains dirty, and the enemy can build a home in that dirt. As I have said, our understanding of God's economy is limited, and the particulars of this process (getting dirty, getting clean) are not fully known. However, we absolutely see greater enemy strength and influence where the dirt is piled higher. Bottom line, "dirt" gives the enemy legal rights which have to be broken.

Note: There are sources of dirt which are brought on externally, separate from our personal sin. We will talk about these.

Important: Underlying this discussion of the enemy's tactics and working with folks who have "dirt" on them, the focus must be overwhelmingly on displaying *love*: the love extended by the Father, Jesus, and the Holy Spirit to us all. We are obliged to try as best we can to reflect that love to those victimized by the enemy. For most, exposure to the demonic is rooted in ignorance, like exposure to cancer-causing asbestos. The person has no clue of the danger, nor of what has gotten in or on them.

Empty Wells

The prophet Jeremiah provides a revealing example of the type of error which leaves us vulnerable to enemy incursion: *"For My people have committed two evils: They have forsaken Me, the fountain of living waters, And hewn themselves cisterns—broken cisterns that can hold no water"* (Jeremiah 2:13). The "broken cisterns," or "empty wells,"[33] are places of brokenness (sin, failure, spiritual poverty,

---

[33]From the *Gospel of Wholeness*, a recommended audio teaching series by Danny Meyer, Founding Pastor of Vineyard Church of Delaware County (Ohio). Danny serves in the Association of Vineyard Churches as Regional Leader for much of Ohio and Western Pennsylvania. He is

Warfare Basics and Recognizing the enemy

self-reliance) resulting from turning away from God's plans for life and fulfillment, and pursuing personal solutions instead. The broken wells, which cannot hold anything enduring, are places of deviation from God's plan for the prayee's life – and places where the enemy can dwell without being disturbed.

Inner Healing Needs

Needs for inner healing (emotional healing, heart healing, healing of the memories) must be dealt with in the deliverance prayer process. The "right" or stronghold the enemy has in his attachment to a person is most often, at the root, an emotional wound or inner healing need, very often from childhood or youth. Covered in depth in Chapter 5, it is mentioned here as an area which must be probed in assessing how to pray and in identifying areas where the enemy has set his "hook."

The power of generational sin and curses must be broken too. This will be discussed in Chapter 8.

Preparatory Prayer and Interview

It has been emphasized that time spent in prayer makes a demonic presence uncomfortable. After the need for deliverance prayer has been determined, however, protracted prayer is also needed for:

- healing of the underlying emotional wounds (the enemy can hang on to these);
- revelation (What powers of darkness are at work?);
- wholeness;
- a real sense of Jesus' presence and love; and
- whatever the Holy Spirit reveals.

When deliverance prayer is called for, it is important that the prayee be interviewed in detail, as prompted by the Holy Spirit.

---

also a leader for the Vineyard USA Philippines Partnership. For information about the *Gospel of Wholeness* (including CDs, DVDs), visit http://vineyardcdc.org/#/sermons-resources/gospel-of-wholeness.

THE DEVIL IN THE BACK PEW

Probe the prayee's personal history, upbringing, life experiences, relationships, sin patterns, hurts, fears, emotional issues, education, employment and generational history, and so forth. Strongholds and ground given to the enemy will become apparent, and these *must be resolved* in the deliverance prayer process.

Why Can't You Simply Command a demon Out?

Indirect references have been made to this question, and more will be said later, but a few comments are appropriate at this point.

- As stated, you cannot drive a dark spirit out until you remove its right to be there. That right must be exposed and broken. Legal rights are an integral part of the spiritual/eternal realm (see Chapter 12, "A Legal Reason May Exist," p. 251).

- Occasionally you can drive out weaker spirits quickly, and sometimes a lesser demon will be released by a greater demon, as a distraction.

- Dark spirits hide! And they try to trick the prayee into helping them hide. Be encouraged; when they show themselves, it is a last resort in their defenses.

- Sometimes people seem to want to keep them hidden. Really!

I had an amusing life experience some years back which provided an accurate object lesson of hiding from the enemy. Returning home from an errand one evening, I pulled into our open garage and, staring at me from a shelf, eye-to-eye, was an opossum. I turned the ignition off and sat still in the car, waiting to see what this critter would do. It began, over the next 90 seconds or so, slowly rotating a tiny amount at a time, until its rear-end was pointed towards me. I waited many minutes and it never moved again. It could not see me, so it was content; out of sight, out of mind! This, unfortunately, describes how too many people deal with indicators of dark spiritual activity.

Warfare Basics and Recognizing the enemy

Kris Vallotton tells the story of how he was preaching on one occasion, and in his message, he mentioned that he often has the ability to discern a demonic presence in a person when he touches them. Now it so happens that the auditorium at Bethel Church has two main rear exits, one which leads out to the parking lot and a second which exits to a hallway inside the building. It is typical practice at Bethel that the person who preaches does not "close" the service, but leaves the final prayer to another, so he/she can get to the parking lot door to greet folks as they depart. Normally, the vast majority of attenders exit via that door. Perhaps you guessed it. After Kris divulged that he discerns dark spirits by touch, the majority, uncharacteristically, exited by the door opposite where Kris was shaking hands![34]

Surely certain people do not want to confront a demon or dark presence out of fear, either fear of the unknown, fear of not knowing what to do, or even fear of uncontrollable manifestation. Others may not want to confront a spirit because it would mean they would have to change a belief or behavior. Yet others, likely most, do not know the "problem" *is* a demon:

- Perhaps they do not know what to do and just want the problem to stop;
- Possibly they are protecting a "favorite" sin, like porn or credit card abuse;
- Maybe they do not want to face it or deal with it; or
- Like Derek Prince's wife's claustrophobia, they have gotten used to it. They know how to manage it.

The secular saying, "the devil you know versus the devil you don't know" may be an apt description of the mind-set.

---

[34]Kris Vallotton, *Spirit Wars* (Chosen, a division of Baker Publishing Group, Grand Rapids, MI, 2012), 175.

THE DEVIL IN THE BACK PEW

The Inherent Tension

When confronted with a person who is oppressed, demonized, or otherwise emotionally wounded, a pray-er can feel rather ill-equipped. There are many variables, complexities, and possibilities, and prayer strategies may not be clear.

Importantly, prayer properly executed does not follow a strict set of instructions, but rather the loving lead of the Holy Spirit. Regardless of the prayee's desperation or the gravity of the need, a restful bathing in the Spirit should be the first order of business. The pray-er must avoid inclinations to be over-controlling and rather gently lead the prayee toward Biblical truths and a God-ordained state of peace, hope, and trust. But it is important to understand that, for someone who struggles with demonic torment or deep wounds, the covering of peace and so forth, real as it is, may be short-lived. The enemy is quite adept at planting seeds of doubt and at creeping back in. Nevertheless, as inner healing needs are dealt with, and as demons are ejected, the prayee will continue to advance.

The assumption throughout this book is that a concerted effort should be made to speak the blessings and truths of God over the prayee, then to deal with the worldly dirt which is exposed. To that end, when barriers like the "Serious Issues of the Mind and Emotions" (discussed above) are encountered, the pray-er should peacefully press on into *blessing* the prayee as best they can. And leave the outcome of those words of blessing to the Lord. Also leave the psychological counseling to the professionals.

When a Prayee Impedes Success

For me the most frustrating aspect of deliverance prayer concerns the individual who has freedom within reach, but will not do what is necessary to take hold of it. Such a person typically chooses to *stop receiving prayer* when they get close to areas they deem too painful. Virtually every such circumstance that I have encountered, and there have been many, involves a person who either will

Warfare Basics and Recognizing the enemy

not let go of unforgiveness, will not resolve an unholy behavior, or will only deal with their "problem" in one self-defined way (which they see as easier, but which has never worked). In these cases, there is compelling evidence of demonization, but the prayee is too fearful or deluded to face his or her "stuff," and they remain in denial that change is necessary, or even that a demon could be harassing them. Their life is one of woundedness and often sadness, bitterness, victimization, and isolation. They tolerate their circumstance while striving to bury their suffering.

In some other cases, a prayee may choose to *curtail* a fruit-bearing prayer and deliverance process only to *return* months or years later to continue. Whether we felt an interruption was prompted by the Holy Spirit or not, God has always shown Himself faithful to meet the person where they are. In one circumstance, we prayed for a young man for a few months, realizing a measure of breakthrough and deliverance, when he chose to stop meeting with us. After not having spoken with him for many years, he contacted us and we reconnected. The subsequent deliverance prayer sessions were very successful, even more so than those in the past. I do not mean to imply that the multiyear break was God's idea, or indeed that it was not. But God *did* redeem it all, and for that we celebrate!

Deliverance Prayer Requested But Not Needed

Some feel they are in need of deliverance because they are having difficulty overcoming a sin or bad habit when direct demonic presence is not the issue. In a sense, dealing with (or blaming?) a demon might be easier than resolving the problem by facing it directly.

Years ago, a likable fellow whom we knew well came to us for "deliverance" because of his difficulty controlling his anger. He was certain a demon was causing his angry outbursts. Now, I have no doubt the enemy was harassing him (planting thoughts, stirring his desire to control), but after some prayer, we did not per-

87

THE DEVIL IN THE BACK PEW

ceive a demonic presence. He did not enthusiastically agree with our opinion, but he was willing to accept some friendly advice on being intentional about controlling his reactions when his anger was stirred (while driving, for example). Over a little time, he has made vast strides in self-control. We never saw evidence of demonization related to his anger.

PART II

Countering
the enemy's Tactics

Chapter 4

The enemy at Work

This chapter considers the destructive practices of the enemy in four discussions: temptation, oppression, demonization, and "possession."

Note: These categories serve more to facilitate the conversation than to highlight the distinctions between them. The aim is to expose the enemy's varied tactics so that he can be more easily overcome. In reality, many of his efforts overlap rather than fit clearly into one of these categories.

Surely satan attempts to influence *all* aspects of our human existence. It is important to understand the *progressive nature* of his plan for destruction, and to recognize his work at the various stages. Though his methods vary, there are common elements to his efforts:

- *Lies:* fundamental untruths; deceptions – satan is the *"father of lies"* (John 8:44 NIV).
- *Accusations:* guilt; condemnation – satan is the *"accuser"* (Revelation 12:10).
- *Hopelessness:* desperation; despair – satan doesn't want people to know the power of the cross, *that their sins are already paid for.* Victory is attainable and available!

A few simple strategies for combating these enemy attacks will be

The enemy at Work

mentioned in context, with the topic covered extensively through-out the remainder of the book.

Temptation

In Chapter 1, I mentioned the Ephesians 2 reference to "the world, the flesh, and the devil." Most of us can relate to being tempted by the world and the flesh. We may strongly desire a material object, such as a 60-inch TV, chainsaw, new pair of shoes, or even a big, new house. Or we may long for an ice-cream cone or a pizza. These can be, at one extreme, typical (Western) human wants or, alternatively, they might represent compulsions far beyond mere preferences. Most of us know of situations where people have been wildly excessive in spending, eating, or uncontrolled fleshly desires and have brought great harm to themselves. Short of that extreme, though, we can still do damage to ourselves, our finances, or our relationships. Perhaps some readers can relate to experiences I have had, mostly pre-Christ, thankfully, where I was so driven to satisfy a worldly or fleshly desire that I made a bad decision. When desire is out of control, or defies good sense, something else is likely going on.

In the Sermon on the Mount, Jesus advised that willful desire for that which is sinful is sin, irrespective of whether the desire is acted upon. *"[W]hoever looks at a woman to lust for her has already committed adultery with her in his heart"* (Matthew 5:28). Jesus' example may be one of simple fleshly desire, or it may be greater and represent direct enemy influence. Regardless, assent to sinful temptation is itself an act of sin, and such sins of the heart are door-openers for enemy involvement.

Temptation, on different levels, is part of life. We pray "lead us not into temptation," but we daily face the lure of billboards, TV commercials, and internet ads. The marketers want us to believe we *need* their stuff, much of which is really okay. We do need toothpaste, right? So, how do we recognize the line we do not want to cross?

91

THE DEVIL IN THE BACK PEW

Channels of Temptation

Bad Thoughts

Where do they come from? At the beginning of Chapter 2, I discussed the topic of intersecting thoughts, those which come out of nowhere and are likely externally planted. When Jesus taught the parable of the sower (Mark 4:14–20), He explained that the parable was about spreading the Word of God and how the Word bears fruit, though some do not receive it. In the parable's first example, Jesus said that it was *"[s]atan"* who came and took *"away the word [i.e., the truth] that was sown in their hearts"* (v.15). We know from this and other Scriptures cited that the enemy can plant thoughts and desires in us. Some real-life examples:

- Several years ago, I was riding my bicycle alone on a sunny summer day. Biking is both exercise and therapy for me, and I often spend time in thought, talking to God, or enjoying nature. As I was traveling through gently rolling hills in a rural area, I noticed that, on this certain stretch of road, I could see no houses or barns or anything man-made to spoil the natural beauty. It was very scenic, like a painting. I remember thinking, "Wow God, that's beautiful ..." And as I passed a small wooded area on my left, I heard a voice in my mind, as clear as if someone was riding next to me, say, "That would be a good place to hide a body ..."

  Aloud, I immediately exclaimed, "What!?" My reaction was one of amusement; I knew who was talking, and laughed at such a ridiculous attempt at temptation or dark suggestion. Just for the record, I confirm that I had not been having any desire or thoughts about "getting rid of" anyone. This was a totally random intersecting thought, completely out of the blue. Who was speaking to me? Is there any doubt whatsoever?

- A long-time Christian friend of ours shared how she, also out of the blue, heard the enemy speak to her, "Smoke!" as

The enemy at Work

if she had been presented with an irresistible enticement. Now this woman has never smoked in her life, has no history of being around smokers, and has never been tempted to smoke, yet she got a clear intersecting thought suggesting it.

- Another Christian friend told how, while driving one day, she took notice of an elderly woman walking along the adjacent sidewalk. Immediately a clear thought came to her mind, "You could beat up that woman ..." The response of my friend was to laugh out loud. She immediately recognized the source and the absurdity of the comment. And, of course, rejected it.

In his book, *Living Above the Snake Line,* author and teacher James Maloney distinguishes between *thoughts of evil* and *evil thoughts,* the former being those the enemy deposits and the latter those which arise within our hearts. In either case, they must be recognized and rejected. Our discernment of what thoughts must be tossed necessarily comes from our knowledge of the Word of God and from the Holy Spirit's revelation.

I can confirm that it is a rare day when I do not "hear" some sort of word or thought of temptation which can only be linked to the enemy of my soul. When the solicitation concerns something I absolutely do *not* want in my life, what (who) else could be the source? Am I subject to an increased barrage of thoughts just because I have been sensitized to this stuff by involvement in spiritual warfare? I think not. That might help explain awareness of the enemy's tactics, but not the enemy's pursuit of my destruction. Remember, he comes to steal, kill, and destroy.

Unhealthy Feelings and Desires

I will begin with two personal examples of what I will call enemy-prompted cravings. These roots of desire relate to my pre-Christ history and behaviors, happily forsaken decades ago. The aforementioned philosopher, Blaise Pascal, stated that each human has

93

THE DEVIL IN THE BACK PEW

on the inside a "God-shaped emptiness" which nothing but the Lord Himself can satisfy. Confirming his hypothesis, I was the classic case of one pursuing any and every distraction and pleasure to fill that void. That is, until the Lord revealed Himself to me.

- For several years of my young adult life, a highlight of my week was going to happy hour at one of several bars I frequented. Alcohol flowed, there were many smokers (permissible then), there was much flirting and suggestive behavior, conversations were loud and coarse, and generally it was wall-to-wall young professionals. I loved it. And, for the record, I much more love the fact that such behavior in no way interests me now.

  Five years or so after giving my life to the Lord and forsaking the former ways, I was a happy, church-attending, God-loving husband with a wonderful wife and two fun young boys. We were returning from a family vacation at the ocean, and I needed to make a phone call. As this was before cell phones were widely in use, I stopped at a restaurant beside the road to use the pay phone. The phone was in the entryway to the bar area of the restaurant, so I stood there to make the call.

  The bar was very crowded and was precisely the kind of place where I used to spend a lot of time. What happened next was a total surprise. A very heavy, tangible feeling of longing and desire came over me; I wanted to go into that place! Really badly! I was drawn by this intense tug inside of me to go in and "party" like so many times before.

  This did not make sense. I knew the error of my former ways, and I knew that true freedom and happiness was with God and with my family, so I started asking myself some questions. Do I really want to go in there and drink? No. Do I want to go inside and smoke? No. Do I want to be loud and coarse? No. Do I want to flirt with girls? No. Do I want to choose the bar over my gorgeous family in

The enemy at Work

the car? Of course not! As I "talked" myself through these thoughts, the heavy draw of the illusion diminished and left. Wow! This whole experience was very real and very intense, but it was also based 100% on lies and the influences of the enemy. I really did not want any of what was going on in there, but the overall tug, pull, or draw was independent of the reality. I learned an application of a Scriptural truth: the enemy's deceptions include *his ability to deposit feelings and desires*. (See Chapter 1, "What the Scriptures Say About satan and his demons," p. 22.)

- Another example of the enemy planting a desire occurred several years ago. I had occasion to observe an educational law enforcement officer display drug paraphernalia, the origin of which was a drug arrest. As I took a closer look, the unmistakable scent of marijuana wafted my way. I insert here my admission to ancient experience with this and other drugs, though it has been many decades since I have partaken of any. And I have no wish whatsoever to use them now. However, the truth is that, when I got close to the exhibit and picked up the scent of the officer's marijuana, it actually smelled *good* to me! Yes, good! It was an excitement or tug or draw similar to the appeal of the happy hour bar scene in the prior example. Believe me, I do not want to get high on marijuana any more. I have chosen Jesus and His far superior ways. This second example speaks to me of the enemy's skill at planting a feeling of, or desire for, something which is actually distasteful to me.

Note: We must be wary of our feelings; we must test if they are really ours.

- A general comment about enemy-planted desire. Perhaps you, like me, have, on occasion, wanted something so bad that you were not rational about it. I gave the example earlier of a person wanting a big-screen TV. Such a desire could be a simple want but, especially if the desire is a real *compul-*

95

THE DEVIL IN THE BACK PEW

sion, and you think you just *have* to have it, and you are truly excited inside at the thought of it, it may be an enemy-planted feeling and not your rational desire. After all, who among us has not wanted something intensely and, after having it for a few days, seen our thrill diminish significantly? The enemy is skilled at "piling on" to simpler wants.

The Most Insidious Incursion

The *Oxford Dictionary* defines *insidious* as "proceeding in a gradual, subtle way, but with very harmful effects." The majority of the topics discussed in this "Channels of Temptation" section, when followed to their natural consequence, fit that description well. But *most* insidious, I believe, best describes those thoughts (temptations) which attempt to create distance, or a blockage, between us and God. And particularly when we are seeking to connect with Him in some way, like: prayer, worship, Bible reading, meditation, reverential singing, or merely attempting to quietly rest in the Holy Spirit's presence.

A planted thought or feeling, and the verbalization of submission to it (i.e., agreement, confirmation), might look like one of these examples:

- When in a church worship service:
  The enemy whispers: "You *really* don't feel like standing and singing today!"
  Person mumbles/thinks to themselves: "Boy, I don't feel much like worshiping today ..."
- When praying at the start of the day:
  The enemy whispers: "You've got too much to do – you *can't pray* this morning!"
  Person mumbles/thinks to themselves: "I just can't take the time to pray today ..."
- When reading the Bible:
  The enemy whispers: "You're tired. If you read the Bible, you won't remember *one thing!*"

The enemy at Work

> Person mumbles/thinks to themselves: "Wow. I'm so tired. I can't concentrate now …"

In these examples, the thought or feeling planted by the enemy is rooted heavily, if not fully, in the power of suggestion. Do we not routinely yield to, or reject, all sorts of thoughts and feelings which come to mind? I believe that most of the enemy's efforts follow such an approach. It is an integral part of the enemy's scheme of temptation – and it is doubly damaging when it interferes with our connection with the Lord. What better battle tactic against us than to interfere with our worship of God, our prayer life, or our study of the Word?

I give a personal example which opened my eyes to the subtlety of this insidious influence of the enemy. For many years, it has been a habit of mine to read a few chapters of the Bible daily. Before I retired from fulltime work, it was occasionally difficult to do, but now I am able to read most days. Still, the enemy selectively battles me. He periodically, most often in a whisper, plants a variety of thoughts and feelings to tempt me to shortcut my time or skip sections of Scripture.

Some time ago I noticed an increase in thoughts/feelings suggesting that I already know a certain section of Scripture, thinking, "Why bother reading it again?" And more recently, when coming to a Gospel chapter detailing the passion of Christ, I could sense the enemy trying to plant *feelings* of boredom (more so than words) – as if to make me think I've read this story "*so many times before.*" And, "Don't I know it well? Do I really need to read it again now?"

Candidly, my personality (flesh?) is such that, at times, I have to battle procrastination, but this was a new twist. I recognized how divisive, and how potentially dangerous to my Christian walk, such a mind-set could be. And this was a true temptation, in the purest form. No, I was not fooled and led to skip reading what I had intended to. I saw through the lie and recognized who was behind it. But it would have been so easy to yield. It was so subtle.

THE DEVIL IN THE BACK PEW

This sort of temptation shows itself in all kinds of ways: skipping Sunday church; foregoing daily prayer or quiet time with God; staying home from my Bible study group; not bothering to help a neighbor in need; holding back on giving because "money's short right now;" and so forth. I don't wish to be legalistic or put anyone on a guilt trip (we all get sidetracked at times), but let us recognize how much of the thought/feeling is enemy-planted.

In the personal example above related to skipping the passage on the passion of Christ, my actual response to the dark urge was to read more slowly than usual and get all I could out of it. This seemed appropriate given that the enemy didn't want me to read it. To be clear, my decision to read more contemplatively was based on what I perceived the Holy Spirit would have me do. I was *not* doing so in a stubborn attempt to do the opposite of the enemy's suggestion. He is clever, and an automatic contrary response could be a manipulation (think negative psychology). When the enemy is speaking, don't analyze it. Focus on the Holy Spirit.

Bottom line, satan is relentlessly trying to cut us off from all sources of truth, overcoming power, and intimacy with God. Otherwise, he is beaten – and he knows it. Don't let your guard down!

There is another aspect of this type of enemy intrusion (again, a temptation to distance us from God's truths or his people), regarding being hypercritical of Christian teachers, teachings, and the like.[35] Too often we are inclined (or tempted by the enemy) to reject the whole when it's most appropriate that we just "spit out the bones." That is, take and hold onto the good and Godly, and ignore that which we are, in good faith, uncomfortable with.

Marital Tension

Below are two Scriptural examples of vulnerabilities pertaining to the marital relationship. In his first letter to the Corinthians, Paul writes:

---

[35]When taken to the extreme, this can open the door to harassment from divisive, dark religious spirits.

"Let the husband render to his wife the affection due her, and likewise also the wife to her husband. The wife does not have authority over her own body, but the husband does. And likewise the husband does not have authority over his own body, but the wife does. **Do not deprive one another** *except with consent for a time, that you may give yourselves to fasting and prayer; and come together again* **so that [s]atan does not tempt you** *…"* (1 Corinthians 7:3–5, emphasis mine)

Paul states explicitly that marital partners are to be submissive to each other sexually, and that not doing so opens the door to satan's temptation.

Likewise, in his letter to the Ephesians, Paul warns against ending a day angry (probably most relevant to married couples) and thereby giving rights to the devil: *"Do not let the sun go down while you are still angry, and* **do not give the devil a foothold"** (Ephesians 4:26–27 NIV, emphasis mine).

It is significant that, in each of the above situations, Paul specifically mentions satan's participation. Bottom line, each party should remain aware that these are prime areas of enemy attack (i.e., channels of temptation), and that husband and wife must each be guided by the Holy Spirit and by selfless love.

A Peculiarly Common Intersecting Thought

Kris Vallotton speaks all over the world. He tells how he often takes an informal poll at his meetings asking, "How many of you have been driving down the road, minding your own business, when out of the blue you have the thought that you should crash your car into something …?" Having asked this question of many thousands of people, he attests that about two thirds raise their hands and acknowledge having had this experience.[36] Two thirds! It is true that one of our most basic human instincts is self-preservation. A clear thought, so destructive and of such consequence,

---

[36]Vallotton, *Spirit Wars*, 48–49.

THE DEVIL IN THE BACK PEW

can only be attributed to the enemy of our souls. Again: steal, kill, and destroy ... If the thought comes into your mind, spit it out. If you have similarly destructive thoughts, recognize the source, recognize the voice(!), and refuse them.

The enemy Can Speak (and Tempt) Through People

... when permitted to do so. With a little Christian discernment, we can occasionally "hear" the enemy speaking through people. It is as if the demon whispers in the person's ear, and the words come out of their mouths – completely unfiltered, and with zero thought. Our enemy satan and his demons are masters at this.

Perhaps you are able to recognize the literally anti-Christ comments of some public figures, celebrities, or television talking heads. Perhaps also you have heard the enemy speak through a rebellious teenager or an unbeliever. If this occurs, be careful what you say in return. A quick, accusatory reply might be the enemy trying to fool *you too,* to jump into the fray.

Now, the mirror. Have you ever thought about this? That a thought you had, or a word you spoke, may actually have been enemy-planted? Do you think you are above this possibility? I confess I have noticed enemy-planted thoughts too late, i.e., after they have come out of my mouth. Sometimes, *a long time* "after." I also wonder about the ones I have *not* noticed. There are relevant Scripture-based recommendations in the paragraph 'Indispensable in Battling Temptation' below.

A practice which we have seen that works successfully with folks tempted to speak too quickly (the enemy is good at zingers and gotchas) is to count to two before saying anything. And especially when we wish to disagree.

Welcoming Dark Thoughts

Does our personal entertainment or do our conversations glorify any of the following: materialism, greed, revenge, broken marriages, broken families, belittling people, lascivious behavior (one-

100

night stands, affairs, porn)? What about movies, TV shows, or books with unholy themes? Also: willful sin, fantasies, porn (near-porn), which feed unholy desires, or desires which are unholy *for you* (e.g., catalogues which excite weaknesses toward clothes, power tools, sports equipment, etc.).

These identified "Channels of Temptation" highlight types of thinking which may be sinful, are sinful, or may lead to sin or oppression. That which becomes a persistent problem generally starts small and gains strength over time. To break propensities which have become strongholds, we must get to, *and deal with*, the root cause or entry point.

I regularly pray, "Lord, show me the devil's tricks and protect me from his lies." Keeping an attitude of needing the Lord's help, as instructed in the Lord's prayer, motivates me to keep my guard up. And as confirmed by Scriptures cited earlier, satan and his demons are real, they are skilled, and they do not give up.

Indispensable in Battling Temptation

Take Every Thought Captive

Take full responsibility for what you do with whatever enters your mind. If it is not pure, holy, and constructive, reject it. *"[W]e take captive every thought to make it obedient to Christ"* (2 Corinthians 10:5 NIV). As thoughts precede activity, refuse to engage in bad thinking or the subsequent steps of submission. For example, if you are married, do not become vulnerable to or interact (flirt?) with, an individual who is attractive to you.

Much of what the enemy speaks are lies to accuse, to demean, to distract, to belittle. When you "hear" the lie, immediately take your stand and vocalize intolerance – aloud, if surroundings permit. Say, "That's a lie!"

Be Careful What You Say

Foundational to the Scriptural admonition to watch our tongue, as well as to the spiritual warfare message of this book, is the verse:

THE DEVIL IN THE BACK PEW

"Death and life are in the power of the tongue ..." (Proverbs 18:21). This truth is critical to harnessing God's power for our lives and for victory in spiritual warfare. The following quotations are from the book *Spirit Wars* by Kris Vallotton:

> *"One of the worst things we can do when we are battling the enemy's onslaughts and our minds are under siege is to speak. I do not mean we should avoid asking for help or grow silent in some corner; I am talking about verbalizing the demonic thoughts, speculations, or lofty things being propagated against us. Articulating these poison arrows only helps assimilate them into our hearts and live them out in our souls."*[37]

Negative words spoken in times of distress must be renounced, and forgiveness from the Lord sought, or they will "live" in us and open the door to demonic oppression, dark thoughts, fears, and destructiveness. Such proclamations can be referred to as "negative covenants." Kris gives an example of a woman who, in a stressful situation, uttered: "I could just die in peace and this would all be over ..." and was thereafter plagued with thoughts of suicide.[38]

> *"Besides a lifestyle of sin and believing lies, negative covenants are one of the most common ways Christians invite demonic oppression into their lives."*[39]

Related to this is another comment I have heard Kris make on more than one occasion: "The entire spirit world operates by faith – if you believe it, you empower it."[40] It is appropriate to add, "If you speak it, you empower it." More on this topic in Chapters 7 and 8.

Temptation, when yielded to consistently, can lead to a sin stronghold, which may open the door to the next level: oppression.

---

[37]Vallotton, *Spirit Wars*, 103.
[38]Vallotton, *Spirit Wars*, 153.
[39]Vallotton, *Spirit Wars*, 154.
[40]Many of Kris Vallotton's teachings are available online at www.bethel.tv.

Oppression

Oppression, in the context of personal spiritual warfare, can be described as:

- A sense or feeling of: defeat, entrapment, despair, helplessness, hopelessness, strong emotion, or lack of control – often accompanied by an intense, though still possibly subtle, heaviness or dark presence. Significantly, this can be so familiar and ingrained that it is virtually not perceived by the person oppressed, or at least not as a matter of present consciousness. The person accepts their situation as normal; they learn to live with it: they think it is who they are (e.g., a "victim" persona), *or*
- A *very* strong temptation, perhaps accompanied by a dark presence.

In this book, I will identify oppression as a demonically rooted attack which is *without* externally visible demonic manifestation, while demonization is much the same (though likely more intense) but *with* externally visible demonic manifestation. Regarding the mechanics of the enemy's assault – whether a demon is *in* a person, *on* a person, *next to* a person, *doing drive-bys*, or *actively influencing* a person – I neither know how to determine with certainty, nor believe it is relevant. And whether the situation is an oppression or a demonization, the pray-er's objective is the same: to get rid of the demon! As stated, the distinction between these two types of attacks is helpful to facilitate the discussion.

Roots of Oppression

- "Dirt" from virtually any sinful behavior can lead to oppression by the enemy. As the dirt accumulates, the enemy's rights, and power and influence, increase.
- An oppression related to strong temptation may result in a perceived lack of self-control for, or overwhelming heaviness upon, the person victimized.

THE DEVIL IN THE BACK PEW

- Physical or emotional trauma is a common root of both oppression and demonization. These may or may not be linked to the prayee's sinful behavior or to a temptation vulnerability, but the intensity can be severe and the distress debilitating.

Trauma

We begin with some general observations about trauma:

- Trauma can result from actual physical hurt or distress, like a bodily injury, a battle with disease, an auto accident, or a violent occurrence, or from witnessing such an event.
- Trauma can be a consequence of emotional hurt or loss: pain, shame, anger, humiliation, fear, rejection, etc., from virtually any negative experience.
- Trauma often stems from a hurtful childhood event or environment, where the memory is connected to overwhelming pain or a feeling of helplessness. Significantly, the painful memory can be tied to the intensity of *a child's perception at the time*, perhaps even more so than to the hurtful occurrence itself. Further complicating the trauma, children often internalize emotional hurts and blame themselves.
- Trauma is the result of the perceived experience of the victimized person. What may not be traumatic to one may be devastating to another.
- Trauma can lead to the creation of self-protective emotional walls.

Evidence of trauma might be an elevated sensitivity or overreaction when a triggering situation or emotion is encountered, resulting, for example, in a red face or instant anxiety or inner turmoil. Importantly, the oppression is not the abhorrence of the experience or the loathing of the memory, it is the internal upheaval related to contemplating it. And it is precisely in this upheaval

104

The enemy at Work

where the enemy is comfortable to camp. It might be thought of as "piling on."

Examples of Oppression

These are similar, in that the hurts are both parent-sourced, but the examples show differing consequences:

- A fortyish person we prayed for a few years ago had an unfortunate relationship with his parents. Though loving and supportive in many ways, they were very disapproving of his wife and would criticize her incessantly whenever speaking with him alone. They stopped short of encouraging him to leave her, but they regularly voiced their many "reasons" why he would have been better off with someone else. Without doubt, the son and his wife were happy in their marriage and pleased with the direction of their lives. From the son's viewpoint, he knew the criticisms were unfounded, and he defended his wife when the barbs flew. But as time went on, he was increasingly plagued with thoughts of the unkind words. As a Christian, he perceived a spiritual heaviness after these condemning conversations, and the heaviness increasingly overshadowed his thoughts, eventually dominating them for weeks after each conversation. Deriding thoughts which replayed in his mind involved: the harsh comments about his wife; the parents' controlling demeanor; the hurt he felt for his wife; the feeling of being treated like a child; the lack of love displayed by his parents' behavior; the parents' refusal to acknowledge that the couple was happy; the misrepresentations; and more.

  I would describe this post-conversation, persistent battering of undesired and painful thoughts as classic enemy oppression.

- Another situation concerns a single woman in her thirties

105

THE DEVIL IN THE BACK PEW

whose mother was a controlling personality. As an elementary student taking music lessons, her mother disapproved of her being creative or playing kinds of music kids like, even though she won the praises of her instructor for showing initiative. In high school, she was badgered for not following her mother's suggestion to pursue science-related studies in preparation for a medical career. In college, she chose to study information technology, again not yielding to her mother's repeated complaints. Finally, after years successfully employed in technology, she is still subject to her mother's ongoing criticism: telling her she does not make enough money; suggesting she quit and seek employment elsewhere; proposing she go back to school to change careers; advising that her older brother could find her a better job; and so on. When we began praying for her, she acknowledged that she continues to be confronted with the critical thought, "Will Mom approve?" for virtually every big and little decision she faces, even inconsequential choices of daily life like which bath soap to buy or what to eat for dinner.

These persistent, pestering, enemy condemnations are a form of oppression, intended to undermine personhood and individuality.

Freeing Yourself from Oppression

It is quite clear that there was an oppressive enemy "piling on" in each of these accounts. I emphasize, though, that the oppression is not the parent's behavior per se, however reprehensible it may be. It is the accusing dark spirit continuing to badger the child victim long after the offending confrontation is over.

Important: Freeing yourself from this type of oppression does *not* require that the offending party change. That is a common deception of the enemy. Freedom comes from turning away from the enemy's accusations and accepting the truth of God's promises.

106

The enemy at Work

Briefly, victory over an oppressive spirit of this type is a two-step process. Step one, as explained in the prior section on Temptation: the victim must take the enemy-planted thoughts captive (i.e., the reminders of the condemning and disapproving words), and purposely and forcefully toss them out. Reject them. Refuse them. Treat the thoughts as the lies that they are (and, as is often the case, as the sin that it is to accept them),[41] and forbid them to be a part of their life.

Now, note well, the critical step two: the enemy's rights have to be broken. To the degree that there is unforgiveness toward the parent – the offender in these examples – he/she *must be forgiven*. This is a non-negotiable. Forgiveness is a Biblical mandate. It does not mean what was done was okay; it means you are turning the judgment over to God alone, which is what He demands. Holding onto the unforgiveness gives the enemy permission to continue doing what he is doing. Forgiving the offender breaks that right (see Chapter 6). This takes a degree of persistence and tenacity on the victim's part. But, without doubt, if we are right with God, we have the authority over these attacking spirits.

If there is a more severe demonic attachment resulting from this type of harassment (quite common), other methods may be required. (Discussed in "demonization" below and in Chapter 9.)

Oppression Related to a Cancer Battle

The two previous examples of oppression could be attributed to the emotional trauma of the situations. My cancer battle of a few years ago resulted in two separate experiences of enemy attacks on me, i.e., beyond the cancer itself. Both seemed to have resulted

---

[41]People often encounter situations where the oppressive voice of the enemy is speaking lies. Accepting this is, in fact, a denial of what God speaks to each of us who follows Him. Such false accusations or condemnation, even when from the mouth of a parent or other authority figure, must (at least internally) be refused, believing God instead. To accept such lies as truths is to disbelieve what God says about you. And that is sin.

107

THE DEVIL IN THE BACK PEW

from a combination of physical and emotional traumatic events.

Regarding the overall experience, I am blessed to be cancer free now and have tested favorably for several years. But it was a brutal experience: two surgeries, weeks of super-nauseating chemotherapy, thirty-three radiation sessions, forty hyperbaric oxygen "dives," three months of eating via a stomach feeding (PEG) tube, and about ten months of oxycodone for pain (over 200mg per day for most of it). I lost 55 pounds of body weight in the process.

- The first instance of oppression involved the radiation treatments. To prepare for the actual therapy, I was custom fitted with a skin-tight containment "mask" which, when in place, rendered me totally unable to move from the shoulders up (the cancerous growths had been in my throat and neck). The mask was bolted to a table, and the table was rolled into a radiation "tube" for each session. Subsequently, everyone left the room, and I was alone and locked down inside this very noisy, "banging" equipment for just under twenty minutes. My first session, when the mask was initially molded to my upper body and I was attached to the radiation table, was for me off-the-charts ugly and loathsome. My revulsion to the physical discomfort and to being severely restrained, combined with the almost morbid (to me) atmosphere of the radiation environment, apparently opened the door to a demonic presence, a tangible heaviness over me of fear and dread.

Of all the actual demon-confronting situations I had experienced in the prior ten or so years, none was as intense as the oppression I felt in radiation therapy. It was totally debilitating, and I was both overwhelmed and surprised by it. On arriving home after the first session, Patti and I immediately sought the help of scores of prayer partners and church leaders, explaining what was going on and seeking their fervent prayer support. I pulled no punches in describing the severity of the spiritual attack. I strug-

The enemy at Work

gle to find accurate words, even now, to explain what happened after the cry for prayer. In the thirty-three following radiation sessions, the oppression was "beaten down" by the presence and power of God. It was a true exchange. He took the oppression away and left me with His sweet presence. I had requested the radiation staff "blast" an intimate worship CD for me during the treatments. It had to be very loud to overcome the roar of the equipment, and the Holy Spirit overwhelmed me, completely displacing the demonic heaviness so dominant before. There were occasions when I found myself so absorbed in the worship, that tears of joy from the presence of God rolled down my face in the midst of the treatment. On at least one occasion, I remember thinking as the session ended, that I did not want it to stop, because I did not want the "presence" to lift. Amazing. All of this Goodness in the midst of one of the most unpleasant experiences of my life.

Now, years later, when I call to mind the radiation treatment room and the whole experience, I think of it as a dreadful battlefield made peaceful and victorious by God's grace. This was oppression overcome by much supportive prayer and the presence of God.

• The second instance of oppression was much different and came on me so gradually that I was unaware what was transpiring. The experience was remarkable to me, and I hope an alert to the reader, for one huge reason: despite my years of experience in dealing with all aspects of the demonic, including supernatural manifestations and talking to demons, *I did not recognize that a demonic presence was actually on me*. That is, until it abruptly left!

It appears that the oppression built up over time as a result of many distinct, unpleasant and stressful (i.e., at the root, traumatic) experiences. No surprise to anyone, a cancer diagnosis is a big jolt. The treatment process began the next day

109

with a cube of flesh cut from my throat, through my mouth, for biopsy purposes. After the lab results confirmed two doctors' diagnoses, my oncologist opined my chances of survival were "a little better than 50%." Then came installation of the stomach feeding tube, surgery to excise the tumors, the beginning of strong pain meds, as well as concurrent chemotherapy, radiation treatments, and IVs. Many chemo drugs have the side effect of making the patient nauseous; per the doc, the drug I was given was "off the charts" in this regard. Thankfully, a combination of two anti-nausea drugs helped. As a result of all of this (which required daily treatment visits for nearly two months), I was left extremely weak, unable to eat, mentally slow, and fighting severe pain 24 hours a day. Mostly due to the chemo drugs, which are toxic by design, but also from heavy radiation, I felt just awful throughout the treatment and for many weeks after: like I had been poisoned and my body was shutting down.

I insert here that, though I battled against pain, fear, and despair (was my life really ending?), I continued to have wonderful personal prayer times and connection with God. I admit, my prayers were often weak and my mind unclear, and at times I slept 15+ hours a day, but I regularly worshiped, rested, and cried out with the Psalms. The Psalms comforted me, gave me an outlet for my emotions, and were a source of God's sweet presence and promises. I had a string of them that I would go through continually to calm me and give me hope. I confess, though, that this cancer battle showed me that I was not as tough as I thought.

In the few months after the intense treatment, I continued to feel physically beat up, poisoned, and weak, and the pain was severe. Spiritually, though, in spite of the closeness I felt with God, I was overshadowed by a heavy "gloom and doom" feeling. I did not like it and would fight it with Bible reading and prayer. And it would ease. But

The enemy at Work

it seemed to remain in the background, returning after a short time. The uncertainty continued, "Am I going to make it?" Though I fought to remain positive and hopeful, each doctor's visit for a checkup was preceded by anxiety and a battle against fear and enemy-planted thoughts.

At one checkup, about five or six months after the first surgery, the doctor examined me and confirmed there were no signs of cancer recurring. It so happens that local recurrences of the kind of cancer I had are best assessed by visual examination. Though this type of cancer sometimes returns even a few years afterward, the first few months are most concerning. So his report was obviously good news. Patti and I left the office very relieved, and we headed for home. I retreated to my favorite chair in our den, and I sat and thanked God for the good report. I sensed peace and rest roll over me; it was sweet.

Suddenly, with no notice or prior indication, I felt what I can only describe as a strong *"Whoosh,"* and a tangible, palpable heaviness abruptly lifted off me, upwards, with a force which was almost violent. I immediately felt and knew that the heaviness, which had built up over half a year, was completely gone. The freedom I felt physically was unbelievable. It was like all of the darkness that came along with the cancer ordeal was gone.

Note: I still dealt with great pain, another surgery to come, and many more treatments, but the oppression, the darkness, the heaviness – and all that comes with it – were gone!

This last example of oppression, which I believe beyond any doubt was demonic in nature, resulted from an accumulation of tough experiences, or traumas. Again, the most surprising aspect of this experience, to me, is that I did not recognize what/who the source was. I have seen similar attacks many times on many people, but I did not recognize it on me! I got tricked. So, once again, I remind myself, "Don't let your guard down. Ever."

111

THE DEVIL IN THE BACK PEW

What caused the demonic attacker to leave? I am certain it was the truths of Scripture, layered over with the truth spoken by the doctor when he pronounced, "No cancer." The spirit world – God's world – is ruled by truth, and when an oppressive or demonizing spirit clings to a lie, it loses all rights when that lie is exposed. The nonbeliever doctor shined the light of truth on the enemy's lies, so the enemy lost his foothold and his power to hang on. As I thanked God and confirmed the doctor's words, the enemy quickly disappeared. The power of truth is one of the greatest sources of strength in personal spiritual warfare.

What I described in the "Whoosh" experience above, is very similar to the descriptions folks use when manifesting demons leave (are cast off) them.

This section began with a definition of oppression, and a statement that I am differentiating between oppression and demonization mainly by what is externally observable. Regarding each of the examples used, deliverance prayer may be required, or it may not. The presence of a dark spirit can, at times, be expelled by persistent, faith-filled prayer and resistance. Irrespective, it is appropriate to probe and pray.

An additional important point: An apparent case of oppression, like clinical depression, can be the result of physical problems (hormone imbalance, hypoglycemia). Professional medical treatment should be sought, as appropriate.

demonization

As stated in the discussion on oppression, when a person "has" a demon, there is often a manifestation of that presence, though that manifestation may be very subtle or intermittent. When a demon behaves in a manner which indicates that it is, in fact, "there," this is good news. The spirit is desperate, making its final effort to hang on.[42]

---

[42]An exception to this is described in "Speaking to/with dark spirits," p. 212.

112

Three Examples of demonic Manifestations

Below are specific details about demonic manifestations observed during actual deliverance encounters. Each differs in degree of intensity of manifestation, while in the third example, there was initially no manifestation whatsoever until a demon was specifically sought.

- In the first case, we were praying for a wonderful, bright woman (an entrepreneur in her forties), when she became mildly agitated. Suspecting demonic activity but still unsure, Patti and I in turn looked into her eyes and attempted to engage: "In the name of Jesus, you tormenting spirit, leave now! I command you. Leave." After repeating that a few times, and with little more effort, she slightly convulsed, paused contemplatively for several seconds, then exclaimed, "I can't believe it! I've had that with me all of my life! ... And it's gone!"

  A dark presence, which was so familiar it seemed to be part of her personality, was completely lifted off. Almost instantly, and with very little struggle. Her description was not unlike the "Whoosh" experience recounted above. She raved, celebrated, and thanked God; it was awesome to see how joyful she was, and how significant this was to her. More dark spirits were ejected in that and another session or two, but her physical response was minimal throughout. With one of those spirits, she stated she saw it close-up, face-to-face (describing it by holding her open hand flat about two inches in front of her nose), then it vanished. With another, she saw it departing as a "ball exploding out" of her chest. To us observers, though, she remained calm and barely disturbed.

  Note: The initial subtle evidence of her agitation could easily have been dismissed without pursuit.

- At the other extreme, several years ago, Patti and I, at the request of a concerned parent, prayed for a young man of

college age. He was raised in the church and had periods of fruitful relationship with God, but also times of lapsing into alcohol, drugs, and wild living. He carried many deep wounds, including being betrayed by people in church leadership. He was, at the core, quite broken. His is a long story with many struggles and victories, but we were only praying for him for a few minutes when a demon (or demons) began barking thoughts/complaints quite boisterously. Indeed, this young man told how he had trouble keeping the demons quiet as he went through daily life. Short of actual shouting, it was loud, pushy, obnoxious in demeanor, and had a penchant for speaking in another language, possibly German. The demonic presence revealed itself with virtually no prompting.

- In this last example, a woman in her late thirties came to us for prayer, seeking spiritual growth as well as healing for emotional hurts. After praying with her a time or two, we learned she was a well-grounded Christian. She prayed regularly, read the Bible, sought God's will for her life, served actively in the church, and had regular connection with other Christian believers. At one point, while recounting her family history, the subject of her sister came up and she visibly soured, muttering about the disdain she had for her. This was shockingly out of character and inconsistent with all her other commentary. She quickly transitioned to speaking of others with no further hint of difficulty or negativity. To be clear, there was no indication of dark spiritual activity related to her thoughts about her sister, though her reaction did not fit with what we might expect from a stable Christian. And since there was a possible stronghold of some kind, we continued to probe. Commonly, when there is an indication of a sinful mind-set or the like, we stop to deal with it – so we began to pray about the relationship with her sister, beginning with her forgiving her sister's

114

offenses. After a short time, she began to shake, a dark presence showed in her eyes, and her face contorted. The spirit was confronted and expelled in just a few minutes, and she was freed. Frankly, this was a surprise; no one present expected a manifesting demon harassing this wonderful Christian woman, but it certainly was.

This example shows a demonic presence successfully hiding until it was confronted with deliverance-type prayer. To be clear, if we had not asked about family history and the subject of her sister had not come up, and if we had not begun praying healing on their relationship, it is unlikely the demon would have been exposed. And it definitely would have remained!

Variations in Intensity

In our experience, when there is a demonic manifestation, prayees differ widely in both physical reactions and in what they sense is going on within them. That which is evident externally may parallel what's going on inside, but it may not.

If a demon is revealing itself, we might observe a range of manifestations:

- from twitching, uneasiness, restlessness, unwillingness to look you in the eyes, inability (or difficulty) to pray or to speak Jesus' name, desire to leave the prayer session, spoken feelings of dislike/hostility to those praying; to
- more extreme shaking, foot-stomping, grunting, groaning, coughing, sweating, contorting, moaning, crying; to
- demon(s) speaking: "He/she wants me here," "I have a right to be here," "You can't make me leave." Also: severe agitation; making the prayee feel ill (headache, nausea, pain); or various threats/hints of violence. Forbid or denounce these immediately, in Jesus' name; to
- supernatural manifestations (beyond demons speaking).

THE DEVIL IN THE BACK PEW

I once saw a man's face grossly distort to the appearance of a gargoyle. A Bible school teacher told me he saw a person's face physically change to the visage of a monkey. I also heard a well-known Christian teacher tell of a person's body bending in a place where bones should not permit; this same person has also seen people levitate under the influence of demons.

So, what do we do when we encounter demonic manifestations while praying for someone? In Matthew 10:8, Jesus tells us to *"cast out demons."* This is not a limitless authority, but if we have permission to pray for someone, we should follow the Scriptural command. I believe that, if God lets me encounter a demon while praying for a person, He wants me to exercise His authority over that demon. I deal with the situation. I engage as necessary, and initiate the process of expelling the spirit(s).

"Possession"

Is the Term "Possessed" Accurate?

I begin with a discussion of the word "possessed," as used in Scripture. Firstly, the underlying Greek word, *daimonizomai*, has historically been rendered "demon-possessed" in most versions (translations) of the Bible. Some more contemporary versions use terms like "demon-afflicted," "demon-oppressed," "demoniac," and the like, but "possessed" remains in the vernacular, and is commonly used to refer to demonization.

Strong's Concordance defines *daimonizomai* as: "To be under the power of a demon" and adds the following explanatory comment:

> *"In the NT [New Testament], these are persons, afflicted with especially severe diseases, either bodily or mentally, (such as paralysis, blindness, deafness, loss of speech, epilepsy, melancholy, insanity, etc.) whose bodies in the opinion of the Jews demons had entered, and so held possession of them as not only to afflict them with ills, but also to dethrone the reason and take its place themselves; accordingly the possessed were*

116

The enemy at Work

*wont to express the mind and consciousness of the demons
dwelling in them; and their cure was thought to require the
expulsion of the demon.* "[43]

Strong's remark suggests a profound level of dark spiritual influence and authority.

It is noteworthy that no Bible account of casting out demons gives clear indication as to the victim's state being beyond "having" a demon. And since not all demonization is of a magnitude that it is even easily recognizable, the term "possessed" is arguably too broad, or at least an overstatement. Throughout this book I give examples of people *in the church* and *in Christian ministry* who have had demons expelled from them. To use the term "possessed" to describe them or, frankly, *any* of the hundreds of other demonized people we have prayed for, would be simply incorrect. Is the demonized person influenced by the enemy? Yes. Is the demonized person secretly harassed or persecuted in some way? Most certainly, yes. But to say they are "possessed" would be an exaggeration.

In his book, *They Shall Expel Demons*, Derek Prince makes the following observation: there is no basis for Bible translators to render *daimonizomai* as "possessed," for the original Greek "conveys no suggestion of ownership."[44] Indeed, foundational to the concept of the English word "possession" is the ability of the possessor to assert his or her right any time they wish, or even *all* the time.

Further, I have been unable to find, from teachers or authors on deliverance, any example of a *complete or full* "possession." I have seen such referenced by an individual affiliated with the Catholic Church, but no detailed evidence or witness was provided. Virtually all other modern-day authors and teachers prefer words like "demonized" or "having a demon." In the account of the Gadarene demoniac (Mark 5:1–17), the most severe Gospel example of demonic infestation, Scripture states the demonized

---

[43]Online Bible Edition 4.42.
[44]Prince, *They Shall Expel Demons*, 16.

THE DEVIL IN THE BACK PEW

man *"ran and worshiped"* Jesus (v.6) when he saw Him from afar. It is difficult to argue that possession, ownership, or complete control comport with such behavior.

Although Francis MacNutt states that he believes possession is possible, though very rare, in his book *Deliverance from Evil Spirits*, he challenges the appropriateness of using the term "possession." He states that thinking in such terms "blocks rather than helps our understanding," because "the need for deliverance is common."[45]

In spite of all the prior arguments, I nevertheless retain usage of the term "possession" (in quotes) for the title of this last, most severe category of enemy attack, principally because it's recognizable and familiar to the general, as well as the Christian population. Were the term not so entrenched and well-known, I likely would call this level "extreme demonization."

Catholic Church Practices

I return briefly to the practices of the Catholic Church because of its many documented examples of intense exorcisms. Whether we agree with their approach or not, the Catholic Church, at least doctrinally, does not shy away from what they call "possession." Under the pope and the church's worldwide organization, dealing with the issue is a matter of approved, if not discreet, ministry, including a documented "rite"[46] and strictly defined practices. Because of the worldwide presence of the Catholic Church, there is a measure of influence and consistency which surpasses that of virtually all other Christian denominations. And the Catholic Church seems to have institutionalized the terms "possessed" and "exorcism."

---

[45]Francis MacNutt, *Deliverance from Evil Spirits: A Practical Manual* (Chosen, a division of Baker Publishing Group, Grand Rapids, MI, 1995), 67.

[46]Rite of Exorcism, http://www.catholicdoors.com/prayers/english/p01975b.htm.

The enemy at Work

In Chapter 2, I mentioned the Catholic Church's restrictions on who may pray exorcising prayers and what words must be spoken. It is interesting that, just a few years ago, it was estimated there were merely fourteen Vatican-certified exorcists in the entire U.S. Given such a small number available to help, it stands to reason only the most severe cases find their way to a church-authorized exorcist. Further, Catholic sources indicate that similar "thin" coverage appears the norm worldwide, even in and near Rome.

I do not wish to debate Catholic vs Protestant faith differences (e.g., interceding through Mary or the saints), but I question the Catholic Church's restrictive controls over the exorcism process. Beyond limiting what can be prayed and by whom, there is a requirement that a psychological review affirm that an exorcism is necessary before prayer can begin, though some priests have challenged this practice. Further, some Catholic exorcists assert there is danger in praying a prayer of exorcism if it is not needed (also questioned by many in the Catholic Church), even adding that you should never speak with a demon, except as modeled by Jesus in Scripture. Additionally, there are expectations of the need to physically restrain the prayee, of the possibility of injury to the prayee or others present, and of demonstrations of superhuman strength. Though I have observed threatening behavior during deliverance prayer, I have never seen a situation where it could not be satisfactorily contained by verbal command, exercising God-given authority.

The supernatural manifestations described by Catholic exorcists are some of the most intense recorded. Surely, because of its notoriety in this regard, the Catholic Church sees a high volume of cases, including those which arise very rarely, say, the one-in-one-thousand occurrence. In the event that I encounter one of these difficult situations, do I need a worldwide church organization telling me precisely what to do and what to pray? My fallback, always, is that if God allows me to enter a situation which is extreme, He will provide me with what is needed to accomplish

119

THE DEVIL IN THE BACK PEW

His purposes, if indeed He wishes me to do anything at all. And, of course, He guides the "easier" encounters as well. My responsibilities are to remain humble and obedient, to keep my heart pure, and to acknowledge that all good that comes out of the situation is because of Him.

It is my contention – relevant to all Christian churches, and a principal reason for this book – that *many* demonized individuals are not freed because their cases are not extreme enough to warrant attention. Yet these lesser situations still involve believers suffering *daily* torment.

Three Situations of "Periodic Possession"

Below I cite two cases of egregious behavior which appear to involve some degree of lost personal control, but in both cases, there is also evidence of personal discipline and restraint. I also give details of a demonic confrontation involving a woman who was severely demonized, but who was nearly always able to suppress the dark spirits' outbursts and urgings. In these three situations, demonic activity is clear, yet the term "possessed" doesn't fit. However, one might legitimately question if there is not some degree of intermittent demonic control, or "periodic possession." Irrespective, the terms "demonized," "having a demon," or "extreme demonization" are more descriptive.

Two Public Examples

In 1989, an infamous serial killer, rapist, kidnapper, and necrophile by the name of Ted Bundy was executed in Florida. Shortly before his death, after a decade of denials, he confessed to killing thirty young girls and women. The actual number remains unknown, and many expect it was much higher. Bundy's case received significant media attention, and his last defense attorney described him as the very definition of heartless evil. But Bundy did not always wear that face. He was charming, presentable, and bright. One judge, after an early court proceeding where Bundy

120

The enemy at Work

represented himself, admonished him for his life choices, stating that he was exemplary in court and could have made an excellent attorney.

Dr. James Dobson, the founder of Focus on the Family and the public face of that organization at the time, sat with Bundy the entire night before his execution. Their time together was videotaped, and a production of it was later offered on television. Though appearing surprisingly calm, intelligent, thoughtful, and communicative, when he was asked a question about what he did to the young girls, he became visibly shaken and his immediate response was, "I can't think about it." And he changed the subject. Surely psychologists have terms for such behavior, but the stark contrast between his monstrous deeds and his peaceful demeanor, in the context of an abhorrence of the truth, forces one to consider intermittent demonic influence. Possibly temporary or occasional "possession?"

Many years ago, I was watching a PBS documentary which included a segment on pedophilia. I insert here that, for me, there are few things I find more repulsive than the sexual exploitation of children. Having that mind-set, I watched while an off-camera interviewer questioned an incarcerated, nice-looking man in his late twenties about his sexual crimes against children. I was taken aback by his spoken disgust with seeking sex with kids, and I was frankly shocked when he stated that his overwhelming feeling when caught was *relief*, "because then I knew I would never do it again." How is it that a seemingly lucid, intelligent-sounding young man does despicable, unconscionable things he hates? Could this represent a temporary "possession?"

Rachel

An additional example of extreme demonization concerns a woman that we prayed for about fifteen years ago, and out of whom were driven in excess of one hundred demons. Though the degree of her torment was immense, her behavior never extended to breaking

121

laws or bringing harm to others. Most would have described her, at her worst, as antisocial or irritable. She was avoided by many, and the brunt of the spiritual attack seemed to be directed at her.

I use a dialogue from a deliverance session with Rachel to show the interruptibility of a manifesting demon. Were she actually "possessed" (controlled or "owned"), I do not believe the spirit could be easily interrupted and Rachel, the person, would not be free to quickly divulge information so helpful to expelling the spirit. Admittedly, there was extreme dark influence, but the word "possessed" does not accurately describe her either.

More generally, in our many experiences with demons actively tormenting their victims, there has never been one where the dark manifestations were not to some degree intermittent: they would intensify then relax, ebb and flow, as the prayer proceeded. Situations or events at times seemed to trigger flare-ups, but nevertheless a cycle was always apparent.

Our experience with Rachel might appear at odds with Catholic exorcism-related accounts of a prayee being in a trance for most of or a whole prayer session. I assume the prayee remains in the "disconnected" state because the Catholic rite of exorcism is less of a dialogue and more a pronouncement of prayers. The prayee isn't "pulled out" of that state until the effort is completed or the exorcist ends it. In all the exorcism accounts I have read, whether Catholic or not, there is never any difficulty exiting the "trance-like" state.

Patti and I had been praying for Rachel for some months. She had a very unfortunate childhood, and we had cast out scores of demons. This exchange, somewhat abbreviated here, shows typical deliverance prayer dialogue.

The context is that we had connected with and were challenging a demonic presence. I was seated opposite Rachel, face to face, looking her in the eyes. Patti was sitting next to her with her hand on Rachel's shoulder. This particular demon was not yielding to

The enemy at Work

commands to leave. I pick up the conversation at that point:[47]

JK: In the name of Jesus, you must leave now. (Repeated several times.)

D: [No response]

JK: What gives you the right to be here? I command you, in the name of Jesus, to tell me and to tell the truth. (Repeated a few times.)

D: I came in when her neighbor molested her when she was twelve.

This was an event we were not aware of, so I paused and directed my question, not to the demon, but to Rachel.

JK: Rachel, I need to talk to you. Let's talk now. (Paused for a moment.) Rachel, are you there?

R: Yes, it's me.

JK: Is that you, Rachel? (Verifying.)

R: Yes, it's me. It's Rachel.

JK: Rachel, is it true – did your neighbor molest you when you were twelve?

R: Yes, he did.

We paused the demon confrontation and chatted briefly. Rachel told us how this man from next door had molested her and how it was so shocking and traumatic to her. We then gently prayed healing for the "little girl" Rachel (Jesus is not restricted by "time"), specifically that the confusion, the emotional hurt, the broken trust, the embarrassment, the violation, the violence, the painful memory, would all be healed by the sweet love and presence of Jesus. We prayed this way for a little while, until we felt the Holy Spirit release us. Next, the indispensable prayer of forgiveness: we led Rachel in a prayer forgiving the neighbor for this horrible act against her. (See Chapter 6 on forgiveness.)

Then, back to the demon, speaking face to face with Rachel:

---

[47]D = demon speaking; JK = the author; R = Rachel.

THE DEVIL IN THE BACK PEW

JK: OK, we're back. In the name of Jesus, I forbid you to hide. Come out, I'm talking to you.

Looking Rachel in the eyes, I sensed I had engaged the dark spirit.

JK: Now, I command you, in the name of Jesus, leave. Go. You must leave; you cannot stay. Your time is up. (Repeated a few times.)

R: [No response, but her countenance slowly relaxed – shifting from a cold, stern appearance to one of peace and calm.]

JK: Is it gone, Rachel?

R: Yes, I think it's gone. (Pause for a few seconds.) Yes, it's gone.

As explained, this dialogue exemplifies how a significantly harassed person being prayed for remains easily reachable in the midst of active interaction with a demonic spirit. Again, I have never encountered or heard of a deliverance prayer situation where this was not the case.

Other Extreme Cases

Father Gabriele Amorth, a well-known Catholic exorcist, tells the story of a man who was delivered of twenty-seven legions of demons over several years.[48] Exhibiting severe demonization for decades, it was revealed that he had been forced to drink the blood from a black mass at the age of four. With much deliverance prayer, family support, and personal prayer, he was fully freed when he was in his forties.

Many of the most severe accounts of demonization directly involve satanism. Fr Amorth tells of a nun whose father exposed her to satanic rituals as a child. After nine years of weekly exorcism prayer, she continued to suffer.[49] In another case, Dr. Ed Murphy tells of a struggling Christian missionary out of whom were

---

[48]Amorth, *An Exorcist Explains the Demonic*, 80.

[49]Matt Baglio, *The Rite: The Making of a Modern Exorcist* (Doubleday Religion, an imprint of the Crown Publishing Group, a division of Random House Inc., New York, 2009), 133.

The enemy at Work

driven over one thousand demons over a period of years. Extensive prayer and counseling sessions (with Murphy and a professional) revealed she was a victim of satanic ritual abuse and had in excess of one hundred alter personalities within her.[50]

Numerous accounts of exorcisms mention bizarre manifestations, including prayees levitating, showing unnatural strength, or vomiting objects which were not ingestible. Fr Amorth asserts that, when a demon identifies itself with a known Biblical name, it is much stronger and more difficult to dislodge.[51] We have seen demons give their names as "satan," "lucifer," "beelzebub," "leviathan," and "jezebel," to name a few, and affirm that they are among the most resistant.

How Common is Extreme demonization?

In his decades of praying the Catholic rite of exorcism, Fr Amorth estimates he has prayed for thirty thousand people. Further, he states that only ninety-three[52] of those cases were sufficiently severe to warrant the description "possessed" as he applies the term, or "extremely demonized," in my words. His experience equates to approximately three per thousand (about one third of 1%), which is roughly the proportion of *extreme* cases we've seen over the years.

One qualification, however: Amorth explicitly states that demons speak only in cases of "true and complete possession."[53] My experience is of demons speaking in situations far less intense than what I would describe as "extreme demonization." Rather, I have seen them verbally communicate in perhaps 15% to 20% of all deliverance encounters – and that, implicitly, is a frequency forty-five to sixty times higher(!) than that described by Fr Amorth.

From my research of Catholic exorcisms, there seems a wide

---

[50]Murphy, *The Handbook for Spiritual Warfare*, 471–476.
[51]Amorth, *An Exorcist Explains the Demonic*, 102.
[52]Amorth, *An Exorcist Tells His Story*, 169.
[53]Amorth, *An Exorcist Tells His Story*, 79.

THE DEVIL IN THE BACK PEW

disparity of views on the wisdom, or correctness, of speaking with demons – with many strongly opposing the practice. I am not reluctant to verbally engage these spirits if doing so may be helpful, and I often initiate such communication, should progress slow. Perhaps this accounts for the vast difference we've observed in the numbers of those spirits which communicate verbally.

Chapter 5

The Need for Inner Healing

In this book, I use the expression "inner healing" to mean the healing of emotional hurts, those non-physical wounds of the heart stemming from personal loss, painful memories, unpleasant life experiences, and even trauma. The terminology is in common use today, though in some cases more broadly, even encompassing New Age beliefs. For our purposes, the reader should think of inner healing as *Christ-centered emotional healing*.

The discussion in this chapter is top-line and in the context of exposing and breaking the enemy connections with these wounds. The significance of the link between emotional hurt and demonic activity cannot be overstated. It is therefore appropriate that this topic be given special attention in a separate chapter. Many wonderful books on inner healing and related subtopics are available from Joyce Meyer,[54] Judith MacNutt, and others.

The call to minister inner healing is quite clear from Scripture:

> *"The Spirit of the Sovereign LORD is on me, because the LORD has anointed me to **preach good news to the poor**. He has sent me to **bind up the broken-hearted**, to **proclaim***

---

[54]I particularly recommend the devotional version of Joyce Meyer's *Battlefield of the Mind*. The format gives brief, foundational lessons of truth and encouragement for daily victory.

freedom for the captives and release from darkness for the prisoners, to proclaim the year of the LORD's favor and the day of vengeance of our God, *to comfort all who mourn, and provide for those who grieve* in Zion—to *bestow on them a crown of beauty instead of ashes, the oil of gladness instead of mourning, and a garment of praise instead of a spirit of despair.* They will be called oaks of righteousness, a planting of the LORD for the display of his splendor." (Isaiah 61:1–3 NIV, emphasis mine)

What Does an Inner Healing Need Look Like?

People with heart wounds often find themselves in emotional prisons, at times seemingly constructed by others, but generally self-made. Inner healing invites the true self, the chosen child of God, to come out into the light – to shed the damaged self-image, or false self, in favor of God's truth.

In many situations, the false self:

- has difficulty maintaining real relationship (keeps others at a distance, even a spouse);
- avoids the risk of rejection (and may work too hard to please others);
- can hide behind a "Who cares?" attitude;
- rejects others before they can be rejected; and
- misrepresents and pretends in order to hide the hurting false self (instinctively, without conscious thought).

Most of us need some measure of emotional or inner healing.

In Judith MacNutt's opinion, there is a demonic element in about two thirds of the people who have need for inner healing.[55] In my experience, the proportion is that high or higher. Emotional wounds and hurts of the heart are places where demonic spirits thrive. The powers of darkness work to *steal* lives, to *destroy* lives;

---

[55]From the video by Judith MacNutt, *Inner Healing and Forgiveness Prayers* (Christian Healing Ministries, Jacksonville, FL).

The Need for Inner Healing

Jesus has come so that we may *"have life, and ... have it more abundantly"*[56] (John 10:10). Inner healing prayer is speaking blessing and healing and truth over the brokenness on the inside, allowing the love and peace of Jesus to wash over those enormously painful hurts. And God is *so* faithful in lifting the heaviness. No, the memory does not disappear, but the Holy Spirit spreads a sweet, unexplainable balm over it.

We pray, therefore, for prosperity of spirit, of soul, of mind, of body, of family, of relationships, of aspirations, of work, of rest. Of every facet of existence. Unhealed inner hurts can cripple a person emotionally, and be a barrier to a rich, full life, to a God-*filled* life. They can also lead to destructive, even sinful, overcompensation to avoid further hurts. For example, a person abused as a child can be overprotective of their own children, to the extent that it is stifling and harmful.

Note: In deliverance situations, it is always necessary to pray for inner healing. At the core of virtually every enemy attachment is a deep, emotional hurt of some kind. Conversely, when an inner healing need is uncovered, it is always appropriate to search for a demonically seeded root. It is in this context that Judith MacNutt's two-thirds estimation proves out.

Common Symptoms of the Need for Inner Healing

- Unforgiveness – perhaps not even acknowledged. From my experience, Christians can be quite self-convincing in their denial of unforgiveness. (See Chapter 6.)
- Persistent fears – both large and small.
- Inflexible behaviors and attitudes (gotta-dos/can't-dos/ compulsions) – versus preferences and peaceful choices.
- Excessive focus on self-protection.
- Uneasiness – in general, and when prayer triggers an emotional response; reluctance to let others "in."
- Painful memories.

---

[56]See Appendix II: "The Poverty Mind-set."

THE DEVIL IN THE BACK PEW

- An unhealthy need (compulsion) to control.
- Shame – a deep belief that you are a bad person or significantly flawed, versus a conviction about sinful behavior, which can be confessed and forgiven.
- Depression.
- Indications of oppression or demonization.

Common Root Causes

- Loss of a family member due to death or divorce. A child perceives this as abandonment or rejection.
- An adopted child's sense of rejection by the birth mother, irrespective of the adoptive parents' care.
- Harassment by siblings, peers, or classmates.
- Physical disability; dissatisfaction with physical appearance or skills.
- Belittlement; feelings of inadequacy (not as smart as brother; not as pretty as sister).
- Physical or sexual abuse; rape; emotional and verbal abuse.
- Physical or emotional trauma, or witnessing the same.
- Fear or experience of inadequate food, shelter, clothing or safety.
- Dysfunctional, negative childhood environment.
- Poor life choices.

Discipling Away the Lies

If there is a call for inner healing, there are virtually always *lies* that need to be uncovered and quashed. In earlier chapters, I have made the case that lies undermine faith and the power of Scriptural truth, and that the enemy is empowered when we believe lies. On several occasions, I have heard Bill Johnson address the subject with these words: "Any place in your life where you have no hope is under the influence of a lie." That is a profound truth. Exposing the lie often reveals the place where inner healing is needed.

How do we approach this? In simple terms:

130

The Need for Inner Healing

- Probe for lies that have been believed.
- Show the truth.
- Proclaim the promises of Scripture.

There are several instances in this book where I mention *discipling* as part of the overall warfare process. Though discipling is a broad term, it is an apt description for the three steps described above. Jesus' pronouncement: *"[Y]ou shall know the truth, and the truth shall make you free"* (John 8:32) is 100% relevant to inner healing and deliverance. Often, the prayee's heartfelt belief of the truth of Scripture, and the concurrent acknowledgement of satan's lie, is all that is needed to open the door to emotional healing and complete victory. This is not an exaggeration!

Practically speaking, a wounded person may have difficulty discerning an actual truth because their feelings concerning a painful experience seem to get in the way. Feelings are often deceptive, and the enemy is quite adept at planting thoughts and feelings to further his destructive purposes. When an unhealthy struggle with feelings occurs, compassionate discipling can help close the gap.

It may also be that believing a particular lie is contrary to God's Word and is actually sin. If this is the case, it should be confessed and renounced. For example, "Forgive me, Lord, for believing the lie that I am worthless. I am a unique child of God, and I am fearfully and wonderfully made. I renounce self-condemnation." The prayee then has the responsibility to take the accusing thought captive, and reject it, whenever it returns. And it likely will, as this is a common tactic of the enemy. As mentioned earlier, a quick, faith-based retort to enemy-planted thoughts is, "That's a lie!"

Inner healing sometimes feels incomplete *solely* because the enemy repeatedly brings a hurtful incident to mind. Several years ago, a sweet, young mother came to me for prayer related to memories of her grandfather sexually abusing her. Her issue was not difficulty dealing with unforgiveness (he had passed on, and she had totally released him), but the enemy kept bringing it up constantly. She was genuinely healed and free of the original hurt,

131

THE DEVIL IN THE BACK PEW

but the big-mouthed enemy of her soul kept telling her she was not. We prayed about what the enemy was doing, emphasizing that he had *no* rights. She embraced the truth and rejected the lie. I did not pray for her further, but her ongoing acceptance of the responsibility to take the thought captive will assure her freedom.

One final comment pertaining to *lies believed.* It is not uncommon that a prayee may feel that their sin or situation is just too bad or too evil for God to tolerate. Statements like, "You don't know what I've done ..." or "No one could accept me given what I've been through ..." are heart cries of despair and shame. And classic enemy-planted rubbish! My reply to these dear people is always the same: "The cross is *good enough!* The cross is *big enough! Jesus paid for it all! All!*"

If a person struggles with accepting this depth of forgiveness, my follow-up question, posed gently but soberly, is, "And what is it about Jesus' sacrificial death that is inadequate to cover *your* sin or situation?" I do not recall ever having been pressed beyond that point, but if it should happen, my recourse would necessarily be to probe the person's perceived self-importance, i.e., their pride. Much brokenness and distorted thinking would be likely. The implication would be that they feel beyond the reach and power of God.

Relevant Principles

- Many hurts at the core of inner healing needs stem from traumatic childhood experiences. As unpleasant memories are carried into adulthood, often the *perception of the pain,* or the fear of recurrence, *remains* as it was comprehended when it was originally experienced by the child. It is as if the feelings of helplessness, hopelessness, or vulnerability, for example, continue to be carried at the child's level of maturity and not at the level of the adult to whom you are ministering. Judith MacNutt, in her video teachings, makes an analogy to a restricted elephant, where an adult

The Need for Inner Healing

elephant continues to be bound by a weak chain used when it was quite small. The adult does not test the strength of the chain, which it could certainly escape, but yields to the memory of the chain's ability to restrict.

In addition to unhealthy fears and sensitivities being carried into adulthood, *poor modeling* has its own consequences. For example, a child victimized by abuse from excessive discipline may struggle in disciplining their own children, or one who was sexually abused might suffer from sexual brokenness later in life. Trauma terrifies, shocks, and can cause extreme emotional pain; inner healing prayer brings Jesus and His truth into the situation.

- Probing inner healing needs has been compared to peeling an onion. There are *layers* of hurts, damaged emotions, and distorted self-image, which must be stripped away one at a time. Then subsequent deeper layers are revealed. And there are tears.

- Whatever is in darkness must be brought into the light of Christ. The enemy (the Bible calls him the *"accuser"*) is quite adept at reminding us of our unpleasant past, then suggesting we must keep it secret. In truth, *secrets* can keep us in bondage to enemy lies.

- *God heals, not us.* We ask the Holy Spirit to lead and to touch the deepest parts of the wounded person. Human love is important, but God's love transforms. And the more we focus on who we are in Christ, the less it matters who we were in the past. For genuine healing, a person must fully yield to Christ and acknowledge that, on their own, they are powerless.

- A basic objective of inner healing prayer is *restoration of union* with God and others. The enemy works to isolate the individual and to sow seeds of doubt and hopelessness.

- Often a prayee is fearful or reluctant to face a memory, confront a personal misstep, forgive, or seek healing, because

THE DEVIL IN THE BACK PEW

doing so is perceived to be *too painful*. It is critical that the prayee understands Jesus will gently help, heal, and lift the pain – and remove the deeply hurt portion of the memory.

Important: If the situation is not dealt with, the prayee will live with the hurt and consequences *until they deal with it*. Or until they die!

- A special *trust* is established when a person shares their innermost thoughts. The wounded person must feel safe, and they must be able to trust you. Author, counselor, and pastor, Danny Silk, speaks of the importance of trust when ministering to hurting people:

  "People who cannot trust will not show the truth of what is going on inside of them to anyone. They feel safer keeping the 'broken spot' concealed. It takes a safe place to expose a vulnerable place, an area that needs healing. It matters ... [most] ... that the one who is scared believes he or she is cared for and protected."[57]

- A large part of the healing process may be in the *telling of the story*. Many times, while praying for someone, I have heard them say, "I've never told that to anyone before."

- Often the *reaction* to an event, and not the event itself, is the problem. For example, a person might pridefully refuse to let go of a negative attitude, cling stubbornly to unforgiveness, or find misguided relief by embracing a victim persona. These coping methods are dead ends.

- The prayee should be led to see that, in God's Kingdom, we do not just put bad things out of mind, but rather we:
  - face and admit the hurt or offense;
  - take it to God;
  - let go of the hurt, and release/forgive the person who is the source of the hurt;

---

[57]Danny Silk, *Culture of Honor* (Destiny Image Publishers, Inc., Shippensburg, PA, 2009), 182.

The Need for Inner Healing

- o repent, confess, and renounce, as necessary; and
- o exchange our brokenness for His wholeness, our hurt for His peace.
- Compassion and love are key to praying for inner healing. Ask to have God's heart for anyone you pray for. Every person is a child of God, including the demonized and the unlikable.
- God is not restricted by *time*. He can enter and bring His healing to memories of past painful experiences. When we ask to see a memory through God's eyes, the memory does not change, but the pain of it can be removed.
- As appropriate, query the person's *image of God*. Oftentimes the wounded person attributes, for example, an earthly father's harshness or intolerance to our Heavenly Father. Help the prayee dispel false images of God.

Praying for Inner Healing

For those inexperienced in praying for inner healing needs, sample wording is offered below. These are not presented as words to be repeated, but rather as indicative expressions of compassion, gentleness, and restoration. Without striving, let the Holy Spirit speak through you.

- Lord, we ask that you heal [person's] broken heart.
- Jesus, lift off the heaviness of the painful memories.
- We pray the hurt of the memory be completely removed.
- We break the enemy's lie that [this situation] defines you.
- Holy Spirit, let your love and peace entirely displace the pain of [this memory].
- We reject the lie that [person] can never get past this.
- Lord, pour your love over [person].
- Lord, renew [person's] mind regarding who [he/she] is.
- Jesus, let your sweet presence wash away every hurt and pain.
- Loving Father, give [person] a sense of how a *real* father

THE DEVIL IN THE BACK PEW

loves, provides, and protects.

- We break the enemy's lie that [person] caused this situation.
- Bring Your perfect peace between [person] and [other].
- Teach [person] that there are many people who are trustworthy and strive to be good.
- Spirit of [fear/regret/shame/condemnation], begone!
- Lord, we speak blessings over every facet of [person's] life – over [his/her] family, work, finances, etc.

In the many teachings I have heard from Christian Healing Ministries, it is regularly advised that, "You should not pray for anyone unless you know God's love for them." This is a foundational truth that should guide all prayer efforts. God's love is truly at the root of everything good that can, and will, happen in this ministry.

We said that God is *so* faithful in lifting the heaviness of emotional wounds. When that pain and memory have been turned over to God, a process is begun whereby the enemy loses all rights to hang on. Again, this is not a science, and we don't understand how it all works, but inner healing prayer can render the enemy powerless. God's truth sets people free! It is glorious, and a foundational step in expelling demonic influences.

Chapter 6

The Need to Forgive

Forgiveness was of great significance in the life and teachings of Jesus. When Jesus taught the Lord's prayer, He told the disciples to pray: *"[F]orgive us our debts, As we forgive our debtors"* (Matthew 6:12). And *while* Jesus was hanging on the cross, He spoke the words: *"Father, forgive them, for they do not know what they do"* (Luke 23:34). These Scriptures show, in the first case, what God's standard is and, in the second, how forgiveness remains paramount, even while we are feeling the pain of the offense.

Texts and teachings on healing and deliverance prayer virtually all deem forgiveness indispensable to victory. My personal experience since early ministry days bears witness to this, and I add that the most difficult challenge in the healing prayer ministry remains persuading the deeply wounded both to acknowledge and to deal with their unforgiveness. Left unresolved, *unforgiveness is an insurmountable barrier to freedom.*

Retribution and Revenge

Though it is not sin to be sinned against, the reaction to abuse may become sin if it moves into resentment, unforgiveness, bitterness and other negative emotions.

It is notable that much of North American culture celebrates

THE DEVIL IN THE BACK PEW

retribution and revenge, which is portrayed as "justice." Perhaps, like me, you enjoy movies with complicated plots where clever bad guys are overcome by smarter good guys. Good over evil is noble and right, and it feels good! But when it enters our personal space, the desire for this can become twisted before God. He has a different agenda for our hearts. No one can escape the hurts of life which, for so many, lead to "offense" – but clearly offense is a trap of the dark realm.[58] We can quite easily cry, "It's not fair!" and justify unbiblical behavior and attitudes.

This next Scripture passage addresses the topic from several perspectives:

> "**Do not repay anyone evil for evil.** Be careful to do what is right in the eyes of everybody. If it is possible, as far as it depends on you, **live at peace with everyone.** **Do not take revenge**, my friends, but leave room for God's wrath, for it is written: '**It is mine to avenge; I will repay**,' says the **Lord.** ... Do not be overcome by evil, but **overcome evil with good.**" (Romans 12:17–19, 21 NIV, emphasis mine)

There are dozens of Bible verses which speak a similar message, and not one permits mankind's unforgiveness. A simple Google search will reveal large compilations of forgiveness-related verses from myriad sources. Of course, there is punishment and retribution for unconfessed wrongs, but God alone judges. And repays.

Forgiveness and Unforgiveness

Is forgiveness optional? According to the Bible, simply, no! I mentioned Jesus' instruction in the Lord's prayer: we are forgiven *as we forgive.* Jesus knew this was going to be tough. Significantly, when He taught the Lord's prayer, He only saw fit to repeat one part of it:

---

[58]See Bibliography for a foundational teaching on this subject – John Bevere, *The Bait of [s]atan.*

138

The Need to Forgive

*"For if you forgive men their trespasses, your heavenly Father will also forgive you. But **if you do not forgive men their trespasses, neither will your Father forgive your trespasses.**"* (Matthew 6:14–15, emphasis mine)

Scriptures on Forgiveness

The Scriptures on forgiveness highlight the following principles:

- Forgiveness is to be from the heart:

  After telling the parable of the unforgiving servant, and describing how the servant's unforgiveness would result in him being *"delivered ... to the torturers,"* Jesus said: *"So My heavenly Father also will do to you **if each of you, from his heart, does not forgive** his brother his trespasses"* (Matthew 18:34–35, emphasis mine).

- Repeated offenses do not change the standard:

  *"Then Peter came to Him and said, 'Lord, **how often shall my brother sin against me, and I forgive him?** Up to seven times?' Jesus said to him, 'I do not say to you, up to seven times, but **up to seventy times seven**'"* (Matthew 18:21–22, emphasis mine).

- Unforgiveness is an impediment to prayer:

  *"Therefore I [Jesus] say to you, whatever things you ask when you pray, believe that you receive them, and you will have them. And **whenever you stand praying**, if you have anything against anyone, **forgive** him, **that your Father in heaven may also forgive you** your trespasses. But **if you do not forgive, neither will your Father in heaven forgive your trespasses**"* (Mark 11:24–26, emphasis mine).

- Jesus' instruction from the Sermon on the Plain (Luke 6:20–49):

  *"Judge not, and you shall not be judged. Condemn not, and you shall not be condemned. **Forgive, and you will be forgiven**"* (v.37, emphasis mine).

- We are to love our enemies:

THE DEVIL IN THE BACK PEW

"But I [Jesus] say to you who hear: **Love your enemies, do good to those who hate you, bless those who curse you, and pray for those who spitefully use you**" (Luke 6:27–28, emphasis mine).

Simple Truths About Forgiveness

- Forgiveness is a transaction between the offended person and God. The perpetrator of the offense has no role in this transaction.
- Forgiveness is an act of the will. A choice.
- Forgiveness is a gift, unearned and undeserved, just as our salvation is unearned and undeserved.
- Offering forgiveness does not mean you are saying that what was done to you was okay.
- Conditional forgiveness is not Biblical forgiveness. Requiring the offender's apology or any other restorative action is not part of the transaction. It may be appropriate in some cases to seek a measure of restoration, but forgiveness is not true if offered subject to some condition.
- Forgiving someone may open the door to ongoing communication and terms of peace, including a personal expression of forgiveness. Or it may not. Where danger exists, contact may need to be avoided. A person in such a situation should prayerfully seek Christian counsel. Also, an offending party may not have the ability, the willingness, or even the understanding necessary to receive an offer of forgiveness. Paul advises: *"If it is possible, as much as depends on you, live peaceably with all men"* (Romans 12:18).
- Forgiveness means letting go of the offense. Continually speaking of the offense might be evidence of a refusal to fully release the offending party, or to forgive from the heart.
- Oftentimes forgiveness is a process, and necessarily dealt with one step at a time. When forgiveness is required in order to continue a relationship, as in a marriage, daily

The Need to Forgive

living can be a challenge. We might rightly demand evidence of trust and proper behavior. In the circumstance of a spouse who has been betrayed, for example, the offended party must demand marital faithfulness. Yet forgiveness before God for the offense (i.e., the transaction with God) is not optional. Bottom line, forgiveness must be offered unconditionally, but the continuation of the relationship will be dependent on the errant spouse's behavior. Wise Christian counsel should be sought when working through the complexities of marital unfaithfulness.

- To completely lift the emotional hurt caused by others, pray for them daily: "Jesus, I ask You to give [person] your best blessing today, the very best You have." This gets easier over time and actually becomes a sweet blessing as it spills back on the person praying. Such is God's way.
- Forgiveness is like saying, "Lord, I am not pressing charges."
- Letting go of unforgiveness, and confessing *your* sin of unforgiveness, is saying, "Forgive *me*, Jesus. I will not try to play *God*. I will let *You* be God."
- Forgiveness cuts the rope that keeps you tied to that old hurt.
- Carrying unforgiveness is like drinking poison and hoping the other person dies.
- "Forgiveness is not an occasional act; it is a permanent attitude." – Martin Luther King[59]
- A daily prayer: "Lord, hold nothing against anyone for what they have done to me."

Is Unforgiveness a Big Deal?

According to the Bible, refusing to extend forgiveness to another means we are not forgiven. It is crystal clear. Does this extend to the forgiveness we need for salvation? Some say "yes," and some

---

[59]http://www.azquotes.com/author/8044-Martin_Luther_King_Jr/tag/forgiveness.

THE DEVIL IN THE BACK PEW

say "no." The only arguments I know of for unforgiveness not applying to salvation are tied to the belief in eternal security (i.e., once saved, always saved) and the doctrine of election. I am not a theologian, and will not attempt to build a case for or against such beliefs, but an obvious weakness of any position permitting unforgiveness is the fact that there are *many* Scriptures explicitly against it. I can find *absolutely none* explicitly for it. Such logic involves taking a general tenet of faith and using it to negate or ignore a specific Biblical prohibition.

Since I have a long history of sin, there is no way I would ever permit myself to stand before God harboring unforgiveness toward *anyone!* If this is a point of struggle for you, I ask: Is holding on to your justification for unforgiveness really worth the risk?

Extreme Offenses that Hinder Forgiveness

Quite often, a person may sincerely wish to forgive, but thoughts about the related hurts and wounds persist. Helping folks navigate through issues peripheral to forgiveness is frequently necessary, especially when the underlying injury is great. Daily life can continue to be impacted by memories of events which occurred years or decades prior, even when forgiveness has been offered. Some examples of the more difficult hurts include:

- sexual assault;
- physical trauma;
- murder of a loved one;
- childhood abuse or abandonment;
- loss or death of a loved one during childhood;
- betrayal; and
- gross shame.

These types of extreme hurts frequently leave lasting wounds, and those wounds often have the faces of the offending persons on them. The emotions (fear, shock, grief) related to each memory can repeatedly come to mind, triggered by simple heartache, by

The Need to Forgive

events of life, by enemy-planted thoughts, or by the direct consequences of the offense itself. In the last case, for example, a person
may find themselves in daily financial straits because they were
cheated by a business partner; or someone may have unrelenting
physical pain due to injury caused by a drunk driver. The daily
struggle serves as a constant reminder.

Note: Children commonly perceive a death or divorce as abandonment or rejection, leaving a deep hurt and, in some cases,
requiring a form of forgiveness.

Forgiving small offenses should not be difficult for the Christian believer. The process of dealing with great hurts, though, can
be most difficult. There actually are two distinct steps to getting
past a big offense:

- The offended person must *choose* to forgive the offender,
  before God, as sincerely as he/she can.
- The offended person must learn how to constructively *deal
  with the residue* of the event or situation, or they can undo
  the forgiveness offered to God in the first step.

Understanding and facing this "residue" is most important, for
incidents will have different characteristics, depending on the
nature and gravity of the offense. We might, for example, whole-
heartedly forgive before God, but unwittingly allow the unpleasant memory to resurface and fester, so that we gradually return to
wallowing in unforgiveness. A necessary follow-up step, is to:

- Seek God's peace and restoration for the loss suffered.

I cannot overemphasize the importance of this step. It is absolutely
essential to give the hurt and pain to God, and to obtain the peace
He promises. We must beware: the enemy is quite adept at "reset-
ting the hook" of unforgiveness. The goal must be to allow God to
heal (completely remove!) the deep hurt of the painful memory.
The memory remains, of course, but the horror, the emotional
pain, goes. In the difficult situations of extreme offense, assuredly
the enemy will attempt to trigger the memory. The response is a

THE DEVIL IN THE BACK PEW

simple, rest-filled rejection of the thought – that is, a rejection not based on striving, but rather on peaceful trust in God. It is also helpful to remind ourselves who it is that is planting the thought, and to reject it out of hand for that reason alone. Recognize the enemy's voice, and refuse anything he says.

Attaining this level of overcoming victory can be greatly helped by compassionate, inner healing prayer. I encourage the reader: permitting the Holy Spirit to truly lighten the load of emotional hurt does not require a special anointing or advanced training. If the Lord is made welcome, He will do His work. *Remember, we are talking about the emotional aftermath.* The burden on the prayee is merely to do his or her part, to let go of the offense and to offer forgiveness. Long-endured enemy attachments (of all intensities) can then be broken. We have seen this work wonderfully countless times!

enemy Harassment that Hinders Forgiveness

Experience has shown us that stubborn unforgiveness has an *"enemy"* component. In the case of a person willfully and purpose-fully hanging on to an offense, it is clear this is a choice against God's will and is sin. As discussed earlier, sin gives the enemy the right to hang around, harass, and plant unpleasant thoughts.

In other cases, however, a person may sincerely wish to for-give, and offer it, yet still fall short of full release from persistent thoughts, feelings of heartache, or the pain itself. Such a struggle is not evidence of unforgiveness. Rather, it reveals a need for *inner healing* and/or *improved spiritual warfare skills*. Battling the pain-ful memories should be approached as we deal with any other enemy attack or temptation: take the thought captive and toss it out – *every time*. And be careful what you speak. (See Chapter 4, "Indispensable in Battling Temptation," p. 101.)

Again, ridding a person – or ourselves – of this type of enemy harassment is a two-step process:

- sincerely offer forgiveness; and

144

The Need to Forgive

- steadfastly refuse the enemy's reminders.

It may require dogged persistence, but it is absolutely doable.

Forgiving Ourselves? Forgiving God?

It is not uncommon to hear people talk about the need to forgive themselves. Indeed, I have heard this suggested by rather prominent Christian teachers. Such a thought can feel quite natural; most of us have done things we are ashamed of, feel guilty about, or otherwise regret. And, not surprisingly, the enemy is quite adept at reminding us of our mistakes. Again, the Bible calls him the *"accuser."* The attendant harassment can take the form of temptation, oppression, or even demonization, but these all can be dealt with as discussed throughout this writing.

Regarding forgiveness of oneself, though, there is no Biblical basis for this. We cannot "pay" for our sins, neither are they "lifted off" if we offer an excuse or explanation for our behavior. We simply do not have the spiritual authority to forgive ourselves. If we did, we would not need a Savior! Of course, the emotional pain should be confronted and dealt with as we deal with hurts from other types of heart wounds. That pain or regret, though, is simply not something resolved by *forgiving* yourself. When folks seem stuck on this thought, I like to shift the focus to their putting trust in God and receiving the forgiveness Jesus bought for us on the cross.

More rarely, in my experience, is the suggestion that a person forgive God for unfortunate circumstances or occurrences in their lives. Exploring this in depth is beyond the scope of this writing, but I would suggest that anyone inclined to think that God needs to be forgiven has a fundamental misconception of God. I would recommend counsel from a respected pastor or Christian leader.

Chapter 7

Blessings and Curses

What are Blessings and Curses?

In the secular vernacular, a "blessing" might be a polite response to someone's sneeze, a prayer before a meal, or an approval for a considered course of action. The term "curse," on the other hand, is commonly used to mean a vulgar four-letter word or a coincidental string of bad luck. Biblically speaking, however, these involve God's favor or judgment, or the works of powers of darkness.

Blessings and curses, in their various meanings and contexts, are mentioned over six hundred times in the Bible. In simple terms, we might think of a blessing as the *exercise, or verbal release, of Godly spiritual authority, and good.* Conversely, a curse would be the *exercise, or verbal release, of dark spiritual authority and evil, or of God's judgment.* An expanded definition of a curse is the dark spiritual power tied to words – written, spoken, or thought – which proclaim negative, undesirable, or unbiblical circumstances upon a person, situation, or place. A curse might also describe the dark spiritual residue that clings to a person from sinful behavior. In his excellent book on blessings and curses, author Derek Prince states:

> "*Both blessings and curses belong to the invisible, spiritual realm. They are vehicles of supernatural, spiritual power. Bless-*

146

ings produce good and beneficial results; curses produce bad and harmful results. Both are major themes of Scripture.[60]

Though society today might dismiss blessings and curses as subjects of fairy-tales, to the spiritually inclined or sensitive, evidence indicates otherwise. That which is released in the spiritual realm, and that which is spoken, is important and carries consequences! Jesus stated:

> *"But I say to you that for every idle*[61] *word men may speak, they will give account of it in the day of judgment. For by your words you will be justified, and by your words you will be condemned."* (Matthew 12:36–37)

Significantly, this is not just about God judging us for mouthing harsh or uncharitable words, it is about the consequences of those words:

- Did we speak life, or did we speak death?
- Did we speak mercy or judgment?
- Love or hatred?

Though God's judgment is absolutely relevant to mankind, our study will focus on relieving curses, specifically those:

- brought on by our own actions or words;
- from external sources; and
- passed on generationally (see Chapter 8).

God promised Abram: *"I will bless those who bless you, And I will curse him who curses you …"* (Genesis 12:3).

Speaking Blessings Rather Than Curses

Decades ago, I heard a well-known Pentecostal teacher's sermon on speaking blessings. He shared a clear example from his own

---

[60]Derek Prince, *Blessing or Curse: You Can Choose* (Chosen, a division of Baker Publishing Group, Grand Rapids, MI, 1990), 32.
[61]NIV: *"careless."*

THE DEVIL IN THE BACK PEW

experience of how we may choose to bless versus disparage or curse. Traveling to a northern city for a speaking engagement, he was picked up at the airport as a winter storm entered the area. The roads were snow-covered and hazardous, and his young driver was proceeding cautiously. Suddenly a car aggressively passed them and sped down the road without apparent concern for the difficult conditions or for anyone's safety. The teacher confessed he muttered judgmentally to himself about the reckless way this person was driving, but was quickly corrected by the grace of his young chauffeur's quiet prayer, "Lord, help that guy to not hurt himself or anyone else." The teacher humbly admitted his youthful driver's response revealed a heart attitude purer than his own.

For several years, my drive to work took me past an adult book store. Many, many times I used the occasion to curse that business. Some of my rants were in the nature of, "satan, get your work out of my community," or "Lord, shut that place down. Let them go broke," or even "Lord, let that place burn, never to reopen." I was quite creative in my condemnations. There were also words of judgment uttered toward the "perverts" whose cars were parked there. Where I am in my Christian walk now, recalling my words makes me shudder! How about this approach: "Lord, bless those broken people who are in that place now," or "Lord, heal the sexual woundedness of the folks who stop here," or "Lord, speak Your love and truth to the owner of that place. Let him see satan's lies."

We can speak life, or we can speak death, light or darkness, grace or condemnation. *Or blessings or curses!* In this chapter, I hope to show how blessings and curses are integrally related to the battle against the enemy of our soul. As quoted earlier, our foundational Scripture, Proverbs 18:21, states: *"Death and life are in the power of the tongue."*

Far beyond the impact of a disapproving tirade from an unreasonable boss or teacher, spiritual weight and authority accompany those words. We will discuss *recognizing curses*, their *power*, and their *sources*, and we will show *how that power can be broken.* An

148

Blessings and Curses

indispensable and integral part of that process is the *proclamation of God's blessings* over the individual or situation.

Recognizing a Curse

Most of us know folks who seem to live under a shadow of gloom, sometimes affecting only facets of their lives (like relationships or finances), while others face persistent difficulties in multiple areas. Could a curse be at work? Such uncertainty is not untypical when dealing with dark spirits and spiritual mysteries. At times, a prayer effort seems a puzzling search to uncover what lies behind the discomfort or loss or torment being experienced by the victimized individual.

Derek Prince lists seven Bible-based problems indicating a curse may be at work in the individual or in their lineage:

- "Mental and/or emotional breakdown
- Repeated or chronic sicknesses (especially if hereditary)
- Barrenness, a tendency to miscarry, or related female problems
- Breakdown of marriage or family alienation
- Continuing financial insufficiency
- Being 'accident-prone'
- A history of suicides and unnatural or untimely deaths"[62]

For clarity, I would add *oppression* and *demonization* to this list. We might say they are inherently included or "beneath" the evidences listed, but often they are the most noticeable indicator. Further, though these problems are not always the result of curses, when they are evident, the possibility should be explored.

The Curse of Death

Since Eden, the curse of death remains upon mankind – and will until such things cease when the New Jerusalem descends from

---

[62]Prince, *Blessing or Curse*, 45.

149

THE DEVIL IN THE BACK PEW

heaven: *"Then I, John, saw the holy city, New Jerusalem, coming down out of heaven from God ... And ... there shall be no more death ..."* (Revelation 21:2, 4). In the meantime, our fleshly bodies deteriorate, and eventually we die.[63] This inevitability, a universal overarching curse of sorts, can be compounded by other curses.

Untimely Deaths

I begin with two examples, where strings of untimely deaths seem so far beyond normal expectations, that it is difficult to imagine that an unseen power is *not* at work. To be clear, I am not suggesting, in either case, that I know what the *nature* of the curse is, or was, at that time. If this is knowable, it would be a revelation of the Spirit, or information possessed by those personally involved. Irrespective, the facts speak for themselves.

The first case concerns the number of tragedies and untimely deaths experienced by the family of U.S. President John F. Kennedy (JFK). I identify each event by referencing the family relationship to JFK:

1941   JFK's sister, Rosemary, intellectually disabled and subject to mood swings, was given a secret frontal lobotomy leaving her unable to walk or speak well. The surgery was arranged by her father without her mother's knowledge. She was thereafter institutionalized until her death sixty-four years later.

1944   JFK's brother, Joe Jr., was killed when his plane exploded on a wartime mission.

JFK's brother-in-law (sister Kathleen's husband) was killed

---

[63]The notable exception to the universality of bodily death is described in 1 Thessalonians 4:17 where, on the Lord's return, *"we who are alive and remain shall be caught up together with them in the clouds to meet the Lord in the air. And thus we shall always be with the Lord."* Otherwise, the Bible (in the Old Testament) identifies only Enoch and Elijah as individuals who did not experience physical death.

150

Blessings and Curses

in battle. They had been married just four months.

1948   JFK's sister Kathleen died in a plane crash in France.

1956   JFK's two-day-old daughter, Arabella, died of an infant lung ailment.

1963   JFK's two-day-old son, Patrick, died after his premature birth.

JFK was assassinated in Dallas, TX.

1964   JFK's brother, Ted, was involved in a plane crash in which his aide and the pilot were killed. Ted suffered a broken back and other serious injuries.

1968   JFK's brother, Bobby, was assassinated in Los Angeles, CA.

1969   JFK's brother, Ted, ran his car off a bridge on Martha's Vineyard, resulting in the death of a young female colleague.

1973   JFK's nephew, Joe II, was the driver in an accident which left his female passenger paralyzed.

1984   JFK's nephew, David, died of a drug overdose in a Florida hotel room.

1997   JFK's nephew, Michael, died in a skiing accident in Colorado.

1999   JFK's son, John Jr., his wife, and sister-in-law were killed when the plane he was piloting crashed into the Atlantic Ocean near Martha's Vineyard.[64]

All the preceding involved JFK, his brothers and sisters, or their-

---

[64]www.infoplease.com/spot/kennedytimeline.html; www.pbs.org/wgbh/ americanexperience/features/timeline/kennedys/; en.wikipedia.org/wiki/ srv/national/longterm/jfkjr/timeline.htm; en.wikipedia.org/wiki/Kennedy_ curse.

THE DEVIL IN THE BACK PEW

children. This is quite a small circle for such extreme calamity. In addition to the above, there were numerous other situations of tragedy and heartache impacting the JFK clan.

The second example I cite concerns a remarkable situation of directly related family members dying on the same calendar date in different years. A Christian friend of mine had a very close relationship with his great-uncle Andrew. Their friendship and connection were so strong that my friend invited Andrew to serve as his best man when he and his wife were married. When he was in his eighties, Andrew, who had been a hardworking farmer, began to develop heart problems. As he came under a doctor's care, he shared with my friend a belief that he would die on September 27. It so happened that, a few years earlier, his brother had died on September 27 … and both their father and their grandfather had also died on September 27! He believed, and stated, it was his destiny to also die on that date. As his condition grew worse, Andrew was hospitalized and under close observation. Significantly, the attending doctor shared with the family that there was no physical reason for Andrew to be doing so poorly. Nevertheless, Andrew continued to decline, and he died on September 27.

Statistically, odds are 365 to one (ignoring leap year) against any person dying on the same date as another. If you add a third and a fourth person's identical death date to the calculation, odds increase to over forty-eight million to one against this occurring randomly. What was going on? Information is scant on Andrew, and nothing is known about the deaths of his brother, father, or grandfather. Andrew himself was an energetic, peace-loving person who always seemed young despite his age. He and his wife had no children, but otherwise their lives were not unlike those of others of his time. But he carried a belief which cast a shadow over him. How can a spoken expectation of death on a certain date, with no intervention, lead to it actually happening?

Two additional examples of untimely death involve people I have personally known. One has to do with a tragic self-curse, and

Blessings and Curses

the other a bizarre preoccupation with death. In the first case, this bank executive was educated, talented, and successful. He became careless with alcohol, however, and it took over his life, leading him to lose his family, career, and all for which he had worked. During the downward spiral, it was peculiar to me that he continued to maintain an ability to work, perform competently, and be 100% temperate when required, operating as some might call a "functioning alcoholic." At one point, while lucid and sober, he predicted to a coworker that he would likely drink himself to death. Unfortunately, that is exactly what he did. He was found dead of alcohol poisoning on the floor of a cheap apartment. At the time, years ago, I grieved for him, but was not aware of the power behind a self-curse. Though still able to control his drinking when he put his mind to it, he yielded to what he verbalized was an irrepressible destiny.

The second situation concerns a guy who was, in most ways, a typical, all-American kid. He had interests and likes typical of most youth of his day, and no one thought anything unusual about him. Unbeknown to most, he did have an almost macabre fascination with death. He would talk privately about details of death, embalming, cadavers, funerals, and coffins with a strange curiosity and enthrallment. Sadly, I did not have a sense of surprise or shock when I heard that both he and his wife died of physical ailments in their thirties. Was this a self-curse? Or did he open a door to darkness? Only God knows. But beyond all doubt, I would strongly discourage verbalizing ungodly affection for death, as I heard him do on so many occasions.

These cases show, in differing ways, the consequences of a dark influence on each of the situations. We certainly do not have full understanding but, importantly, we have Biblical truths to reflect on.

The Power of Words

Perhaps you have heard someone say "knock on wood" or "touch wood," and even reach for an object of wood, after speaking of a

THE DEVIL IN THE BACK PEW

bad possibility they wish to avoid. For example: "Oh, it might rain for our picnic tomorrow. Knock on wood, I hope that doesn't happen!" as if knocking on wood negates the possibility of the words coming to pass. To be clear, belief in any power related to such "safety solutions" is superstition, the validity of which I adamantly and fully reject. But again, Scripture tells us: *"Death and life are in the power of the tongue"* (Proverbs 18:21). We must watch our words so that we do not give powers of darkness any permissions over our lives.

In many years of meeting and praying with folks struggling physically or emotionally, we have seen countless examples of careless words given life, as it were, by the verbal proclamation of lies, fears, and enemy-planted thoughts. I truly believe it is impossible to overstate the importance of this issue to the subject of this book and to the maintenance of spiritual, emotional, and even physical health. What we speak matters! Statements like, "I'm never going to find a man I can trust," "I'll probably get prostate cancer just like my dad and brother," or "Everybody in our family struggles financially," give permission to the enemy to impact our lives in these areas.

The Bible tells us we are to bring our thoughts into *"captivity"* (2 Corinthians 10:5) and make them obedient to Christ. That plainly means rejecting those which are *not* Godly! Be aggressively intolerant of them. I once advised a woman to treat believing the nagging, painful thoughts and memories of her mother's incessant criticism as sin, because to dwell on and accept those condemning words was to deny God's acceptance of her as His child. That she is special in His eyes. That she is *"fearfully and wonderfully made;"* that all her *"days [were] fashioned"* before she was born (Psalm 139:14, 16).

Derek Prince recounts an experience of praying for a woman who had come to him for deliverance. She had a history of occult involvement and was seeking God, but she had not yet been fully freed of her old ways. At one point during the prayer session, she

154

Blessings and Curses

stated to Derek, "I see you in a car and it's wrecked against a tree." He immediately recognized that a demon was speaking, and he took his stand. Speaking to the enemy, he proclaimed, "[s]atan, I refuse your destiny for my life. I shall not be in any car that's wrecked against a tree!"[65] This event took place thirty years earlier, and he thanked God that he was alert enough to reject the curse the dark spirit was trying to put on his life.

His response is a model for us all. Biblical descriptions of the enemy were cited earlier (satan comes to steal, kill, and destroy; he prowls around like a roaring lion; he is an accuser and the father of lies), and we know these truths. Paraphrasing Philippians 2:9–10, every knee shall bow and every tongue confess that Jesus is Lord, of those in heaven, on earth, and under the earth.

The enemy of our soul has no power over us unless we give it to him. If you have unconfessed sin, deal with it, and be made righteous. *"If we confess our sins, He is faithful and just to forgive us our sins and to cleanse us from all unrighteousness"* (1 John 1:9). Then take your stand against the dark plans for you. When a future-focused accusatory, fearful, or sinful thought or temptation comes to your consciousness, renounce it and confidently proclaim: "satan, I refuse your destiny for my life. I follow the Lord and choose *His* direction for my future." And give it no further thought. If you catch yourself saying something you wish you had not said, renounce it and ask God's forgiveness for your idle words, then speak God's favor into the situation.

As unfitting words often result from stress, frustration, and the like, a great help in dealing with these is to repeatedly pray the words of Psalm 19:14 (NIV): *"May [the] words of my mouth and [the] meditation of my heart be pleasing in your sight, [O] LORD ..."* And allow God's peace to rest on you.

Some years ago, my wife, Patti, and I gave each other full permission to correct the other when one of us utters anything unscriptural or that opens a door to the enemy. And yes, this per-

---

[65]Prince, *They Shall Expel Demons*, 116.

THE DEVIL IN THE BACK PEW

mission is still exercised from time to time. We *all* have difficulty controlling our tongues!

The Sources of Curses

Though there are different sources of curses, importantly, Proverbs 26:2 tells us that *"a curse without cause shall not alight,"* stating that neither God's judgment nor dark spiritual authority comes upon us on its own. There is a cause or source or reason. The derivative message of this verse is that, if there is a cause, that cause can be identified and fended off, refused, removed, or otherwise rendered null and void. We therefore seek to identify the source or cause of any suspected curse.

God's Curses

Does God really curse? The Bible clearly tells us that there is a penalty for sin. We know we serve a God of mercy, but He is also a God of justice and judgment. Were judgment not necessary, Jesus would not have submitted to death on the cross.

It is clear throughout the Bible that there are consequences to our behavior. Two New Testament verses confirm this simply and clearly: *"[T]he wages of sin is death"* (Romans 6:23); and *"[W]hatever a man sows, that he will also reap"* (Galatians 6:7). Related, simple observation of humanity reveals the unpleasant outcomes of ungodly life choices and behavior, many examples of which are cited in this book.

Paul continues: *"For he who sows to his flesh will of the flesh reap corruption, but he who sows to the Spirit will of the Spirit reap everlasting life"* (Galatians 6:8). And James adds: *"[W]hen desire has conceived, it gives birth to sin; and sin, when it is full-grown, brings forth death"* (James 1:15). Though the Old Testament goes into great detail about blessings promised for obedience, and curses resulting from disobedience, should our new status in Christ not relieve us of the end result of confessed sin? It is apparent a degree of "tag along" residue, or "curse" can remain.

156

Blessings and Curses

In Deuteronomy 28, there is an extensive list of blessings and curses spoken to the nation of Israel. About these, Moses wrote: *"[I]f you diligently obey the voice of the LORD your God, to observe all His commandments ... all these blessings shall come upon you ... "* (Deuteronomy 28:1–2), but, *"[I]f you do not obey the voice of the LORD your God, to carefully observe all His commandments and statutes ... all these curses will come upon you and overtake you"* (v.15). Derek Prince summarizes this detailed Bible text as follows:

- Blessings:
  - "Exaltation
  - Health
  - Reproductiveness [of lineage, livestock, crops, investment, etc.]
  - Prosperity
  - Victory
  - God's favor"[66]

- Curses:
  - "Humiliation
  - Barrenness, unfruitfulness
  - Mental and physical sickness
  - Family breakdown
  - Poverty
  - Defeat
  - Oppression
  - Failure
  - God's disfavor"[67]

There are more specifics in this Scriptural narrative but, ultimately, the curses (or judgments) are generally the unfavorable opposites of the blessings. It is important to understand that the Bible offers no direct third option to the blessings-curses "rule." We have the choice to submit and obey, and be blessed, or to disobey and suffer

---

[66]Prince, *Blessing or Curse,* 42.
[67]Prince, *Blessing or Curse,* 43.

THE DEVIL IN THE BACK PEW

the unavoidable consequences. Since Eden, the enemy has been trying to convince mankind that we can elude submission to God with no downside. This is certainly not the case. God will not be mocked. Again, we *will* reap what we sow!

Now, despite the foregoing, there is an additional, overriding truth which is relevant here. The atoning sacrifice of Jesus can cover our sins! And neutralize them, and *"cleanse us from **all** unrighteousness"* (1 John 1:9, emphasis mine). Irrespective, it is undeniable that, even if we turn to Christ and are cleansed of sin, further cleanup is most often necessary.[68]

The Judgment of God: False gods

It is foundational that we serve a loving God. He is the Creator, Provider, and Source of all that is good. He has given us literally *everything* that we have, and He has made, through Jesus Christ, a means of everlasting relationship with Him. But He rightfully requires of us that we put nothing before Him. The following are excerpts from the ten commandments:

> *"I am the LORD your God … You shall have no other gods before Me. You shall not make for yourself a carved image … you shall not bow down to them nor serve them. For I, the LORD your God, am a jealous God, visiting the iniquity of the fathers upon the children to the third and fourth genera- tions of those who hate Me … You shall not take the name of the LORD your God in vain. Observe the Sabbath day, to keep it holy … "* (Deuteronomy 5:6–12)

For the context in which the commandments were listed, Deu- teronomy 4:24 states: *"[T]he LORD your God is a consuming fire,*

---

[68]A simplified example of the nonremoved consequences of sin is the confession of a drunken binge. The sin is surely forgiven, but the hango- ver remains and must be dealt with separately. Likewise some measure of dark spiritual residue can remain after confessed sinful behavior. Indeed, this book is written to help overcome the stronger aspects of this residue, i.e., that not dealt with via personal sanctification.

a jealous God." The writer of Hebrews also states: *"[O]ur God is a consuming fire"* (Hebrews 12:29) and further warns: *"It is a fearful thing to fall into the hands of the living God"* (Hebrews 10:31).

God is quite clear in His message – putting anything or anyone before Him will not be tolerated: it will lead to disfavor in this world and destruction in the next. All forms of idol worship, satanism, occult practices and the like will result in God's curse extending as far as the fourth generation of descendants.[69] Specifically, witchcraft (dark power), divination (knowledge from a dark source), and sorcery (dark-sourced influence, from "good luck" activities, charms, amulets, drugs, dark music) each attempt to replace the legitimate authority of God with that of satan. In our Western culture, the dark root of these activities is often not flaunted, but represented as harmless fun, and described with benign-sounding words like "new age," "white witchcraft," or "paranormal activity."

Note: It is quite common for churchgoing folks, both in ignorance and willingly, to have dabbled in some of these dark practices in their pasts. But freedom awaits!

The Judgment of God: Forbidden Behavior

The Bible identifies ungodly, immoral, and uncharitable conduct as behavior which results in curses.

- Deuteronomy 27:16–26 forbids:
  - Mistreating parents
  - Perverting justice owed to neighbors, strangers, orphans, widows, or the unfortunate
  - Sexual activity with family members, in-laws, or animals
  - Disobeying God's law

  New Testament listings cite similar sinful activity.[70]

---

[69]This is discussed more particularly in the next chapter.
[70]See Romans 1:28–32, 1 Corinthians 6:9–10 and Revelation 21:8.

THE DEVIL IN THE BACK PEW

- Trust in human nature (self-reliance; independence from God):

"Thus says the LORD: 'Cursed is the man who trusts in man And makes flesh his strength, Whose heart departs from the LORD. For he shall be like a shrub in the desert, And shall not see when good comes, But shall inhabit the parched places in the wilderness, In a salt land which is not inhabited.'" (Jeremiah 17:5–6)

- Trusting in obedience to Biblical law (i.e., thinking of yourself as doing no wrong and, for that reason, not needing Christ to remove the curse):

"For as many as are of the works of the law are under the curse; for it is written, 'Cursed is everyone who does not continue in all things which are written in the book of the law, to do them.'" (Galatians 3:10)

Of course, Christ is the promise of the New Testament:

"Christ has redeemed us from the curse of the law, having become a curse for us (for it is written, 'Cursed is everyone who hangs on a tree.')" (Galatians 3:13)

- Teaching a distorted or false gospel:

"As we have said before, so now I say again, if anyone preaches any other gospel to you than what you have received, let him be accursed." (Galatians 1:9)

- Taking what is not yours or swearing falsely:

"'I will send out the curse,' says the LORD of hosts; 'It **shall enter the house of the thief And the house of the one who swears falsely** *by My name. It shall remain in the midst of his house And consume it, with its timber and stones.'"* (Zechariah 5:4, emphasis mine)

Note: As this curse is explicitly said to *"remain,"* it has last-

Blessings and Curses

ing consequences. *The Message* gives a clear New Testament perspective on ill-gotten gain: *"You thought you were piling up wealth. What you've piled up is judgment. ... The groans of ... [those] you used and abused are a roar in the ears of the Master Avenger"* (James 5:3–4 MSG).

- Robbing God

  "Will a man rob God? Yet you have robbed Me! But you say, 'In what way have we robbed You?' In tithes and offerings. You are cursed with a curse, For you have robbed Me ..." (Malachi 3:8–9)

  Significantly, this warning of a curse is followed immediately by explicit promises of blessing, if a choice is made to be obedient:

  "'Bring all the tithes into the storehouse, That there may be food in My house, And try[71] *Me now in this,' Says the LORD of hosts, 'If I will not open for you the windows of heaven And pour out for you such blessing That there will not be room enough to receive it. And I will rebuke the devourer for your sakes, So that he will not destroy the fruit of your ground, Nor shall the vine fail to bear fruit for you in the field,' Says the LORD of hosts; 'And all nations will call you blessed, For you will be a delightful land,' Says the LORD of hosts."* (Malachi 3:10–12)

  I have heard it argued by some that tithing is an Old Testament concept and is no longer required. Jesus made an indirect, though quite clear, statement regarding tithing in a corrective declaration to the Pharisees: *"But woe to you Pharisees! For **you tithe** mint and rue and all manner of herbs, and pass by justice and the love of God. **These you ought to have done**, without leaving the others undone."* (Luke 11:42, emphasis mine)

---

[71]NIV: *"test."*

161

THE DEVIL IN THE BACK PEW

- Anti-Semitism (dislike of, or negative behavior toward Jewish people). When God chose Abraham as the father of His people, He promised:

   "I will bless those who bless you, And I will curse him who curses you." (Genesis 12:3)

Curses by Authority Figures

Throughout the Bible, the authority of a father to bless is emphasized and celebrated. Derek Prince states:

   "The blessing of a father is considered second in importance only to that of God Himself. Implicit in the authority to bless, however, is the authority also to curse. Blessing and cursing can never be separated from one another, any more than heat from cold or day from night."[72]

Below, I quote an extended narrative of a parental curse experienced by a Christian couple with formal ministry involvement. It details both the husband's and the wife's perspective. As you read, note:

- The evidence of the curse: the frustration and "lack" which permeated their lives
- The power of words spoken by someone with authority
- The step-by-step process needed to obtain freedom
- The importance of controlling our thoughts
- The enemy's lies
- The sovereignty of God

"Husband

   *"Living under a curse is like living in a vapor. The effects can be seen, yet it is without clear form and substance. Even though you may experience success, you feel only **frustration and hopelessness.***

---

[72]Prince, *Blessing or Curse*, 107.

162

Blessings and Curses

"For me, the blessings of God always seemed somewhat remote and unattainable. I often knew the Lord's presence and moved in the spiritual gifts, yet satisfaction in ministry and life always seemed just out of reach. My wife and children had nagging health problems, and finances were continually short (even though we tithed, gave regularly and lived frugally).

"Though I knew clearly the ministry to which God had called me, I could not move into it. Most of my work seemed to end with just a measure of fruitfulness. I could start things, but couldn't complete them. I seemed to be facing some kind of invisible resistance.

"This struggle went on for years. Then one day I found myself explaining the situation to a group of fellow ministers, including Derek Prince. They discerned a curse coming on my family from my mother-in-law. I will let my wife explain:

"Wife

"Early in my marriage I spent two days in prayer and fasting. I felt the Lord showed me that there was a curse in my family. My husband and I were newly baptized in the Holy Spirit and had never even heard of such a thing as a curse. Our experience, as we have sought to become free, could be compared to peeling layers off an onion.

"This curse revolves around a spirit of witchcraft that has operated through the women in my family, especially my mother. My family was churchgoing, moral and quite 'normal,' but the witchcraft worked subtly to undermine the authority of the men in our family, while manipulating the other family members.

"I was not aware of the extent of my mother's control until I became engaged. As my loyalty began to switch to my future husband, I could sense her growing resentment. That was when my mother said, 'He'll never make any money and you'll have to work the rest of your life.' All through the years of our marriage I have labored against that 'curse.' I was

163

determined to 'show her' by not working in an outside job, but I was, in fact, controlled by it because I wasn't free to have a job! Also, my husband and I could never visualize ourselves as prosperous, and we have had continual financial problems.

"Then, shortly after I married, my mother said, 'You know you're not a strong person physically.' I felt as if someone had hit me on the head! What she said was such a shock to me because I had never perceived myself as a weak or sickly person. On the contrary, I had always been healthy and athletic. So I began to think that perhaps I had been wrong, and really wasn't strong physically ... Subsequently I have battled a lot of physical ailments, some of long duration.

"I also struggled because I was responding to my own husband and children in some of the same ways my mother did. This left me with a sense of hopelessness. How could I get completely free from this curse? Witchcraft had exercised control in several generations of my family. It seemed the spirit associated with it truly believed it had the right to dominate me and, in fact, it believed it **owned** me!

"Whenever I would be ministered to for deliverance this spirit would whisper to me that I couldn't really be completely free. I blamed my mother ... Through a slow, 'layer-by-layer' process of revelation and deliverance I came to see that my enemy is not my mother. I have forgiven her, and acknowledged the curse of witchcraft that had been influencing both of us.

"Since having ministry specifically to break these curses, I have had to learn to battle old thought and habit patterns. Now I daily confess with confidence: 'Through the sacrificial offering of Christ on the cross I have been purchased out from under the curse and have entered into the blessings of Abraham, whom God blessed in all things' (Galatians 3:13–14). **Christ has redeemed me from the curse!**

Blessings and Curses

"Husband

"After prayer for breaking of curses, there was a distinct 'clearing of the air.' The changes have been neither dramatic nor immediate, but they have been real. There is a sense of **direction** *in my life.*

"There is **progress***. I feel that I have a Scriptural degree of control over my life and that I can take my rightful place in my family. I can also see productivity and fruitfulness as a result of my labors.*

"Most important to me, there is hope. The nebulous darkness of the future has been replaced by excitement and joy at what God is doing. The 'fog' is clearing!"[73]

The quotation, viewed in its entirety, might prompt us to question how a loving mother could make such scarring statements. It would not be surprising, however, if the mother was not even aware of the magnitude of what she said, or indeed if she even remembered speaking the hurtful words. Likely the mother heard similar discouragements from her own parents, and perhaps was raised in an environment of negativity. Possibly there was a generational history of such talk.

We may more easily speak dispiriting words than we wish to admit. How many parents, in frustration over a less-than-responsible teenager, have snapped, "You're never going to amount to anything!" or "You're never going to make the team!" or something worse? This can be spoken so easily, thinking you are merely trying to wake up your child to the truths of life, or encouraging them to be diligent about practice. Less obvious are the casual remarks youths may overhear their parents make: "She's not as pretty as her sister," or "He's not as smart as our other children." Though these latter examples may not be as extreme, they also can be the roots of shame and the beginnings, or building blocks, of an enemy stronghold – and lifelong stigmatization. Quite insight-

---

[73]Prince, *Blessing or Curse*, 114–116. Used by permission.

165

THE DEVIL IN THE BACK PEW

fully, exorcist Fr Gabriele Amorth states: "[C]ursing ruins the climate of a home, which is the center of our lives."[74]

Curses by authority figures, however, do not only arise in the home. There are many types of rightful and legal authority in our lives. As Paul states: *"Let every soul be subject to the governing authorities. For there is no authority except from God, and the authorities that exist are appointed by God"* (Romans 13:1). Additionally, we may be under the rightful though limited authority of a sibling, boss, coach, teacher, pastor, or even, as Paul asserted, a politician, lawmaker, or public servant. And some requirements of that authority may be inescapable, like taxes, for example.[75] While it is beyond the scope of this book to analyze the New Testament's many explicit and implied comments about submission and authority, negative pronouncements and actions of an authority can amount to a curse.

An additional aspect of curses by authority figures concerns medical diagnoses. While I would never suggest dismissing a bad medical report just because we do not want to hear it, clearly not all are accurate or certain. Nor are all prognoses correct. Occasionally a doctor, nurse, or practitioner may offer a comment or prediction which is tantamount to a curse. If this is the case, you might privately wish to refuse – not to "receive" – the enemy's destiny regarding the statement. And, in faith, look to God's promises.

Negative Proclamations and Lies

Two of the examples in the earlier section, "The Curse of Death" – the spoken expectations of dying on a specific date and of drinking oneself to death – clearly are self-curses. In the section, "Be Careful What You Say" (Chapter 4, p. 101), a foundation was laid relative to the power of our words. An example was given there of a woman opening the door to oppression by her careless

---

[74]Amorth, *An Exorcist Explains the Demonic*, 56.
[75]*"Render therefore to all their due: taxes to whom taxes are due, customs to whom customs, fear to whom fear, honor to whom honor."* (Romans 13:7)

166

Blessings and Curses

words about dying. This also was a self-curse. The previous section, "The Power of Words," further expands the importance of what we speak.

Words uttered in anger, despair, frustration, pain, heartache, or idly, can carry dark spiritual power. Often what is said gives direct rights to the enemy or is the equivalent of a vow, which verbally binds us like a promise to some pledged act or condition. Once again, what we speak matters! A few examples of careless utterances include:

- "I'll *never* trust a man [woman] with my heart again."
- "I'm *never* going to let someone cheat me like that."
- "I'll *never* take this weight off."
- "My memory is just horrible. I *always* forget important things."
- "*I'm* scatterbrained."
- "I *can't* stop using my credit cards."
- "I'll *never* get out of debt."
- "I'll *always* be alone."
- "I'll *never* find someone to love me."
- "*Everyone* in my family suffers from health problems."

The common thread in these statements is the spoken *surrender of hope*. I mention again the Bill Johnson quote cited in Chapter 5: "Any place in your life where you have no hope is under the influence of a lie." Proclaiming a statement against God's promises, against hope, or otherwise contradicting God's truths, is reckless and self-defeating and must be undone.

A Scriptural example of restoring truth and victory involves Peter's three-time denial of Christ after He was arrested. When last challenged if He was with Jesus, Peter *"began to call down curses on himself and he swore to them, 'I don't know the man!'"* (Matthew 26:74 NIV). After Jesus had risen, He graciously invited Peter three times to restate his love for Him, which, of course, Peter did. Responding to Jesus' queries, in both verses 15 and 16 of John 21, Peter is quoted saying: *"Yes, Lord; You know that I love You."* And

167

THE DEVIL IN THE BACK PEW

in verse 17 he adds: *"Lord, You know all things; You know that I love You."* That Jesus initiated this dialogue leading Peter to explicitly counter his denials is instructive. Peter's spoken expression of negativity and rejection could not be left to stand unaddressed. We need to "undo" the harm of spoken words:

- Confess the error of what was spoken.
- Renounce or "unsay" what was proclaimed.
- Restate the truth, in faith.

This process is simple, but indispensable. Ground given to the enemy must be retaken. Should I catch myself in an unsanctified slip of the tongue, I immediately confess the error or untruth, renounce it, and speak Scriptural words of hope and truth. And of Christ's victory! The enemy is thereby rendered powerless against me for that careless remark.

But what about all of our faithless utterances made in the past, when we were ignorant of this truth? The fix is simple: make a general confession and renouncement of all unbiblical speech, and proclaim your faith and trust in Jesus. And give it no further thought.

Having so often witnessed the life-ruining consequences of self-curses and of *believing lies*, it would be difficult to overstate the importance of victory in this regard. Virtually everyone who struggles with ongoing, insurmountable fears and hopelessness is believing lies. And satan and his minions gain their rights and their power from lies believed and lies spoken. We *must* seek God's truth or suffer the consequences of error. Again, I quote Hosea 4:6: *"My people are destroyed for lack of knowledge."*

In meeting with folks who are seeking prayer for physical or emotional stresses, identify falsehoods believed and shine the light of truth on them. When a person pessimistically proclaims he/she will remain in the same heartache or pain or illness, the enemy is given permission to continue his work.

Note: I am not suggesting anyone should refuse to be honest with themselves, but there is a difference between saying, "I *have* cancer," and "I am *battling* cancer" or "I have been *given a diagno-*

168

sis of cancer." I believe it is extremely important that we not assert ownership of something contrary to God's best. If the worst case plays out and it is God's destiny, so be it. With His help, we may endure in peace. However, we are better positioned for victory and healing if we stir up our faith, avoid words of surrender, and speak honest, yet positive, expressions of God's best for us.

Curses Spoken Against Us Or By Us

Curses can be spoken against us in carelessness or with malevolent intent. We may be aware of the exact words uttered, or the "curse" event may be wholly unknown, or only suspected. Those involved in witchcraft, for example, may make private dark spiritual pronouncements against your health, marriage, family, church, ministry, or career. Other curses may range from simple wishes like, "I hope he fails!" to expressions of personal contempt like, "Go to hell!" or the non-verbal curse of a middle-finger gesture. Muttering "You idiot!" or the like, when a driver pulls out in front of you, is also a curse. Moreover, careless talk such as, "I hope they get what they deserve," may amount to a curse.

In truth, *I do not want to get what I deserve,* and I am thankful that Jesus has taken away my sin. Perhaps speaking of what someone "deserves" may amount to judgment (which is God's territory) or it may merely be a description of apparent consequences. Our focus should be on what is in the heart, recalling Jesus' admonition: *"For by your words you will be acquitted, and by your words you will be condemned"* (Matthew 12:37 NIV).

Misguided Prayers

The third chapter of the book of James addresses aspects of our unruly tongues and the great harm they can do. Anyone who is honest with him/herself will acknowledge the difficulty of controlling our words. I have heard many sermons on this subject, but I cannot recall anyone ever applying the "tongue" warnings to the subject of prayer. Is this something we need to pay attention to?

THE DEVIL IN THE BACK PEW

Are there really any *bad* prayers?

Generally speaking, misguided prayers are those which speak unbiblically. Prayers that, perhaps, are from *our* sense of what is right and good and needed. Maybe, also, there is a bit of flesh embedded in them. In the worst case, these can be actual curses.

Sometimes, though, a misguided prayer may just be a reflection of the clumsiness of our humanity; our hearts are right and our motives are pure, but our theology is a bit off. In this latter case, I have a hard time believing our loving God would not "interpret," in a manner of speaking, our erroneous prayer and hear it the way our hearts intended. Irrespective, we will look at some relevant Scriptures.

King Solomon advised that, for one who turns from the law: *"Even his prayer is an abomination"* (Proverbs 28:9). Further, Psalm 66:18 advises that the Lord will not listen to our prayers if we *"regard"* sin in our hearts. To *"regard"* sin, to give importance to it or, as the NIV says, to *"cherish"* it, means purposely hanging on to the sin, or willingly choosing it, as opposed to trying to deal with it. There is an important distinction here. If I say, "I'm never going to forgive my brother-in-law for what he did!" I am willfully choosing to disobey what the Bible mandates: I am *"cherish"*ing or *"regard"*ing that sin. On the other hand, if I say, "I keep giving my brother-in-law to the Lord for what he did, but the memories keep coming back – and it's a struggle to keep my heart right," that is not making a willful choice against God's ways.

Regarding the efficacy of our prayers, 1 Peter 3:7 (NIV) advises husbands to *"be considerate as you live with your wives, and treat them with respect ... so that nothing will hinder your prayers."* How this warning plays out is not clear from Scripture, but the indication is that such a prayer will not achieve the desired end. Surely this also applies to the way wives treat their husbands.

Also relevant is the truth that the Holy Spirit is our way to the Father. We don't get there on our own! We *"have access by one Spirit to the Father"* (Ephesians 2:18). And

"... we do not know what we should pray for as we ought, but

the Spirit Himself makes intercession for us with groanings which cannot be uttered. Now He who searches the hearts knows what the mind of the Spirit is, because He makes intercession for the saints according to the will of God." (Romans 8:26–27)

Clearly, we must rely on, and yield to, the Holy Spirit in our prayers to the Father. In the context of James' writing on the instance of *"blessing and cursing"* coming from *"the same mouth"* (James 3:10), he adds that *"such ... does not come down from heaven but is earthly, unspiritual, of the devil"* (v.15 NIV). We must watch what we say! Our prayers should always be fruit-bearing, merciful, and positive.

Oftentimes in praying for individuals with deep hurts, we encounter people with unholy pasts. Many problems folks deal with are the direct consequences of their own life choices and result from personal sin. Of course sin must be dealt with, but it is imperative we are not judgmental in the prayers we speak, and that the prayee is shown personal acceptance and the kind of love Jesus displayed. As mentioned in Chapter 5, the MacNutts of Christian Healing Ministries maintain we should never pray for another person without understanding God's love for them. That simple instruction goes a long way toward avoiding misguided prayers.

Rejecting Curses

If you know or believe a curse has been sent your way, refuse it. Reject it. Declare it null and void. With a peaceful and confident attitude, order the powers of darkness out and away, and refuse the enemy's destiny for your situation. If you are uncertain if there has actually been a curse, speak a conditional prayer such as:

"Lord, if there has been a curse of [...] spoken against me, I cut its power now with the sword of the Spirit and declare it of no effect. In the name of Jesus, I command every unclean spirit away. If there is any way in which I have given permission for the enemy to have authority here, I confess my sin of

THE DEVIL IN THE BACK PEW

[…] and I revoke all permissions now."

If you suspect that witchcraft might be the source of a curse, Francis MacNutt suggests you pray specifically against spirits of "earth, air, fire, water, the netherworld [hell], and the satanic forces of nature," because traditional pronouncements (curses) of witchcraft "send" such spirits against people.[76] It is beyond the scope of this book to examine witchcraft or the occult in great depth. More information is available from books listed in the Bibliography.

Author and teacher Bobby Conner suggests the nature of the curse be identified and prayed against. He reminds us of John 8:36: *"Therefore if the Son makes you free, you shall be free indeed"* and suggests a simple prayer: "Father, in Jesus' name, I ask you to break the curse over me [and verbally name it]. I renounce it in the name of Jesus. I am free!"[77]

In different contexts above, I have given examples of dark or unfavorable words spoken against an individual. Regardless of the nature or source of the curse, a first line of defense is simply to decline to receive it. When something spoken or directed your way is life-stealing, as opposed to life-giving, confidently proclaim, in faith, "I don't receive that."

We will deal more fully with breaking the power of curses in the next chapter.

Proclaiming God's Blessings

Early in this chapter, blessing was defined simply as the exercise or verbal release of Godly spiritual authority and good, rather like speaking *"on earth as it is in heaven"*[78] (Matthew 6:10). The subsequent various references to God's promise of blessing, the

---

[76]From the Francis MacNutt video, *Deliverance II* (Christian Healing Ministries, Jacksonville, FL).

[77]Bobby Conner, *Lineage-Line and Legacy* (Eagles View Ministries, Bullard, TX, 2012), 71.

[78]From the Lord's prayer, as Jesus taught it in the Sermon on the Mount (Matthew, chapters 5–7).

blessing-curse "interplay," the Old Testament example of a father's blessing to his firstborn, our speaking of blessing on God's people, and the many other Scriptural uses of *bless* or *blessing*, all point toward the significance of this simple verbal pronouncement. Our words are powerful! They can speak life!

Significantly, the verbalization of blessings is an indispensable element of prayer for individuals or situations, and especially when dark spirits are involved. The release of God's favor creates a stumbling block for the enemy, and strengthens the faith of all who participate. Spoken blessings enfeeble the powers of darkness. They are a weapon of warfare.

Peter's first letter describes our call to be people of blessing:

> "[A]ll of you be of one mind, having compassion for one another; love as brothers, be tenderhearted, be courteous; not returning evil for evil or reviling for reviling, but on the contrary blessing, knowing that you were called to this, that you may inherit a blessing." (1 Peter 3:8–9)

Blessing is God's way!

A Personal Perspective

I can tell you with certainty that, over my three decades of trying to follow the Lord, I have done *many* things wrong. I am not referring here to sinful behavior, but I am speaking of incorrectly doing this or that for God, or this or that for God's people, or taking this or that stance on a Christian belief. My heart was in the right place, but my judgment, wisdom or zeal was, at times, misplaced. There is one thing I know that I did right, though, from my first days as a believer – I sought to be blessed. I always responded (generally meaning walking to the front of the congregation) to any call for those who want prayer for an announced need, even if my need was only loosely tied to the invitation. I do not recall ever letting the whispering enemy deter me. And I am not sure how I would have responded back then if someone asked me why

THE DEVIL IN THE BACK PEW

I so eagerly sought prayer. Now, given the countless times I have had God's people pray for me (at times literally for my survival, at times for far less), I can tell you there is a basic motivation: it just feels good! It feels *really* good to be blessed! Irrespective of what is going on with me physically or emotionally, when people of God pray for me, *speak blessings over me,* I always feel better. Even if, for example, my back still aches, I feel genuinely uplifted and encouraged on the inside. At the core of my being.

I can say with confidence that the folks Patti and I meet and pray with virtually always feel better after being prayed for. And it is not about us. When blessings are compassionately spoken over someone, unless the prayee has a strong spiritual barrier of some sort, they will always feel better, "lighter," more peaceful, hopeful, happier. God is good and He is faithful. Once again, Proverbs 18:21 tells us life is in the power of the tongue. Speaking blessing is speaking life!

Author and pastor Kerry Kirkwood has an outstanding book on the power of speaking blessings, *The Power of Blessing.* The Derek Prince book, *Blessing or Curse,* referenced in this chapter, is also highly recommended.

Chapter 8

Generational Sin and Curses and Dark Attachments

Generational Sin and Curses

In the preceding chapter, excerpts of the passage containing the ten commandments were cited revealing that the *idolatrous* sins[79] of the father impact the children to the third and fourth generations: "*I ... am a jealous God,* **visiting the iniquity** *of the fathers upon the children* **to the third and fourth generations**" (Deuteronomy 5:9, emphasis mine).

Prior to comments about idolatry in today's world, we'll discuss briefly what this verse means in the context of generational sin and curses. Though Deuteronomy 5:9 had been understood in the prophet Ezekiel's[80] time to mean that the children would be punished for their fathers' sin, the Lord spoke through him and gave a new and clarified instruction contradicting Israel's former understanding as revealed in the proverb: "*The fathers have eaten sour grapes, And the children's teeth are set on edge*" (Ezekiel 18:2).

---

[79]In the context of the commandments, idols were principally the manmade objects people worshiped and to which they offered sacrifices.
[80]Author of the Old Testament book of Ezekiel.

175

THE DEVIL IN THE BACK PEW

Verse 3 states: *"As I live,' says the Lord GOD, 'you shall no longer use this proverb in Israel,'"* and specifically adds: *"The soul **who sins** shall die"* (v.4, emphasis mine). Further clarifying, Ezekiel explains that each individual will answer for himself, because a son has a choice *"when he sees the sins which his father has done"* (v.14), and that a person's own action shall determine personal accountability: *"He shall **surely live!**"* (v.17, emphasis mine) or *"He shall **die for his iniquity**"* (v.18, emphasis mine).

Though Ezekiel 18:1–18 resolves the issue of people answering for their own sin, it does not comment upon the residual effect or consequences of that sin on succeeding generations.

In the case of witchcraft and occult activity, which seek power and knowledge from satanic sources and give satan "god"-like authority, these are explicitly idolatry. Worshiping satan is the culmination of this, and evidence may include willful satanic agreement by covenant, consecration, or dedication. In the twenty-first century, there are also many other opportunities to put items and activities ahead of God, in fact, to worship them. I confess to having worshiped a very nice powerboat prior to coming to the Lord. Though in my experience not often preached about, the New Testament also identifies covetousness (greed) as idolatry: *"Therefore put to death ... covetousness, which is idolatry"* (Colossians 3:5).

In general terms, we might consider whatever we give precedence over God as an idol. I once heard a Christian teacher define an idol as anything you have to check with before saying "yes" to God. That is a revealing truth! It is healthy to ask ourselves periodically what we may be tempted to put before God: Golf? Shopping? Money? A TV ballgame? Status? Clothes? Tools? Food? "My" ministry?

Dealing with Generational Sin and Curses

Any observer of humanity surely has seen vices, sins, weaknesses, habits, and the like carry through family lines like shared physical characteristics. Much of the behavior might be learned or emulat-

Generational Sin and Curses and Dark Attachments

ed, such as dispositions toward anger or alcoholism, but certainly not all. There definitely is a sin-based spiritual component, and it must be addressed. An example of an activity which has explicit generational ramifications is involvement in Freemasonry or similar organizations. In Freemasonry, for example, participants make pronouncements and perform rituals diametrically opposed to Biblical Christianity. Such activity must be confessed, renounced, and replaced.[81] Derek Prince comments that a curse can "be likened to a long, evil arm stretched out from the past."[82] We have seen individuals with Freemasonry in their ancestry wonderfully set free from the "arm" of dark, controlling forces permeating their lives.

When there is evidence or suspicion of a generational carryover regarding sin habits, disease, misfortune, or anything short of God's promised provision, specific prayer should be undertaken. In John 10:10, Jesus states that: *"I have come that they may have life, and that they may have it more abundantly."* Jesus is not promising everyone a Cadillac, but He *is* saying you should have sufficiency and peace in your connection with Him, and regarding your basic needs, health, finances, relationships, church community, and the like. (See Appendix I: "The Poverty Mind-set.")

For known or suspected generational curses or generational sin, the spiritual "legal" ground must be recovered. Use the following or a similar approach. In the event the causal activity is unknown, you can pray conditionally, that is, with "If" prayers. Follow as the Holy Spirit leads, and speak aloud:

- Confess known and unknown sins of ancestors (four generations = 30 people)
  - Consider satanic and occult activity, witchcraft, Freemasonry, or any other dark spiritual involvement.
  - Consider divorce, abandonment, adultery, suicide,

---

[81]See "Prayer of Release for Freemasons and Their Descendants" (http://jubileeresources.org/?page_id=650).
[82]Prince, *Blessing or Curse*, 17.

alcoholism, unbelief, etc.

- o Consider sins, the consequences of which may be root causes of current difficulty or deficiencies.
- Renounce each type of sin and ungodly behavior.
- Using words you are comfortable with, proclaim with authority something like this: "I cut [break, declare null and void, sever with the sword of the Spirit] every curse, sin, generational carryover, propensity for wrongdoing, genetic weakness, and dark spiritual right, off me and my family and descendants, in the name of Jesus."
- Speak blessing and God's goodness into your life/lives and into the situation.

In our experience, most people have only limited knowledge of their ancestry. When specifics are unknown, and we are praying against a particular sin or sinful propensity (in the following example, adultery), we might join with the prayee, speaking something such as:

"We confess and cut off all roots of the sin of marital unfaithfulness from Sylvia, from her father and mother, from her grandparents, from her great-grandparents, and from her great-great-grandparents. We renounce and reject every related desire and action, and we speak the blessing of a healthy and happy Christian marriage on Sylvia, her siblings, and her descendants."

It is often helpful for a person to make a simple chart of their ancestry and note instances of various unfavorable occurrences. A beginning list of things to look for might include:

- Abortion
- Accident propensity
- Alcoholism
- Anger
- Antisocial behavior
- Disappearance

Generational Sin and Curses and Dark Attachments

- Disease
- Divorce
- Financial lack
- Ill will
- Imprisonment
- Marital unfaithfulness
- Mental illness
- Miscarriages/birth defects
- Premature death
- Rejection of God
- Renegadism
- Sexual sin
- Suicide
- Violence

We can then address the issues identified and confess, renounce, and pray appropriately. For a more in-depth approach, Christian Healing Ministries currently offers regularly a Day of Healing Prayer, which includes a Generational Healing Service. Their website[83] describes these events and gives detailed aid for completion of a "Family Tree," a tool which helps identify needs for generational healing.

An Example of Generational Carryover

Many years ago, Patti and I found ourselves praying separately, on different occasions and for different reasons, for a mother and her daughter. Third parties had independently asked each of us to join them. Patti had prayed for the daughter, and I had prayed for the mother. The relevant points to this account are:

- Both were practicing Christians.
- Both the mother and daughter were demonized.
- The mother had a root of sin, which she refused to deal with.

---

[83] www.christianhealingmin.org.

THE DEVIL IN THE BACK PEW

- The daughter carried a similar sin attachment, but it appeared neither knew of the other's sin.
- Neither was willing to acknowledge or confront her own problem.
- Neither demonization was, to our knowledge, ever dealt with or resolved.

Knowing the details of the situation, I am extremely doubtful that either of them had any understanding that a dark spiritual link existed bridging mother to daughter. Sadly, I later became aware of some family behavioral issues, and it seems likely that a teenage granddaughter is following a similar path. Is that granddaughter's choice an inevitability? Certainly not, but the vulnerability exists. And without God-sourced guidance and help, I fear a similar path could be followed.

Objects and Places with Dark Attachments

To the extent that we may be in possession of books, objects, jewelry, clothing, or other items related to witchcraft, the occult, Freemasonry, etc., drugs, pornography, or anything involving the demonic, such material must be destroyed. The Bible is quite specific in declaring idolatrous items to be *"abominations."*

Note: The word translated *"abomination"* is the strongest word in the Hebrew language for what the Lord hates and rejects:

> *"You shall burn the carved images of their gods with fire; you shall not covet the silver or gold that is on them, nor take it for yourselves, lest you be snared by it; for it is an **abomination** to the LORD your God. Nor shall you bring an **abomination** into your house, lest you be doomed to destruction like it. You shall utterly detest it and utterly abhor it, for it is an **accursed thing**."* (Deuteronomy 7:25–26, emphasis mine)

There is certainly nothing unclear about God's perspective on that topic! The message is clear: you cannot be involved in occult activities, or possess occult or dark-spirit-related objects, and avoid

Generational Sin and Curses and Dark Attachments

demonic exposure. Or the judgment of God.

Many years ago, my wife and I became aware of the very real connection between Deuteronomy's *"abominations"* and how retaining, possessing, or tolerating ungodly objects opens the door to dark spirits. Accordingly, we destroyed quite a few items which were questionable, spiritually speaking. These included certain CDs and DVDs, some oriental artwork, items with dragon images, books of low moral tone (some with well-known titles), and other possessions from our pre-Christ lifestyle. Frankly, it felt good to destroy and burn it all, and there was a sort of spiritual exhilaration. I sensed I was putting another stake in the ground for Christ in my life.

Another aspect of housecleaning: there is potential for negative spiritual attachment through what might otherwise be a completely harmless item when that object is connected to a sinful memory or situation. An example would be a piece of jewelry which a woman received from a man in a past adulterous relationship. Though the liaison might be confessed and long over, wearing the jewelry, or just seeing it in the jewelry box, may bring a subtle longing to mind once again. On a spiritual level, or perhaps with a back-of-mind awareness, the person may be able to acknowledge that there *is* a dark connection or link of some kind with the object. If so, we must ask, "Is possessing the jewelry worth carrying the thought?" My observation is that the enemy is quite adept at "piggybacking" on the smallest of things. Give him no ground!

In a similar vein, I have known ostensibly happily married women who, by their own admission, still hold on to love letters from a former romance. To be clear, I am not speaking, for example, of memorabilia from a cherished first marriage where the husband has passed away, or from a love tragically lost in a war or accident. I refer to the circumstance where the wife might relive, in some measure, the old excitement with a bit too much yearning or sense of nostalgia. I wish to be neither judgmental nor overly black-and-white, but if we cannot be at peace with God over those old

THE DEVIL IN THE BACK PEW

letters, they are probably better discarded. The downside? Again, it is just a tool the enemy can use to sow tiny seeds of discord or dissatisfaction when the opportune time arises. The enemy is good at doing that too! The question is: What would the Lord have me do?

Retaking What's Yours

In "Examples of Discernment" (Chapter 3, p. 72), I gave an illustration of sensing a darkness in the room during a prayer session. As mentioned, I learned later that the room had been used for immoral activity by neighborhood teens. At the time, the dark presence was easily commanded out, but I make the point here to emphasize that physical locations can be occupied by dark spiritual forces. Sinful activity opens the door to, or grants permission for, such habitation. The approach is simple: retake the area over which you have present authority.

I believe that, once the enemy has a "right" to be present in a physical place, he will likely remain until forced to leave. Therefore, order the enemy out of your "space": home, apartment, property, hotel room, work area, car, finances, and so forth.

Note: If you suspect or have knowledge that your property or your home, for example, was used for sinful, criminal, occult/ pagan, or immoral activity in the past, pray the unclean residue out and God's Spirit in!

Also, physical places can be explicitly cursed by those who practice witchcraft or engage in occult activity. If this is suspected, and you have rightful authority over the space (see Chapter 9, "Understand Your Authority," p. 188), command unclean spirits out, declare their works of no effect, and reclaim the place for God, welcoming in the Holy Spirit. It is also suggested the location be anointed with oil, typically including rooms, doors, windows, and corners of the property, as appropriate. The oil is applied in small amounts with prayers of cleansing, dedication, protection, and even confession, if necessary. Oil, as a sanctifying and cleansing element, will be discussed in Chapters 11 and 13.

PART III

Freedom: The Deliverance Prayer Process

Chapter 9

Practical Aspects of Deliverance Prayer

As we begin Part III, which I have designated "Freedom: The Deliverance Prayer Process" you might think of this as the "battle" portion of the teaching. And it surely is, focusing on principles, techniques, and hands-on tactics for undermining and confronting agents of satan. It is important to understand, though, that the topics and methods discussed in the remaining chapters are relevant to *all* levels of dark spiritual warfare, not just the intense interactions. Let what you learn here aid your war against simple temptation as much as when you deal with a loud-mouthed, rebellious demon.

What Is Needed to Pray for Deliverance?

Be a Christian Believer

The Book of Acts recounts the story of the sons of Sceva, seven brothers who had a difficult time trying to rid a person of a tormenting spirit. The Scripture narrative makes clear that commanding a dark spirit out is not a formulaic recitation of words (again, like "abracadabra"):

> *"[S]ome of the itinerant Jewish exorcists took it upon themselves to call the name of the Lord Jesus over those who had*

Practical Aspects of Deliverance Prayer

evil spirits, saying, 'We exorcise you by the Jesus whom Paul preaches.' Also there were sons of Sceva, a Jewish chief priest, who did so. And the evil spirit answered and said, 'Jesus I know, and Paul I know; but who are you?' **Then the man in whom the evil spirit was leaped on them, overpowered them, and prevailed against them, so that they fled out of that house naked and wounded.** *"* (Acts 19:13–16, emphasis mine)

That must have stirred the gossip in the neighborhood! For the record, I have been threatened and bad-mouthed by demons, but after forbidding their aggression, in Jesus' name, have never seen those attempts at intimidation turn to danger. More on this in Chapter 11. The issue here is:

- who *you* are;
- *Who* is in you; and
- *Who* is in charge.

Because the sons of Sceva were not walking in true connection to Christ, they had no resource for strength against the enemy. It is who we are *in Him* that gives us authority.

Be Free of Gross Sin

In the section on "Misguided Prayers" (Chapter 7, p. 169), I quoted two verses which highlighted the rejection of prayers offered by a person in willful sin. As mentioned there, a difference exists between sin we refuse to deal with, and that which we are working to overcome. Certainly, if we had to be totally sinless to pray, none of us would be praying! Some years ago, I heard author and teacher Graham Cooke make a profound comment on this subject: "The first rule of spiritual warfare is: You can't take ground from the enemy if he has ground in you."[84]

We cannot carry our sin into a prayer session or a potential

---

[84]Graham Cooke, "Crisis and Process" (a presentation at Toronto Airport Christian Fellowship, 1996).

185

THE DEVIL IN THE BACK PEW

encounter with a demonic power and hope to be effective. But, of course, all we need to do is clean up: *"If we confess our sins, He is faithful and just to forgive us our sins and to cleanse us from all unrighteousness"* (1 John 1:9).

I heard of a situation where a noninvolved observer attended a deliverance session, and his sins were announced, by a demon, to all in the room. I imagine he quickly left! I can tell you that, on at least one occasion, a demon has tried to intimidate me by saying, "I know your sins." I ignored the comment and moved on, knowing that my confessed sins are *"[a]s far as the east is from the west"* (Psalm 103:12), and that I have been *"cleanse[d]"* according to 1 John 1:9. The demon did not bring up the subject again. I should add that, if a demon ever brought up an actual uncon-fessed sin of mine, I would immediately confess the sin to the Lord, thank the demon for reminding me of my oversight, and proceed with commanding him out.

Obviously, it is appropriate for the prayee to be free of gross sin as well. As a general statement, when entering a spiritual bat-tle zone (which is what healing prayer is), things will go better if participants are facing and dealing with their sin. But, of course, we all live under the covering of God's mercy and grace.

Rely on the Holy Spirit

Simply put, be a willing servant. Listen to the prayee, but keep your spiritual antennae cocked to sense direction or information from the Comforter. Be interruptible.

Note: I am *not* terribly consistent in my discernment of what the Lord is doing or saying at a given time. Nevertheless, I am totally confident He will give me what I need when I need it. He just does! What a faithful God! And He seems especially compas-sionate toward those who have been beaten up by the enemy.

Extremely important in the deliverance prayer process is pray-ing for areas of emotional brokenness (Chapter 5). Uncovering old, deep hurts is sometimes challenging, not typically because

186

the prayee is consciously hiding them, but because they are buried under layers of trauma or behind walls of self-protection and fear. Patti and I have witnessed countless occasions where the Holy Spirit has revealed only a word, such as "humiliation," which would prompt us to ask the prayee, "Have you experienced humiliation?" A simple revelation like this opens the door to praying compassionately for the related hurt, then confronting and ejecting a tormenting spirit. It is glorious!

Let the expression of Jesus' love for the person, through you, be the foundation for all your efforts.

Embrace the Promises

There are many Bible verses referencing the power of God and His limitless nature. The selected examples below focus on truths supportive of confrontational warfare prayer. As best you can, keep the message of these in your heart, and stir your faith accordingly.

- *"For the **weapons of our warfare are** not carnal but **mighty in God** for pulling down strongholds"* (2 Corinthians 10:4, emphasis mine)
- *"'**No weapon formed against you shall prosper**, And every tongue which rises against you in judgment You shall condemn. This is the **heritage of the servants of the LORD**, And their **righteousness is from Me**,' Says the LORD."* (Isaiah 54:17, emphasis mine)
- *"What then shall we say to these things? **If God is for us, who can be against us?**"* (Romans 8:31, emphasis mine)
- *"[M]y brethren, **be strong in the Lord** and **in the power of His might**."* (Ephesians 6:10, emphasis mine)
- *"He gives **power to the weak**, And to those who have no might He **increases strength**."* (Isaiah 40:29, emphasis mine)
- *"**Be exalted, O LORD, in Your own strength!** We will sing and **praise Your power**."* (Psalms 21:13, emphasis mine)
- *"Now **to Him who is able to do exceedingly abundantly above all that we ask or think, according to the power***

THE DEVIL IN THE BACK PEW

that works in us, to *Him be glory in the church by Christ Jesus to all generations, forever and ever."* (Ephesians 3:20–21, emphasis mine)

Don't Be Fearful or Doubt

When confronting a dark spirit, whether harassing another person or you, it is important that you not be fearful or doubtful. If you are, demons will know it (a faith issue) and will not heed your commands. In "Dispelling Doubt" (Chapter 3, p. 61), we looked at the example of Peter yielding to doubt while walking on the water to Jesus. His doubt undermined the miraculous event while it was underway. If you are fearful of the demon you are encountering, or if you question your authority or effectiveness, you will not have the Lord's overcoming power at your disposal. In the event you struggle with doubt due to your lack of experience, I would just say *press on.* There is much more to share about deliverance prayer but, I emphasize here, I am *repeatedly* in situations which seem new and different. Listen to the Holy Spirit, trust the Lord, stay humble, and try to do what is right. As best you can, leave no room for doubt, and be intolerant of fear. Jesus *is* in control.

Understand Your Authority

As Granted

Throughout this book, I have been referring to our authority to expel demons. See the full context of Jesus' instructions to His apostles after He was resurrected. Note that *all believers* are explicitly given that authority:

> *"He said to them [the apostles], 'Go into all the world and preach the gospel to every creature. He who believes and is baptized will be saved ... **And these signs will follow those who believe: In My name they will cast out demons ...**'"*
> (Mark 16:15–17, emphasis mine)

188

Practical Aspects of Deliverance Prayer

As Limited

In his first letter to the Corinthians, Paul identified the spiritual gifts: *"word of wisdom ... word of knowledge ... faith ... healings ... miracles ... prophecy ... discerning of spirits ... tongues ... interpretation of tongues"* (1 Corinthians 12:8–10). Each of these gifts is, inherently, supernatural – meaning they cannot be explained by science or the laws of nature. Paul states he does not want us *"to be ignorant"* (v.1) about these spiritual gifts, but to *"earnestly desire"* them (v.31). They are given explicitly to facilitate the expansion of the Kingdom of God on this earth! Confirming that, Paul also states: *"[T]he kingdom of God is not a matter of talk but of power"* (1 Corinthians 4:20 NIV).

Note: The Greek word translated *"power"* is *dunamis*, i.e., miracle-working power.

Other than the explicit power of the spiritual gifts, I am aware of no mention in Scripture where mankind is given authority over spiritual or demonic realms. Certainly, in situations calling for deliverance prayer spoken over individuals, we are empowered,[85] but not freely over the entire hierarchy of the dark spiritual kingdom. We see Jesus rebuking the wind and waves during a storm on the water, saying, *"Peace, be still!"* (Mark 4:39), but there was no encouragement or instruction for the disciples to do likewise.

Surely I am not suggesting we should not, as fitting, pray and ask for protection against bad weather or situations of danger. I only state we have not been granted *authority* there. We have not been given the ability or right to *command* nature as Jesus did.

Daniel 10 gives a glimpse into the spiritual realm, the exercise of authority and power there, and the contention with powers of darkness. The narrative below speaks of Daniel's description of a

---

[85]See Mark 16 quotation above. Note also, Jesus referred to casting out a demon as working a "miracle" (one of the 1 Corinthian 12 spiritual gifts). The disciple John said: *"'[W]e saw someone ... casting out demons in Your name' ... Jesus said, 'Do not forbid him, for no one who works a miracle in My name ...'"* (Mark 9:38–39, emphasis mine).

189

THE DEVIL IN THE BACK PEW

glorious "man" (an angel or heavenly being), of combat with the prince of Persia, of archangel Michael's assistance, and of coming contention with the prince of Greece:

> *"I lifted my eyes and looked, and behold, a certain man clothed in linen, whose waist was girded with gold ... His* **body was like beryl,** *his* **face like the appearance of lightning,** *his* **eyes like torches of fire,** *his* **arms and feet like burnished bronze** *in color, and the sound of his* **words like the voice of a multitude.** *... I was left alone when I saw this great vision, and no strength remained in me; for my vigor was turned to frailty in me, and I retained no strength. ... [H]e said to me, 'O Daniel ... I have now been sent to you.' ... 'Do not fear, Daniel, for* **from the first day** *that you set your heart to understand, and to humble yourself before your God,* **your words were heard;** *and I have come because of your words. But* **the prince of the kingdom of Persia withstood me twenty-one days;** *and behold,* **Michael [the archangel] ... came to help me'** *... Then he said ... 'And now I must* **return to fight** *with the* **prince of Persia;** *and when I have gone forth, indeed the* **prince of Greece** *will come.'"* (Daniel 10:5–20, emphasis mine)

It is instructive to consider this passage in a discussion of authority and dark spirits. Significantly, the text reveals:

- There are anti-God "princes" assigned to, or associated with, political states, and they are powerful;
- A rather awesome "being" (per the description) had his hands quite full fighting with the prince of Persia;
- That "being" was dispatched on day one of Daniel's prayer, but met with twenty-one days of resistance until Michael came to help; and
- Daniel ultimately received the response to his prayer.

If we might be inclined to minimize the strength or powers of the dark realm, this text certainly should give us pause. There are obvi-

190

Practical Aspects of Deliverance Prayer

ous levels of power and conflict that we can scarcely comprehend. I believe that to assert a warfare-type authority where it has not been granted is dangerous. To be clear, I am not suggesting a sincere believer should be fearful of satan or any powers of darkness, provided he/she is not in gross sin or outside of rightful authority, or outside the umbrella of protection we enjoy when we walk with God in humble obedience.

Regarding our prayers against the powers of darkness, we likewise have not been given broad authority over them either, but we can pray for God's assistance. We do have authority over those dark spirits which attack what is "ours" – ourselves, families, households, jobs, finances – and over those situations where people have given us permission. But we do not have free authority to command, *as we choose*, *any* demon out of *any* place at *any* time. I believe that, when we overstep our rightful authority, we open the door to satan's attacks. (See Chapter 1, "What the Scriptures Say About satan and his demons," p. 22.)

Since we do not have complete authority over the demonic realm, to pray a demon off someone, we must have the prayee's permission to do so. We should not, for example, stop people on the street and blindly attempt to *command* all darkness off their lives. But gaining permission can be simple; when someone asks for healing prayer, I believe I have been given all the authority I need. And if there is any doubt, I politely and diplomatically ask if I can pray or, more specifically, "pray the attacking enemy away" from them. I don't recall anyone ever refusing.

One final thought related to the granting of authority: I have heard of situations where the person praying seemed to be asking for a bit too much authority over the prayee. I become uncomfortable when:

• Someone asks for broad authority over another person, i.e., more than they need for prayer purposes; or
• When someone willingly grants that authority – exposing themselves, perhaps, to sinister motivations.

THE DEVIL IN THE BACK PEW

I assume this to be an uncommon concern, but I prefer to close the door to *every possible entryway* of the enemy.

Seeking Assistance from Others

It may seem appropriate to ask for help from others when confronting demonic powers. I know of examples where those with greater "church" authority (pastors, leaders) successfully commanded out demons when folks with lesser authority were unable to. One specific case involved a small team of believers, praying deliverance prayers in a church office, who became "stuck" and sought the help of a pastor who was walking by. This senior leader, who was well accredited and had additionally served on the foreign mission field for many years, confronted the spirit and it quickly left. Was this an authority issue? Or could it be a faith issue? In similar situations I am aware of, no lack of faith on the pray-ers' part was obvious. But there is no certain way of knowing. Related, adding prayer team members (praying, worshiping, interceding) appears to increase the power and authority against the dark spirits. Patti and I often call in other believers to help.

Indirectly related, there is much in church history of individuals operating with a significant healing anointing. Roberts Liardon's *God's Generals* tells the stories of many people thusly gifted. Are some folks similarly empowered regarding the confrontation of demons? Possibly, though it would be difficult to prove conclusively. Surely, though, experience in successfully casting out dark spirits is very helpful.

When Challenged by the enemy

Of course the enemy will resist efforts to unseat him. Expect to have your authority tested, either by a demon speaking through a prayee or via negative thoughts planted by the enemy. Pay these distractions no mind. Other examples of enemy resistance will be given in Chapters 11 and 12.

192

Practical Aspects of Deliverance Prayer

Summation – Authority

In this section, I have attempted to build the case that we have truly supernatural authority over powers of darkness, where that authority is rightful and legal. To assert authority (i.e., *to command*) where we do not legally/rightfully have it, exposes us to dark spiritual attack, illness, loss, strife, division, and other negativity. The solution is simple: where you do not have the rightful authority, make your prayer *a request* to God. Save the commands for areas where your rightful authority is clear.

Consider the following:

- The Bible alludes to various levels and skill sets in the angelic realm. Thomas Aquinas, thirteenth-century philosopher and theologian, identified nine categories of angels: seraphim, dominations, principalities, cherubim, virtues, archangels, thrones, powers, and angels.[86]
- Even less clear are Biblical references to fallen angels. Author Ted Montgomery identifies four categories: rulers (or principalities), authorities, powers, and spiritual forces.[87] It is reasonable to assume that some degree of strength or ability possessed by an angel prior to the rebellion is still carried by that spirit after rejecting God.
- satan, demons, and powers of darkness *do* have the ability to harm people and interfere in our lives. Over two dozen Scriptures were cited in "What the Scriptures Say About satan and his demons" (Chapter 1, p. 22), showing, among other things, how people suffer from direct attacks and how doors can be opened to dark interference.
- I revisit here the section entitled "satan is active and purposeful" (Chapter 1, p. 22), to emphasize that the dark

---

[86]http://bartholomew.stanford.edu/onangelsranksthomas/intro.html.

[87]Ted Montgomery, *Creation ... Counterfeits ... and the 70th Week*, Chapter 8, 1998–2016, http://www.tedmontgomery.com/bblovrvw/C_8a.html.

193

THE DEVIL IN THE BACK PEW

spiritual realm *will* strongly resist efforts to dislodge a demonic presence. To the extent that there is sin in the forefront, such as unforgiveness in the prayee or pride in the pray-er, the demon will be able to hang on. As quoted earlier, "You can't take ground from the enemy if he has ground in you."

Remember: difficulties in freeing someone from a demonic tormentor are not insurmountable!

Don't Be Proud

When confronting a demonic spirit, we must faithfully draw upon the authority which has been granted to us, but we must not be prideful. Jesus gave specific instruction when He said: *"[D]o not rejoice in this, that the spirits are subject to you"* (Luke 10:20). The disciples were told not to exalt themselves or relish any perceived superiority over the spirits, even though those spirits were made to submit. We will not defeat the enemy if we carry our pride into a spiritual battle.

Pride in a Confrontation with Occultists

Several years ago, a church in a nearby city invited a well-known guest speaker to share his message of power evangelism. His church in the Midwest was living proof of fruit-bearing ministry in healing, deliverance, the prophetic, and God's presence. This pastor shared a story of a challenging time when his team attempted to deal with dark forces.

It happened that a group of occultists were holding a public event celebrating their way of life. In response, a group of enthusiastic Christian believers decided to go and "show" those folks how occult power was no match for God's power. But things did not go so well.

After many attempts to engage the occultists and show the supremacy of Christ, they found themselves getting nowhere.

194

Practical Aspects of Deliverance Prayer

Retreating to their home turf and seeking the Lord's guidance, it became clear that their motivation was prideful. Instead, they decided to go back the next day and concentrate on simply loving these people – speaking truth, but carrying first a heartfelt expression of God's love for each of them, individually. And yes, the barriers fell and the ministry was fruitful. They were openly received and truth was proclaimed. The lesson, in this instance, is that the tools we believers are given are not for our entertainment or to make us feel good; they are for the furtherance of His Kingdom.

A perspective from Scripture. When the apostles said to Jesus: *"Increase our faith"* (Luke 17:5), Jesus spoke of having the faith of a mustard seed, and told of how servants are to serve their masters. Concluding the narrative, He added: *"So likewise you, when you have done all those things which you are commanded, say, 'We are unprofitable servants. We have done what was **our duty** to do'"* (v.10, emphasis mine). Bottom line, it is about the Kingdom of God; it is not about us!

Pride in a Deliverance Encounter

This section tells of a well-intentioned leader misunderstanding his role in dealing with the demonic. Unfortunately, it was evident at the time he shared this experience that he did not grasp the error of his ways.

A few years ago, I went to a church in another city to attend a conference on deliverance. I like to hear other people's experiences and perspectives. The guest pastor who was instructing was poised and charismatic, and he spoke confidently on the subject. At one point, well into his presentation, he began to recount a story of dealing with a teenage boy who was being acutely attacked by a demonic force. Given his description of what was transpiring, it appeared to me that his discernment was accurate, and that a dark power was actively tormenting the young man. The speaker's reaction, though, surprised me. Becoming visibly angry as he told the story, and with a tone of intolerance and, frankly, self-importance,

THE DEVIL IN THE BACK PEW

he explained how "pissed off" he was at the devil for what he was doing to this kid.

I was really surprised: over the vulgar expression, which I don't use and don't hear from any pastors I know, but more so with the arrogant attitude. If my jaw did not drop physically, it sure did in my mind. The error of his approach was made clear when he told how the boy physically attacked him when he attempted to confront the demon in his office. The instructor's message shifted to, "This deliverance stuff isn't for everybody. You have to be careful what you're getting into."

Well ... God bless that guy! I hope he has come to a better understanding of what to do and not to do in dealing with demons. Unfortunately, I do not recall if anything was shared about how the situation with the boy finally concluded.

What is the lesson here? You cannot take your sin, your pride, your arrogance, into a confrontation with a demon and expect victory. Even the archangel Michael, with his great authority, when contending with satan over the body of Moses, *"dared not bring against him a reviling accusation, but said, 'The Lord rebuke you!'"* (Jude 1:9). Michael modeled humility, and so must we. To repeat, Jesus said we are *"not [to] rejoice"* in our authority over demons (Luke 10:20); we servants must merely do *"our duty"* (Luke 17:10).

To be clear, assuming our authority is not compromised by a prideful attitude or some other gross sin, we *can* effectively command a demon to stand down and behave. I am aware of no cases whatsoever, other than the one just described, of a prayee attacking or assaulting those praying for them in a deliverance situation. Indeed, on several occasions I've heard prominent teachers give examples how they had no problem commanding a threatening spirit to stand down. And this has been my experience as well. See "Verbally Bind the Powers of the demons" (Chapter 11, p. 225) for more on this topic.

In one instance, many years ago, a woman my wife and I were praying for lightly swiped my knee with her hand as I sat facing

196

Practical Aspects of Deliverance Prayer

her, looking into her eyes. I interpreted her response as a lame attempt of demonic intimidation. Her face was contorted in aggression and anger, reflecting the demon's attitude, but I barely felt the contact, it was so slight. And that is the only "hostile" experience I have had. I do not recall, but I likely did not forbid dark spirits to act out.

Pride Undercuts Authority

Authority is a fundamental concept of the Bible, and an unavoidable component of human existence. The rightful exercise of authority can be good, fruit-bearing, and Kingdom-building – as described earlier in this chapter. The abusive use of authority, however, or the attempt to illegitimately seize it, is clearly prideful.

The core sin of satan was pride: *"I will be like the Most High [God]"* (Isaiah 14:14). He wanted power, and he believed he could place himself above all the angels and be like God. The sin of Adam and Eve was also pride: The serpent (satan) said to them: *"For God knows that in the day you eat of it [the forbidden fruit] your eyes will be opened, and **you will be like God**, knowing good and evil"* (Genesis 3:5, emphasis mine). Adam and Eve yielded to their personal desire to lift themselves to a higher level of existence. Following this, it is my belief that pride is at the root of all sin. "I want what I want, and I don't care about anything else!" – whether the choice is disobedience to God's law, disregard for the impact on others, or just plain selfishness.[88]

Psalm 94:11 tells us that the Lord *"knows the thoughts of man, that they are futile,"* or *"vanity"* or *"shallowness"* as the King James Version and *The Message* respectively translate the word *"futile."* Irrespective of which word we prefer, God's assessment of the

---

[88]It is my personal "theology" that all conscious sin has pride at the core. As sin is, by definition, choosing to act against the will of God, such behavior inherently considers *our* will superior to that of Almighty God, and is prideful. In essence, we believe we know what's best and, in fact, are smarter than God.

197

THE DEVIL IN THE BACK PEW

heart of man speaks what most of us know – that our thoughts and hearts are not terribly noble, especially when we have access to power and authority. We need boundaries.

In Luke 9, the story is told of how Jesus sent his twelve disciples to nearby towns to preach the Kingdom of God. The apostles were given several instructions, but Luke 9:1 tells us specifically that Jesus *"gave them power and authority over all demons."* Looking at that verse alone, it appears that the disciples were given rather broad authority over the demonic realm.[89] Luke 10 tells how Jesus then sent out seventy disciples, two by two, with similar instructions. It was upon their return that they marveled: *"Lord, even the demons are subject to us in Your name"* (Luke 10:17). Importantly, Jesus responded by warning them: *"[D]o not rejoice in this, that the spirits are subject to you"* (v.20).

There are a few things to consider here. Human beings have not been created superior to heavenly beings. The Bible instructs us that man was made *"a little lower than the angels"* (Hebrews 2:7). And it was an overt act on Jesus' part, described in Luke 9:1 above, that gave the disciples authority over demons. Related, it is important to keep in perspective the message of Luke 17:10, that we are unworthy servants, just doing *"our duty."* Indeed, in the prior example of reaching out to the occultists, rejecting the prideful attitude and choosing an expression of love was what overcame the darkness and won the day. And in the example of the pastor who was attacked, he became vulnerable when he gave in to his prideful anger against the demon harassing the young man.

Carrying our sin of pride into a spiritual battle does not win God's favor. It distances us from Him! To do so is akin to saying, "My sin of pride isn't as bad as what the devil is doing." That doesn't work in God's economy, and it does nothing to help the afflicted person. I am aware of no situations in Scripture where,

---

[89]From the context of the specific verse (Luke 9:1), as well as in the context of the entire Bible, it is clear that *"all"* refers to those dark spirits which they encounter, not the entire spiritual realm.

198

Practical Aspects of Deliverance Prayer

in His ministry, Jesus became angry or showed haughtiness when dealing with demons. When He came into contact with them, He unceremoniously, yet decisively, commanded them out. We should do likewise. There is no justification for pride, anger, or fleshly behavior.

Sanctified Authority

In spite of previous words of caution, if the Holy Spirit prompts you to pray and speak commands outside of your scope of authority, by all means do so! Of course, we are always to *"test the spirits, whether they are of God"* (1 John 4:1).

I offer a wonderful example of this type of declaratory prayer. In the late 1980s, a number of Christian leaders were encouraged by the Holy Spirit to pray "down" the Berlin Wall. I recall watching a Christian television interview of Dick Eastman, president of Every Home For Christ, where he told how he was specifically prompted by the Holy Spirit to "get on a plane, fly to Germany, go to the Berlin Wall, lay your hands upon it and say five words to it, 'In Jesus' name, come down!'"[90] I also recall him telling how he later learned that other Christian leaders had been led to do the same. Of course, U.S. President Ronald Reagan later famously stood in front of the wall in Berlin and urged, "Mr. Gorbachev, tear down this wall!" And the rest is history.

How Do You Assure Success in the Battle?

The suggestions here are important, not only in the context of warfare-type prayer, but also for our own daily resistance of the enemy. He will *never* stop pursuing us.

Deal with Sinful Habits and Inclinations

- Make sure your sins are confessed. Keep short accounts;

---

[90]Dutch Sheets, *Intercessory Prayer* (Regal from Gospel Light, Ventura, CA, 1996), 289.

199

THE DEVIL IN THE BACK PEW

don't wait until bedtime to reconcile with God.

- Renounce or eject, as appropriate, memories of former sins which come to mind or that the enemy brings to mind.
- Get prayer if there is strength in, or temptation related to, an enemy aggression.

Submit to God and Resist the devil

It is obviously helpful to be able to compel the enemy to flee from you. The verse cited in "We Have Defenses Available" (Chapter 1, p. 24): *"Submit yourselves, then, to God. Resist the devil, and he will flee from you"* (James 4:7 NIV) provides the Biblical approach. Importantly, though, the broader context of this passage of Scripture is a message of faithfulness.

Note: The opening mention of adultery (v.4) is not referring to sexual sin, but to the spiritual equivalent, unfaithfulness to God:

> *"You adulterous people, don't you know that **friendship with the world is hatred towards God?** Anyone who chooses to be a friend of the world becomes an enemy of God. Or do you think Scripture says without reason that the spirit he caused to live in us envies intensely? But he gives us more grace. That is why Scripture says: '**God opposes the proud but gives grace to the humble.'** Submit yourselves, then, to God. Resist the devil, and he will flee from you. Come near to God and he will come near to you. Wash your hands, you sinners, and purify your hearts, you double-minded. Grieve, mourn and wail. Change your laughter to mourning and your joy to gloom. **Humble yourselves before the Lord, and he will lift you up.** "* (James 4:4–10 NIV, emphasis mine)

Our heartfelt faithfulness to God provides the foundation upon which our strength to resist rests. We gain the power to make the enemy flee by living *for* Jesus with sincerity and resolve.

Practical Aspects of Deliverance Prayer

Paul's Thorn

The apostle Paul says:

> "And lest I should be exalted above measure by the abundance of the revelations, a **thorn in the flesh** was given to me, a **messenger of [s]atan** to buffet me, lest I be exalted above measure. Concerning this thing **I pleaded with the Lord three times** that it might depart from me. And He said to me, '**My grace is sufficient for you, for My strength is made perfect in weakness.**' Therefore most gladly I will rather boast in my infirmities, that the power of Christ may rest upon me. Therefore I take pleasure in infirmities, in reproaches, in needs, in persecutions, in distresses, for Christ's sake. **For when I am weak, then I am strong.**" (2 Corinthians 12:7–10, emphasis mine)

This Bible passage reveals a profound truth about our personal spiritual battles. In the narrative, we see Paul being harassed by a "messenger" of satan. As mentioned, the Greek word translated here as *"messenger"* is rendered *"angel"* 96% of the time.

So Paul is dealing with an *angel of satan,* or a demon. Paul asked the Lord three times that this harassing spirit would be taken from him in order that he would not have to contend with it. But the Lord's response was, in essence, "No. You have what you need to handle it." The Lord's words of encouragement: *"My grace is sufficient for you"* and *"My strength is made perfect in weakness,"* along with Paul's response, *"when I am weak, then I am strong,"* all speak the way to victory. The Lord provides us with the knowledge and the strength, but *we* have to do our part.

Now I quote the same passage from *The Message.* Take note how the contemporary wording conveys the point in a more encouraging and positive way:

> "Because of the extravagance of those revelations, and so I wouldn't get a big head, I was given the gift of a handicap to keep me in constant touch with my limitations. [s]atan's

THE DEVIL IN THE BACK PEW

angel did his best to get me down; what he in fact did was push me to my knees. No danger then of walking around high and mighty! At first I didn't think of it as a gift, and begged God to remove it. Three times I did that, and then he told me, My grace is enough; it's all you need. My strength comes into its own in your weakness. Once I heard that, I was glad to let it happen. I quit focusing on the handicap and began appreciating the gift. It was a case of Christ's strength moving in on my weakness. Now I take limitations in stride, and with good cheer, these limitations that cut me down to size— abuse, accidents, opposition, bad breaks. I just let Christ take over! And so the weaker I get, the stronger I become." (2 Corinthians 12:7–10 MSG)

Add to this the great Biblical truth that God will not permit us to be tempted or tested beyond our ability to resist, and we see that we have *all* that is required to overcome: ***"God is faithful**, who will **not allow you to be tempted beyond what you are able**, but with the temptation will also make the **way of escape**, that you may be **able to bear it"*** (1 Corinthians 10:13, emphasis mine).

We do not know what the nature of this harassment or temptation was, nor do we know how long it persisted. It is possible Paul dealt with it for many years! Regarding our personal battles against dark spiritual attacks, the lesson is clear: we have the tools we need. And, importantly, we should never permit the enemy to pull us into anger, frustration, despair, or even impatience. If we do, he wins. I recommend dealing with the enemy's persistence, planted thoughts, and temptations with an attitude similar to that of swatting away an annoying housefly. There's no need to get upset, prideful, or self-righteous. Just peacefully, yet stubbornly, permit him no access.

Francis Frangipane has this wonderful insight: "[s]atan will not continue to assault you if the circumstances he designed to destroy

you are now working to perfect you!"[91]

Rats and Garbage

Author and teacher Charles H. Kraft often uses the metaphor of rats and garbage to explain the basics of demonic harassment. Indeed, I believe every time I have heard him speak on the subject of spiritual warfare, he has stated: "Get rid of the garbage, and the rats will flee." It is a foundational truth relevant to confrontation with the demonic realm. Garbage is, fundamentally, the spiritual or emotional brokenness which provides a "congenial setting for the demonic rats."[92]

Dealing with sin habits, unforgiveness, and other aspects of spiritual brokenness, and receiving blessing and healing for emotional wounds (Chapter 5), removes the "garbage" to which the enemy clings. Garbage empowers the enemy, and gives him a right to stay. Break the "right," then send the enemy packing!

Self-cleansing/Sanctification

I offer a personal example, though the experience is quite common. When we turn to God and begin embracing His ways, darkness begins to fall off. We become ever more sanctified and "clean" as we grow in faith and change our ways. In the Lord's prayer sense, it is akin to being "delivered" from the evil one. The process may or may not feel as confrontational or intense as deliverance prayer, but the outcome is the same.

As a result of my own history of running from God, I accumulated a lot of dirt, garbage, and sinful habits and inclinations. I have no doubt I was heavily oppressed, and likely demonized to some degree. Surely the dark spirits were comfortable in my company. I never received actual deliverance prayer similar to what's described in this book, though I know that much of the demonic

---

[91]Francis Frangipane, *The Three Battlegrounds* (Arrow Publications, Cedar Rapids, IA, 1989), 14.
[92]Kraft, *Defeating Dark Angels*, 120.

THE DEVIL IN THE BACK PEW

fell away over time.

To be clear, I was not following a plan or strategy of purification, because I didn't know one! Nevertheless, I *was* turning to and believing in God. And I *was* getting rid of sinful behaviors, resisting the devil, and getting the garbage out of my life. The demons simply had insufficient grounds to continue to hang on. Certainly I was, and remain, far from perfect. But the big stuff is gone. It was a displacement of sorts; the area formerly occupied by darkness had been filled with light.

Get Help

The book of James advises that when someone is ill, leaders should be called in to help pray. *"Is anyone among you sick? Let him **call for the elders** of the church, and **let them pray over him,** anointing him with oil in the name of the Lord"* (James 5:14, emphasis mine). We might wonder why it is suggested that others be brought in. Can't a Christian believer just pray for him/herself, or get prayer from a spouse or family member?

I offer two examples where self-directed prayer, or praying for oneself, was insufficient, but where breakthrough was then achieved by outsiders. In the first case, my wife and I were the people called in to pray; in the second case, my wife and I were the ones who needed the help of others.

A wonderful woman with whom my wife and I had had several deliverance sessions asked to meet again for prayer. She and her husband, both in formal Christian ministry positions, could not free her of a tormenting spirit which was showing itself rather boldly. We met, prayed, confronted the dark spirit, and ejected it, without a whole lot of difficulty. By any outside assessment, these leaders were far superior to us in position and authority granted them by the church, yet we outsiders brought something that tipped the scale in their favor.

We mentioned in "Examples of Discernment" (Chapter 3, p. 72), our personal experience of sensing a dark presence in our

204

Practical Aspects of Deliverance Prayer

home during my battle with cancer. There were many months of spiritual warfare, and Patti and I were not lax in prayer and crying out to God. Additionally, it is, and has long been, a part of my daily prayer to command powers of darkness out of our house and off us personally, and to welcome the Holy Spirit in. Nevertheless, an identified dark spiritual presence, similarly discerned by two Christian believers, as well as what I might call a spirit of gloom or heaviness, permeated our home. Of course we prayed and had literally hundreds of people praying with us, but relief was not obtained until we had a Godly older couple come and pray through the house. That liberation came in the form of the identified spirit no longer being in the house. This was confirmed by one who originally exposed it, and in the tangibly "lighter" spiritual atmosphere we felt throughout our home. This couple did what we could not seem to do.

Concluding, I have often observed more/better fruit when an outsider prays than when someone who is emotionally close prays. I would never discourage prayer by or from anyone, and certainly pray fervently for those close to me, but there is something brought by an outsider which is special and precious. And, from my experience, powerful.

Confidentiality

Confidentiality *must* be maintained for all private prayer sessions. Vague or anonymous references can unexpectedly reveal private matters to others. I know things about specific people *that I should not know*, but came upon information because a well-meaning believer spoke things they did not realize I could link to an individual.

If a private matter is made public, the offended party typically feels betrayed. And a wounded or unstable believer can be pushed by the enemy into a most vulnerable place: isolation.

205

Accountability

An exhaustive discussion of ministry accountability and oversight is beyond the scope of this book, though some mention is fitting. Experience shows that Christian ministers and leaders who fall into bad practices or sinful behavior often have deficient oversight. Accordingly, I strongly believe a healthy faith walk requires we each have a solid believer who will ask us the hard questions. And this applies to both our personal spiritual lives as well as the soundness of our ministry methods.

If I ever wish to discuss the particulars of a prayer approach, I first seek counsel without giving details. In the rare circumstance which calls for the sharing of private information, I obtain permission first. Following these practices, I have never had difficulty resolving issues satisfactorily.

Chapter 10

Before Praying

The following discussion addresses topics to be considered prior to engaging in deliverance prayer.

Don't Judge a Person Who Has a demon

Your perspective should always be that a demonized prayee is a victim. Speak words of support. Some folks are clearly demonized because they have been exposed to an inescapable, difficult situation, like an abusive upbringing. Others, though, suffer because of "junk" which has been self-inflicted. Without doubt, I do not believe anyone would give ground to the enemy if they truly understood the dark realm. These wounded people, like all of us, have made mistakes. Be compassionate and merciful: *"Mercy triumphs over judgment"* (James 2:13).

- If a demonic presence manifests by some physical response of the prayee, speak words of comfort should they seem embarrassed. The enemy may plant condemning thoughts about how undignified they were. At the root, the battle is against pride: Do you want dignity or deliverance? What drowning person would be embarrassed about screaming for help?
- When a prayee is struggling with any aspect of the deliver-

207

THE DEVIL IN THE BACK PEW

ance process, I like to point out one of my favorite traits or "ways" of God: He so often takes an enemy victory and turns it into a *much greater victory* for the Kingdom and for the person being attacked. Nehemiah gave witness to this when he said: *"[O]ur God turned the curse into a blessing"* (Nehemiah 13:2).

- An encouragement: After Jesus rose from the dead: *"He appeared **first** to Mary Magdalene, out of whom He had **cast seven demons**"* (Mark 16:9, emphasis mine). Mary was clearly very special to Jesus. No one ever needs to be ashamed of having had the need for deliverance prayer.

- Jesus showed His perspective on judging when He rebuked James and John who wanted to *"command fire to come down"* (Luke 9:54) on the Samaritan village which would not receive them. He said: *"You do not know what manner of spirit you are of."* I came not *"to destroy ... but to save"* (v.55–56).

Should You Pray Deliverance Prayers for an Unbeliever?

Jesus warned of the re-entry of spirits "more wicked" than those expelled, when a demon returns to a person and finds him/her open and vulnerable. The Scriptural account is quite clear:

> *"When an **unclean spirit goes out** of a man, he goes through dry places, seeking rest, and finds none. Then he says, '**I will return to my house from which I came.**' And when he comes, **he finds it empty**, swept, and put in order. Then he goes and **takes with him seven other spirits more wicked than himself**, and they enter and dwell there; and the **last state of that man is worse than the first**."* (Matthew 12:43–45, emphasis mine)

This passage raises an important cautionary flag about demonic re-entry. The exposure to the prayee results from the fact that he, in this example, is *"empty,"* that is, not internally "occupied" by a

Before Praying

love for God and by the Holy Spirit. The solution to the problem is simple, yet indispensable: the prayee must be, or become, truly connected to God. Otherwise, the *"empty"* place remains, and it will ultimately be re-occupied by spiritual darkness.

In my experience, Christian teachers discourage praying deliverance for unbelievers. Jesus did, but only as an apparent exception. His stated ministry was to the children of Israel, but He reacted differently on this occasion:

> *"[A] woman of Canaan came … and cried out to Him, saying, 'Have mercy on me, O Lord, Son of David! My daughter is severely demon-possessed.' … But He answered and said, 'I was not sent except to the lost sheep of the house of Israel.' Then she came and worshiped Him, saying, 'Lord, help me!' But He answered and said, 'It is not good to take the children's bread and throw it to the little dogs.' And she said, 'Yes, Lord, yet even the little dogs eat the crumbs which fall from their masters' table.' Then Jesus answered and said to her, 'O woman, great is your faith! Let it be to you as you desire.' And her daughter was healed from that very hour."* (Matthew 15:22, 24–28)

The many other accounts of Jesus casting demons out of people involved the children of Israel.

I would be reluctant to pray deliverance-type prayers over someone who did not have a measure of stability as a Christian. Of course, I would yield to a clear prompting from the Holy Spirit, but I am sure I would reverently "test" what I thought I was hearing. The best approach: be very careful!

Does the Prayee Have a Supportive Environment?

A similar risk to casting demons out of unbelievers exists in the case of persons who are immature in their faith, or who do not have an adequate Christian support system. I believe deliverance prayer should be undertaken only when the prayee is connected to

209

THE DEVIL IN THE BACK PEW

an established Christian community, a dedicated circle of Christian friends, or a Christian family for the following reasons:

- The individual will require prayer, follow-up, encouragement, and likely further deliverance.
- As a pray-er, you may need to step into a spiritual support role for the person.
- Again, it is a mistake to believe that just because a tormentor is gone, it will not try to return.

I often follow up with prayees a day or two after the first time a demon is expelled. They will likely need encouragement and have questions about what happened or what lies ahead. It is wise to schedule the next prayer session as soon as is practicable – to maintain momentum and to encourage the prayee. Experience has shown that, if too much time elapses between initial encounters, ground can be lost and errant beliefs or doubts permitted to creep in (enemy-planted, of course).

Occasionally, we may sense it needful to allow no more than a day or two between prayer sessions.

Managing the Prayer Session

How difficult or uncomfortable can deliverance get? I have heard anecdotal comments about evening deliverance sessions lasting until daybreak, but I have no first-hand knowledge of this. I have also read of exorcists organizing rotating teams of muscular men to hold down crazed, demonized people so the pray-ers could administer multiday deliverance prayer. If that system bears fruit, I cannot criticize it. But we have seen great success employing a less stressful approach.

Our preference is to provide a peaceful, restful environment for both the prayee and the pray-ers, and this approach has consistently borne fruit. Of course, the demons themselves often present a sour or nasty demeanor, but this is to be expected. These spirits are a sad, condemned lot, being driven from their present place

210

Before Praying

of refuge. And they are desperate. Do not feel sorry for them, though!

Note: Their attitude or disposition does not dictate how we manage them.

- Direct the session with expulsion in mind.
- Be relaxed, casual, and comfortable. The battle is not yours.
- Take a break if you feel the need. There is an instructive story in the lore of John Wimber (the first national leader of what is now Vineyard USA) regarding his potato chip break. Some folks were involved in a lengthy deliverance prayer session, when John went to an adjoining room for a snack. One of the other pray-ers, taken aback by a perceived lack of seriousness on John's part, expressed his objection. As the story is told, John sprayed potato chips as he replied, "Do you think the demon's going to get mad and leave?"
- It is perfectly acceptable to "table" a session for continuation later. While it is desirable to continue the prayer until it naturally winds down, at times other constraints prevail. And that is okay. In our experience, deliverance is virtually never accomplished fully in one meeting.
- Proceed as far as seems reasonable and comfortable, following the Holy Spirit.
- Postpone:
  - If help is needed.
  - If the process seems "stuck."
  - If practicalities limit – time, place, fatigue.

When a particular day's deliverance prayer session ends, it is important to order the remaining demons to cease harassment. By command, "bind" all powers of darkness and unclean spirits, naming/identifying them when you can, and forbid them to attack, distract, disturb sleep, steal peace, and so forth. Direct them to "stand down" until dealt with at the next meeting. More in the next chapter's "Cleansing Prayer" discussion (p. 248).

211

Speaking to/with dark spirits

As mentioned, at times a demon will audibly speak through a prayee. When this occurs, it is often the spirit's last, desperate effort to hang on. Still, demons much prefer to stay quiet, unseen, and ignored. From the pray-er's perspective, the initial objective is always to cast spirits directly out. And most demons are ejected without a word on their part, though occasionally they may give out a yelp, a scream, or a subdued moan. Stronger spirits can become vocal as their discomfort increases. But if they begin to talk, they are most likely on the ropes.

There is an exception to this: certain very strong spirits (e.g., religious spirits, occult spirits, or those with Biblical names) often aggressively flaunt their presence and make no apparent effort to hide. From our experience, they are very arrogant and put up a much greater fight. Nevertheless, the spiritual warfare principles of this book apply.

We have seen vocal spirits run the gamut from being brash and boisterous to almost meek. Typically, the meek ones are rather easily expelled. Nevertheless, demons are often verbally aggressive at first contact, trying to intimidate and put forth an air of boldness and strength. Usually there are two general directions things go from the "bold stand:"

- We embark on the verbal confrontation described in the next chapter, persisting until the spirit weakens and departs; or
- We find ourselves unable to gain the upper hand, which indicates there is something that needs to be resolved before progress can be made. The resolution process is normally a combination of the Holy Spirit's revelation, confession of sin, the offering of forgiveness, emotional healing, dismissal of lies believed, and the prayee's faithful determination to move ahead with God.

Then we can once again open conversation with the demon.

Before Praying

Important: As mentioned, some measure of discipling is generally necessary in the deliverance process. Also, it may take a few to several intervening sessions of probing, confessing, praying emotional healing, and the like before the nature of a stronghold is revealed or a right can be identified and broken. At other times, the enemy's right/stronghold can be broken quickly by confessing and renouncing a long-held sin, or offering forgiveness where it has been withheld. In either case, when the underlying issues are settled, the demon has nothing to cling to and can be driven out. We have successfully worked through this cycle many, many times. Don't get discouraged!

Familiar spirits or ancestral spirits

Occasionally, a spirit may represent itself as a deceased loved one, ancestor, or acquaintance. When this occurs, my suspicion is that the spirit gained entry generationally or via an occult attempt to contact the dead.

The common explanations for these spirits are:

- They are demons masquerading as known people who are now dead.
- They are actual spirits of the dead.

Certain Christian denominations believe either explanation is possible, whereas others accept only the first, as do I. Irrespective, they are both handled in the same way: confront the spirit and command it out. Of course, all relevant legal and generational rights must be broken, and if the spirit gained entry via sin (as in an occult attempt to contact the dead), that sin must be confessed and renounced.

The Prayee's Reactions

During deliverance prayer, a prayee may shake, cough, yawn, sneeze, gag, belch, drip mucus, shout, scream, or speak vulgarities. All these are common when a dark spirit is present – and

213

THE DEVIL IN THE BACK PEW

sometimes are concurrent with, and evidence of, a dark spirit's departure.

- Encourage the prayee. Again, be sensitive to feelings of embarrassment.
- As mentioned, forbid speech you don't like, and forbid the spirits to make the prayee uncomfortable, ill, or uncontrolled.
  - o I have never witnessed a prayee vomit matter supernaturally (e.g., nails, large quantities of semen), though there is testimony of this in Catholic exorcisms. On a few occasions, it seemed helpful to permit, and to encourage, a prayee to spit mucous/saliva which was being coughed up.
- Have a lined wastebasket, tissues, drinking water, and anointing oil available.

Be gentle, comforting, and loving to the prayee, but single-minded toward the demons. Keep the focus on Jesus.

Where to Pray

When circumstances indicate a need for deliverance prayer, it is best that it be scheduled separately. For Patti and me, deliverance prayer is typically an integral part of a private soaking prayer session, and we are always prepared should things go that direction. If an apparent need arises spontaneously, keep in mind:

- Scheduling deliverance prayer separately can provide time flexibility.
- Privacy can be assured.
- The "right" prayer team can be assembled (especially if it is a unique situation).
- The prayee can be instructed and comforted, in advance, about the process. This is important. The enemy often will attempt to plant seeds of anxiety, fear, shame, or other discouragement to convince the prayee to back out.

Before Praying

Note: If there's a demonic presence, it no doubt has some level of influence, and it will attempt to use that influence to keep deliverance prayer from even starting.

Regardless of the obvious desire to assure a prayee's privacy, I describe here how I have discreetly confronted and expelled a demon in an open environment.

Some years ago, we had begun attending a church which energetically promoted the spiritual gifts of 1 Corinthians 12. Though the leadership was not terribly assertive about confronting the demonic, there was a designated team to pray for individuals' needs at the end of services. Patti and I had not felt led, at that point, to make a commitment to this church, and we had not joined the prayer team. We had, however, fulfilled their requirement and attended their prayer training classes.

As the service was ending one Sunday, a couple I knew quite well from prayer ministry elsewhere was praying for a woman at the front of the room. Patti and I were preparing to leave when the husband caught my eye and motioned me to come to him. As I drew close, he stated simply, "I don't know what to do." The woman receiving prayer was showing signs of demonic torment (her face reflected extreme dread, hopelessness, sadness, fear, and she was trembling). My friend had never been exposed to such behavior. There, amid several teams actively praying for people, I quietly asked her about her situation. She explained she'd gone through an ugly divorce and was also having severe health problems. We began by praying briefly for healing, focusing mostly on the emotional hurts and the pains of betrayal and abandonment. I then looked her in the eyes, and quickly confronted and expelled one or two dark spirits. She showed immediate relief, and a look of peace settled on her face as she acknowledged what we had discerned: the presence had departed. I believe this interaction took about seven or eight minutes, and I would be very surprised if anyone else knew what was going on. There is more to the story, but I share this portion as an example of how God can free some-

215

THE DEVIL IN THE BACK PEW

one so sweetly and privately in the midst of a room full of people.

Since we had not joined the prayer team or been released by the church to pray for folks, I believed it appropriate to email the pastor and tell what had transpired. As it turned out, we felt the Lord lead us elsewhere, and shortly thereafter began attending another church. That move, though, had nothing to do with this experience.

Despite the success of the deliverance prayer in this rather open setting, I remain most cautious about doing so. In the case mentioned, I felt a sense of peace from the Holy Spirit, and that discernment seemed to prove accurate.

Not all such situations resolve so easily, though. We know an individual whose receipt of after-service prayer turned into a very visible and humiliating experience. Overzealous, well-meaning but misguided pray-ers let the affair become somewhat of a spectacle, with focus more on the confrontation with demons than on loving ministry to the prayee. Years later, when we were told of the event by the prayer recipient, it was still a hurtful memory and required us to fully deal with that old hurt as an inner healing need requiring prayer and deliverance *now*. To be clear, I am speaking of the unrestrained, public deliverance "prayer" itself as the problem.

The lesson: The enemy is quite clever and can even use a deliverance prayer effort to advance his agenda. And even to establish a dark attachment.

Regarding where to pray, generally speaking, privacy is paramount. Should a need for deliverance prayer arise in an open church service or other nonprivate place, you can always check for a nearby office or room. And if no suitable venue is available, I would take it as an indicator that God is not in a hurry.

216

Chapter 11

The Confrontation

People with a degree of spiritual sensitivity recognize temptation is a part of daily life. As discussed, Scripture tells us we are confronted by the world, the flesh, and the devil. Though hopefully few of us yield or are deceived to the extent of becoming demonized, there exists a clear progression: temptation can lead to oppression and demonization. But in addition to this personal source of vulnerability, spiritual torment can also be the consequence of external events. Significantly, there is a fine line between oppression and demonization, and though demonization may seem far worse, someone who is oppressed can suffer horribly. Assertive, deliverance-type commands should be spoken whenever the enemy is tormenting or tempting.

We might suspect that dealing with a dark spirit, manifesting or not, is frightening and intimidating, and perhaps even dangerous. Without a doubt, dark spirits *want* us to feel that way, but the truth is far from that. If we are walking rightly with God (perfection is not required), and if we follow the essence of what is conveyed in this book, there is no reason for fear. There is every reason to expect wonderful fruit from our efforts.

This chapter will discuss some customary approaches to deliverance prayer. Keep in mind, though, that the process will likely

217

THE DEVIL IN THE BACK PEW

not follow an orderly plan. Accordingly, the best way to learn is through apprenticeship. If you can, partner with or observe someone who is experienced. But don't be discouraged if you have no one to hold your hand along the way. Other than my initial exposure to a dark spirit described under "Can a Christian Really Have a demon? – My Experience" (Chapter 2, p. 47), Patti and I saw one video of one ten-minute deliverance prayer session prior to our first direct encounter with a demon. The Holy Spirit is a marvelous Instructor!

Understanding Entry

As mentioned, occasionally dark spirits can be ejected rather easily. The more stubborn ones, though, might require increased effort. Hence, we begin exploring how the dark attachment was established. This information can help us with our prayer direction.

Open Doors

"Open doors" is a commonly used descriptor among those who teach or write on the subject of deliverance. Curiously, on one occasion when I questioned a demon as to how he gained entry into the prayee, his response was an arrogantly spoken, "Open doors."

Sin

Virtually all demonic attachment is rooted in *sin*, either on the part of an individual, or resulting from the actions of a person who sins against them. Sin can open the door, but the specifics of how this happens, or what comprises the "last straw," is certainly not clear. Yet there seems an unmistakably higher frequency of demonic harassment with grievous sin, long-term sinful behavior, and sin which is, in effect, celebrated.

Regarding *personal sin*, Scripture speaks of *enslavement* and giving the devil a "place:"

218

The Confrontation

> *"Do you not know that to whom you present yourselves* **slaves** *to obey, you are that one's* **slaves** *whom you obey, whether of sin leading to death, or of obedience leading to righteousness?"* (Romans 6:16, emphasis mine)

> *"Jesus said ... 'If you abide in My word, you are My disciples indeed. And you shall know the truth, and the* **truth shall make you free**.*' They answered Him, 'We are Abraham's descendants, and have never been in bondage to anyone. How can you say, "You will be made free"?' Jesus answered them, 'Most assuredly, I say to you, whoever commits sin is a* **slave of sin**.*'"* (John 8:31–34, emphasis mine)

> *"'In your anger do not sin': Do not let the sun go down while you are still angry, and* **do not give the devil a foothold**.*"* (Ephesians 4:26–27 NIV, emphasis mine)

Occult Involvement

Likewise, the Bible is quite clear about the gravity of one of the most dangerous open doors, *occult involvement:*

> *"**There shall not be found among you** anyone who makes his son or his daughter* **pass through the fire**, *or one who practices* **witchcraft**, *or a* **soothsayer**, *or one who* **interprets omens**, *or a* **sorcerer**, *or one who* **conjures spells**, *or a* **medium**, *or a* **spiritist**, *or* **one who calls up the dead**. **For all who do these things are an abomination to the LORD** ... "* (Deuteronomy 18:10–12, emphasis mine)

As mentioned earlier, the word translated *"abomination"* is the strongest word in the Hebrew language for what the Lord hates and rejects. Participation in activities related to the occult opens the door to demonic infestation, as does retaining possession of physical objects related to occult practices.

Our experience has shown that *many* church people have dabbled in occult activities, and many quite innocently or, more

THE DEVIL IN THE BACK PEW

accurately, naively. Slumber party ouija board sessions, reading horoscopes, studying astrology, and participating in palm reading or fortune telling are explicitly occult in nature. It could be a big error to assume that, since you have been faithfully following the Lord for a long time, you do not need to resolve an occult exposure from the past. I encourage you to take this seriously and settle old business! Neil T. Anderson's booklet, *The Steps to Freedom in Christ*, is an excellent tool for identifying and resolving spiritual conflicts. We purchase these booklets in bulk, and regularly provide copies to folks we pray for. I cannot recommend it too highly.[93]

demonic Attachments – "Hooks," Strongholds or Sources of "Dirt"

I list below examples of the open doors to which the enemy may cling.[94] Again, the dark spirit's attachment may not be visible demonization but a less obvious, but still life-stealing, oppression.

- Anger, hatred, bitterness, self-pity
- Drugs, alcohol, addiction
- Generational/bloodline bondage – multigenerational or ancestral (Chapter 8)
  - Including negative pre-natal influence. If a baby is not loved or wanted, a spirit of rejection may cling to the child.
- Greed
- Idleness – laziness, unfruitfulness, busybody behavior
- Immorality, sexual soul-ties – the "one-ness" which results from an unholy sexual union: *"the two shall become one flesh"* (Mark 10:8)

---

[93]The checklist in Anderson's booklet identified for me some occult exposures I had not recalled. This is common.

[94]A demonic attachment can be rooted in virtually any sin or failure of mankind. This top-line listing has been compiled over many years and represents both our experience and that of others. As there is much duplication in lists from different authors, I refrain from attempting to name sources.

220

The Confrontation

- Jealousy
- Lust, fantasy of illicit liaisons, both sexual and non-sexual
- Non-sexual soul-tie – a harmful spiritual identification with another; codependence, a dominating or overcontrolling relationship[95]
- Occult activity, false religions, idolatry, satanism – going back four generations (30 people) – whether willing or unwilling, and when thought to be harmless (e.g., satanic rock music)
  - o Divination – seeking hidden knowledge from any source other than God – of people, events, the future, etc.
  - o Sorcery – usage of or dependence on words/objects believed to have hidden power, such as charms, spells, incantations, drugs, potions, amulets, "good luck" possessions/activities
  - o Witchcraft – seeking supernatural power
- Pornography
- Unforgiveness (Chapter 6)
- Willful disobedience, a renegade disposition, habitual lying
- Works of the flesh, as identified in three passages of Scripture:
  - o *"The acts of the sinful nature are obvious: **sexual immorality, impurity and debauchery; idolatry and witchcraft; hatred, discord, jealousy, fits of rage, selfish ambition, dissensions, factions and envy; drunkenness, orgies, and the like**. I warn you, as I did before, that those who live like this will not inherit the kingdom of God."* (Galatians 5:19–21 NIV, emphasis mine)
  - o *"Therefore each of you must put off **falsehood** and speak truthfully to his neighbour, for we are all members of one body. 'In your **anger** do not sin': Do not let the sun*

---

[95]MacNutt, *Deliverance from Evil Spirits*, 127.

THE DEVIL IN THE BACK PEW

*go down while you are still angry, and do not give the devil a foothold. He who has been **stealing** must steal no longer, but must work, doing something useful with his own hands, that he may have something to share with those in need. Do not let any **unwholesome talk** come out of your mouths, but only what is helpful for building others up according to their needs, that it may benefit those who listen. And do not **grieve the Holy Spirit** of God, with whom you were sealed for the day of redemption. Get rid of all **bitterness, rage and anger, brawling and slander**, along with every form of **malice**. Be kind and compassionate to one another, forgiving each other, just as in Christ God forgave you. Be imitators of God, therefore, as dearly loved children and live a life of love, just as Christ loved us and gave himself up for us as a fragrant offering and sacrifice to God. But among you there must not be even a hint of **sexual immorality**, or of any kind of **impurity**, or of **greed**, because these are improper for God's holy people. Nor should there be **obscenity, foolish talk or coarse joking**, which are out of place, but rather thanksgiving. For of this you can be sure: No immoral, impure or greedy person—such a man is an **idolater**—has any inheritance in the kingdom of Christ and of God. Let no one deceive you with empty words, for because of such things God's wrath comes on those who are **disobedient**. Therefore do not be partners with them. For you were once darkness, but now you are light in the Lord. Live as children of light (for the fruit of the light consists in all goodness, righteousness and truth) and find out what pleases the Lord. Have nothing to do with the **fruitless deeds of darkness**, but rather expose them. For it is shameful even to mention what the disobedient do in secret."* (Ephesians 4:25–5:11 NIV, emphasis mine)

The Confrontation

o *"For from within, out of men's hearts, come **evil thoughts,
sexual immorality, theft, murder, adultery, greed,
malice, deceit, lewdness, envy, slander, arrogance
and folly.** "* (Mark 7:21–22 NIV, emphasis mine)

Note: The next three items, though different individually, are
alike in that they can be externally caused or initiated – i.e., the
results of the person's life circumstances or what people have done
to them. They nevertheless need to be fought and renounced as
determinedly as combating willful sin choices:

- Fear
- Trauma – physical or emotional (Chapters 4 and 5)
  - o Accident, violence, assault (sexual and non-sexual)
  - o Hurtful life experiences – want of basic needs, personal rejection (including from adoption), absence of love, etc.
  - o Exposure – e.g., proximity to or witnessing violence; a household member active in the occult; an environment of criticism, persecution, or derision
- Victimization – repetitive persecution, ill-treatment

Of course not all instances of the foregoing result in demonization
or oppression. But, if demonic activity is suspected, it can be helpful to understand a person's history in order to gain knowledge
of strongholds which may exist. Then, emotional wounds can be
prayed for and healed, and demonic rights identified and broken.

The Encounter

General Guidelines

- Do what you can with the gifts and knowledge the Lord has given you. Follow the Holy Spirit and *purposefully* minister love to the prayee.
- Remember that you are totally relying on the Lord. The only righteous strength you bring to the situation is what

223

THE DEVIL IN THE BACK PEW

He provides.

- If you are uncomfortable, get help. Don't get stressed or feel pressured. God's timing is always right.

Deliverance Prayer Basics

Pray for Protection as You Begin, or Beforehand

Note: I rarely feel prompted by the Holy Spirit to do this, but that is because I have a lifestyle of praying protection over myself, my family, possessions, and activities/efforts. It is a regular part of my prayer and, indeed, an explicit part of the Lord's prayer. I am comfortable that I am amply safeguarded by the Lord.

Be sensitive, though, to the prayee's need for prayers of protection. I sometimes begin by praying specifically for the prayee's spiritual and physical safety, not only for the inherent benefit of doing so, but also to allay fear as well as provide an example of praying in this way for themselves. Actually, very many of the prayers spoken in the deliverance prayer process are explicitly prayers of protection.

I add a personal anecdote which I believe is significant in positioning myself in faith and trust to confront powers of darkness. I am wired, if you will, to be thorough – to cross every "t" and to dot every "i" – in things of consequence. And because my Christian walk is certainly of paramount importance, I have always worked hard to get things absolutely right. In classes I have taught or studies I have led, I always strongly recommended praying "on" the armor of God (from Ephesians 6:14–17) *every day.* We want to be protected, right? I confess I may have been somewhat Pharisaical about this, almost implying that missing a day would leave me vulnerable to enemy attack. Not long ago, I got a better perspective from a comment Bill Johnson made when he told of his response to someone who casually questioned, "Did you put on your armor today, pastor?" Bill's reply was, "Nope. I didn't take it off last night."

I couldn't help but smile at my own juvenile rigidity, and at the

Lord's grace and faithfulness. Yes, I do regularly pray protection, but I also have an underlying faith and trust that I won't get clobbered by the enemy due to some ritualistic oversight. Nevertheless, it is entirely appropriate to pray for protection. Also, you may wish to ask the Lord to send His ministering angels to aid and protect in the deliverance prayer effort.

Pray with a Team

I generally prefer a team of two to four people, with one person leading and the others praying along, worshiping, and interceding. It is best when folks are accustomed to praying with one another, yielding to each other's gifting and discernment.

Though some may disagree, I believe it is unwise to engage in deliverance prayer alone. It simply takes more than one to manage it well and to deal with contingencies. I know folks who have done this as a perceived last resort, but they have affirmed that it can get uncomfortable, difficult, and, in a few cases, threatening. I have never encountered a situation which was so urgent that I felt compelled to address it alone. Of course, if the Holy Spirit prompts, I will yield. But then again, God's timing is always right, and I have never seen Him in a hurry.

Minister to the Prayee, Not the demon

Shouting is certainly not necessary. Nor is there any rightful place for anger, arrogance, or pride, as we discussed in Chapter 9.

Verbally Bind the Powers of the demons

Forbid disturbance, discomfort, aggression, illness, and intercommunication between spirits. By command, "cancel" or "declare void" all demonic assignments – orders given to lesser demons by their superiors – which have been sent against the prayee or pray-ers.

Jesus gave an example of "binding" in a confrontation with the Pharisees about His power to cast out demons: *"[H]ow can one*

THE DEVIL IN THE BACK PEW

*enter a strong man's [satan's] house and plunder his goods, unless he first **binds** the strong man?"* (Matthew 12:29, emphasis mine). In a more general discussion about authority, Jesus said: *"[W]hatever you **bind** on earth will be bound in heaven, and whatever you **loose** on earth will be loosed in heaven"* (Matthew 18:18, emphasis mine). Accordingly, a binding prayer might take the form of:

> *"I speak to all dark spirits present, and I bind you in the name of Jesus, you will not make [person] sick, agitated, uncontrolled, or uncomfortable in any way. I bind inter-communication between every dark spirit, and I cancel and declare void every demonic assignment sent against [person]."*

In active deliverance prayer, it is quite common for demons to speak and conduct themselves as if they are superior to you and do not have to obey you. If they become threatening in any way (verbally or by assuming an aggressive posture), command them to stop and demand their submission and obedience, in Jesus' name.

Also, following Jesus' teaching, we should "loose" the Holy Spirit, the Kingdom of God, healing, and grace, as called for in the situation. A simple example: "I loose now the Spirit of God and all His truth into this situation. Overcome, Lord, by Your holy presence and sovereignty."

Proclaim Scripture Throughout the Prayer Session

When Jesus was tempted by satan, each of His three responses began with: *"It is written …"* then He quoted Scripture (Matthew 4:4, 7, 10). The enemy has no weapon against the truth of the Word.

Proclaiming truths of Scripture is tapping the power of God and is indispensable when confronting dark spirits. It is likewise vital to the discipling component of deliverance prayer, for the prayee must believe and take ownership of these statements of faith. See "Power Scriptures" below.

The Confrontation

dark spirits are Not Clones

They have individual characteristics, skills, and levels of strength and authority.[96]

- Jesus gave evidence of this when He told of re-entry of seven spirits *"more wicked than"* the first one (Matthew 12:43–45), and therefore unequal or different.
- The enemy is a deceiver, divider, and master trickster. However, information useful to understanding the nature or source of the enemy's attachment can be gained by intense questioning, and commanding the spirit to speak the truth.
- Some demons are clever, others not too bright.

A few years back, Patti and I, along with two women who each were gifted in discernment of spirits, were praying for folks at the end of a praise and prayer service. A few other attenders were praying for a young woman nearby when she became agitated and began to show stirrings of demonic activity. Those praying appeared uncomfortable with what was going on, so the four of us joined them. We began by asserting the authority of Jesus, and Patti sat facing the young woman, attempting to engage the spirit via eye contact. At times, doing so may take a little while, so Patti was persisting when one of the women turned to me and said, "Joe, that demon's not afraid of Patti, but it's very afraid of you." The other woman concurred, "She's right, Joe. It's afraid of you." Patti and I switched places, and I confronted the spirit while looking into the prayee's eyes. Shortly after engaging, an expression of great fear came over the prayee's face, and the demon departed without a whole lot of effort.

---

[96]I tend to believe their individuality goes even further – perhaps also to the extent of having unique personalities. After all, most believe they are fallen angels, and we humans have personalities, free will, etc. but were made "a little lower than the angels" (Hebrews 2:7). Accordingly, thinking of them as in any way less gifted than us (like brute beasts) carries the risk of underestimating their abilities and insights.

THE DEVIL IN THE BACK PEW

I mention this as an example revealing the individuality of a demonic spirit. What its vulnerability was, or why it was afraid of me and not Patti, I had only a suspicion. I am bigger and physically stronger than my wife, but this is not about bones and muscle. My guess, at the time, was that perhaps that demon was associated with some area of sin or offense over which I have had victory in my life, and that I consequently carried authority there.

That speculation appeared to bear out in a similar circumstance years later. Patti and I, along with another couple, were actively engaged with dark spirits tormenting a young man we'd been praying with for months. As our friends had joined us in praying for this person for the first time, it was fascinating that the young prayee (who was quite sensitive to the spiritual activity within him), stated that the demons "really don't like" Jeff, the husband. I immediately yielded the face-to-face seat to Jeff, and the spirit(s) became *much more* disturbed when he began to command them. When we finished praying for the day and were leaving the building, Jeff mentioned that he had dealt with sinful behavior in his own life similar to that of the prayee, but that he had had victory over it. This seemed a confirmation of my suspicion that our personal victories over sin carry authority over dark spirits connected to like sin patterns.

These experiences encourage a team approach, and a practice of alternating pray-ers (switching out) when directly confronting demons.

Interacting With a demon Can Be Like Talking to a Rebellious Teenager

A pastor I knew had a similar take, saying it is like dealing with a strong-willed two-year-old. Responses are often dodgy, condescending, or defiant. The litany of excuses and deflections spoken are so consistent from demon to demon, you get the impression they follow standard instructions on insubordination. And perhaps they do!

The Confrontation

Yet sometimes I am surprised by what I hear from a demon. Patti and I were praying for a young man with whom we had met many times for deliverance prayer. It so happened that the demons which talked through him were usually very vocal and assertive. They typically spoke in a loud, deep, resounding voice, rather like a Shakespearian actor or a Gestapo-like commander. Patti, whom the demons in the prior example did not fear, was engaging a demon very aggressively. She was staring into the young man's eyes and hammering away at the spirit with a relentless flow of commands and orders when the demon barked, "Woman of God, stop talking to me!" He was really annoyed! And I actually laughed, and still am amused when I recall the words of his complaint. Of course, Patti didn't stop.

The devil is a Liar

Keep in mind, when you are speaking with a demon, that you are in conversation with a liar. Do not accept excuses, deflections, or statements that they do not have to obey you. Understand that you may have to persist through the tactics suggested. Persevere. Only the weakest of spirits will go with little fight.

It may appear that success is achieved by wearing the demon out. In most cases, demonic entry is a process which has taken place over time. We should anticipate resistance and a need for some amount of "dismantling."

Command dark spirits to Tell the Truth

If you want information from demons, command them to speak and to tell the truth. Ask, for example, "What right do you have to be here?" or "How did you get permission to be here?" then, "I command you to speak and to tell me the truth, in the name of Jesus." Keep in mind that a well-entrenched spirit (e.g., a stronger one with a clear right to remain) may not respond, irrespective of commands. I recall on several occasions a spirit sitting undisturbed, displaying an arrogant smirk on the prayee's face. That is,

THE DEVIL IN THE BACK PEW

until the right is identified and broken.

Also, demand to speak with the demon who is "in charge." Often a lesser spirit is at the forefront and may even be "sacrificed," allowing the greater power to remain.

In one situation, we had to be most persistent, over several sessions, to maintain contact with the spirit which was the true superior. There had been much avoidance and deception along the way. When we finally connected with that "boss" spirit, it became apparent, by a slight voice change and spiritual discernment, that a lesser spirit was slipping in mid-conversation so that the senior fellow could revert to hiding. Whenever this occurred, we rejected the subordinate and demanded the return of the true superior. Give the dark spirits no benefit of doubt.

Respond to the Information Obtained from the demon

Respond, as appropriate, to what you hear from the demon. For example, revoke, and have the prayee revoke, rights or permissions revealed during the interrogation.

It may be unclear what, if anything, we should do with the information we receive. As pray-er, you may be uncertain if the information is true or relevant, or if it's just a distraction. Ask the Holy Spirit for discernment, and use your common sense. Something learned may be a valuable fact, usable in a future prayer session with the prayee.

Related, sometimes a dark spirit may speak solely *to* a prayee, that is, not *through* them. Accordingly, the person receiving prayer should be encouraged to share what they are hearing – which is commonly a negative or sarcastic reply of some sort. I deal with such responses in the same manner as if the demon was speaking directly through the person (react to the information, ignore it, or hold it for possible future use).

We have seen this occur both in prayees through which spirits often speak as well as with folks whose demons never respond audibly.

230

The Confrontation

Address demons by "Name" When Possible

It may be helpful to ask a demon its name. Often a spirit's name is equivalent to the nature of its attachment, like resentment or loneliness or anger. My experience is that it is easier to learn a spirit's "name" when it describes its skill/purpose than when it is an actual proper name or Biblical name. In the latter case, they seem more reluctant to disclose it, and dogged persistence may be necessary to compel them to do so.

Leaders I respect have differing opinions on the value of knowing a spirit's name. Some say you don't need to know it, which you often don't, while others feel you have more authority if you can address a demon by name. If, for example, a prayee is tormented by fear, we would naturally address and command out the "spirit of fear" as an initial part of the prayer. We might uncover that the fear is rooted in the parents' divorce when the prayee was young, which could prompt us to pray against a "spirit of rejection," or "spirit of abandonment," or "spirit of poverty," and so forth. Often it becomes obvious what a spirit's attribute or strength is, and therefore its descriptive name or identity, as a prayer session proceeds.

In cases where we have addressed a demon by its proper name (by discernment or by their disclosure), they are typically disturbed by our usage of it, snapping back angrily or even complaining, "Don't call me that!" Of course, that does not deter us. If I know a dark spirit's name, I always use it when speaking to it.

Respond Selectively to Statements or Questions Initiated by demons

In the "Engaging dark spirits" section below, under "Sample Phrases," a few suitable responses to demons are suggested – to be used if relevant and helpful, or if the Holy Spirit prompts. Otherwise, you may wish to ignore what they say to you. A clever demon will attempt to get you off track, to stir your emotions, or to engage you in superfluous dialogue.

I once observed a Christian man who had joined us in a prayer

THE DEVIL IN THE BACK PEW

session get pulled in by a demon who would fling insults his way. This fellow became *really* angry and took what was said quite personally. The demon clearly recognized his vulnerability and piled it on all the more. I counseled the man, whom I knew pretty well, and urged him to reject the bait of the lying demon. What more would you expect from a creature who serves the "father of lies?" If such sour talk can get under your skin, focus on the truth: your identity is in Christ.

If vulgar or inappropriate words are spoken by a demon, by all means forbid it. I have never observed anything close to profane misuse of God's name. I once heard a demon blaspheme by referring to satan as the "most high," but when I immediately objected and asserted that God is the "Most High," he backed down. Curiously, he quickly referred to satan as the "second most high," which I thought rather amusing and still quite wrong, but I was not going to engage in his distraction. If I feel it fitting to remind a demon Who is in charge, I typically paraphrase Philippians 2:10–11 saying, "every knee shall bow and every tongue confess that Jesus is Lord."

Note: Verse 10 identifies, and certainly demons already know, whose knees will bow to Jesus, and that it includes, *"those in heaven, and of those on earth, and of those under the earth."* Anything a demon utters to the contrary is thus inarguably powerless. Again, no demon can prevail over the truth of the Word of God.

Two simple examples of my responses to a demon's statements are shown here in the context of an active confrontation:[97]

D: She needs me.

JK: She doesn't need you or want you; she only needs Jesus. Jesus is the way, the truth and the life (per John 14:6).

D: I don't have to leave.

JK: You must leave now. I command you to go. I've been given power to tread on serpents and scorpions and power over all

---

[97]D = demon speaking; JK = the author.

232

The Confrontation

the power of the enemy (per Luke 10:19). Now, go!

Note: Each of the examples included a Scripture-based authority. I use these when I can, but continue the confrontation unhindered if no Scriptural retort comes to mind.

Often you will not wish to respond to a demon's comments, but at times you can gain helpful information by asking questions (see example in Chapter 4, "Rachel", p. 121). There is no need to be overly concerned about error, though. If you are pulled off track, ignore what the demon is saying and get back to business. You are not obliged to listen politely when in a conversation with a dark spirit. And I would add, engage in *no* conversation with a demon unless it furthers the purpose of ejecting it.

Some typical demonic commentary:

- "I have a right to be here …"
- "I've been here a long time …"
- "I don't have to listen to you …"
- "There are many of us …"
- "I don't want to leave …"

Should You Tell a demon Where to Go When It Departs?

Firstly, when confronted by a servant of God (i.e., a committed Christian), demonic spirits at times reveal their perception of the surroundings. For example, comments can show their understanding of who they are dealing with and their ultimate fate. Some background Scriptures:

- demons recognized Jesus.
  - At the synagogue in Capernaum: *"Let us alone!* **What have we to do with You, Jesus of Nazareth?** *Did You come to destroy us? I know who You are—the Holy One of God!"* (Luke 4:34, emphasis mine).
  - After healing Peter's mother-in-law: *"And demons also came out of many, crying out and saying,* **'You are the Christ, the Son of God!'"** (Luke 4:41, emphasis mine).

233

THE DEVIL IN THE BACK PEW

- o Teaching by the sea: *"And the unclean spirits, whenever they saw Him, fell down before Him and cried out, saying,* **'You are the Son of God.'** *"* (Mark 3:11, emphasis mine).
- demons knew the disciples and their mission:
  - o The slave girl with the spirit of divination: *"This girl followed Paul and us, and cried out, saying,* **'These men are the servants of the Most High God, who proclaim to us the way of salvation.'** *"* (Acts 16:17, emphasis mine).
- demons fear their destiny:
  - o Gadarene demoniac: *"And suddenly they cried out, saying, 'What have we to do with You, Jesus, You Son of God?* **Have You come here to torment us before the time?'** *"* (Matthew 8:29, emphasis mine).
  - o At the synagogue in Capernaum: *"Let us alone! What have we to do with You, Jesus of Nazareth?* **Did You come to destroy us?** *I know who You are—the Holy One of God!"* (Mark 1:24, emphasis mine).

As mentioned earlier, Patti has been addressed by a grumbling demon as "woman of God," an interesting acknowledgment of Who she serves, and of her role in the deliverance session.

In deliverance prayer, it is certainly no surprise that demons are not happy with the prospect of leaving. Scripture speaks of them crying out on departure: *"Then the spirit cried out, convulsed him greatly, and came out of him"* (Mark 9:26). We have, on many occasions, witnessed demons scream, cry out, or groan as they left. Fr Amorth gives possible insight on this. He tells of demons demonstrating "terror toward their leaders," which is not uncommon, but on one occasion a demon actually complained to him: "If I go away from here, my leader, [s]atan, will punish me."[98] Similarly, we have seen demons express fear of the consequences of angering

---

[98]Amorth, *An Exorcist Explains the Demonic*, 140–141.

The Confrontation

their superiors.

In the story of the Gadarene demoniac (Mark 5:1–20), Jesus encountered a man who was demonized and occupied by *"many"* spirits (v.9). Interestingly, Jesus had earlier commanded the unclean spirit to *"come out of the man"* (v.8), but it had apparently not done so immediately. Jesus subsequently permitted the *"legion"* of demons (v.9) to be sent into a nearby herd of swine (v.12). This is the only occasion in Scripture where Jesus sent an unclean spirit, driven out of a *person*, to a particular destination. It is also the only account where demons do not leave immediately on Jesus' first command.[99] We should not be surprised, therefore, that we may be required to persist!

In Luke's account of the Gadarene demoniac, he tells of the demons begging Jesus *"not [to] command them to go out into the abyss"* (Luke 8:31). In Mark's parallel account, the demons also begged Jesus *"earnestly that He would not send them out of the country"* (Mark 5:10). Jesus referred to spirits wandering *"through dry places"* (Matthew 12:43) in His warning about demonic re-entry. However, the phrase *"through dry places"* appears to be a term descriptive of their surroundings, not a specific destination to which they should be directed.

Concerning the issue of "sending" demons to a specific place, authors and teachers I am familiar with have varying opinions. As there are no Scriptural guidelines, my assumption of why the issue is discussed is that others have had the same experience I have had: demons often hang on pleading, "Where can I/we go?" And they stubbornly resist until given an option. I have experimented with both responding to the question and with ignoring it, yet demons seem to depart more quickly if given a directive like, "Go

---

[99]A possible explanation for the need for Jesus' second command is that the demon He spoke to initially was already gone, and Jesus was thereafter dealing with the remaining "legion" or its representative. The text of both Mark's and Luke's (Luke 8:26–39) account seems to permit this interpretation.

235

THE DEVIL IN THE BACK PEW

to Jesus!" so I often command that. Occasionally, a demon may hang on for a while after being directed to Jesus. In this case, my assumption is that the spirit doesn't like that option, but with no other, it finally leaves.

Obviously, an alternative would be to tell them to go to hell or to the abyss, but I am not terribly comfortable issuing a command like that.

What about telling a demon where *not* to go? Jesus did give us an example for that: *"He rebuked the unclean spirit, saying ... 'come out of him and **enter him no more!***'" (Mark 9:25, emphasis mine). It is a standard part of our deliverance prayer that we, by explicit command, forbid a demon's return.

Not surprisingly, when a demon asks, "Where can I go?" it is aware that its time is short.

Comfort the Prayee

Throughout, bathe the prayee in words of encouragement, love, healing, reassurance, and praises to God.

The enemy is quite adept at "piling on" when there are hurts of the heart. And the more profound the pain, the greater the likelihood of demonic activity. When praying for someone with deep emotional wounds, always check for symptoms of oppression or demonization. And vice versa: when you suspect oppression or demonization, probe for evidence of emotional hurts.

The Prayee Must Be a Participant in the Process, Not Just a Recipient

Always enlist the prayee's active involvement. I often advise the prayee that we pray-ers are not here just to slather a coating of goodness or blessing over them. Underneath, foundationally, ground needs to be stirred and recultivated. Certainly, the prayee will need to adjust beliefs, habits, and often their core connection to God.

236

The Confrontation

As You Prepare to Begin, Assure You Have

- A "go" from the Holy Spirit[100] to pray for deliverance or to participate
- Adequate people to pray
- Sufficient time
- An appropriate place available

Initiating the Process

Remember: deliverance is neither science nor art. It is simply God's heart shining through people. Be a conduit!

Be Sensitive to the Holy Spirit's Guidance Throughout

As mentioned, be interruptible.

Probe the Prayee's Personal and Spiritual History

Spend some time discussing the person's life history. As this could take many hours to thoroughly explore, only delve as deeply as necessary to get the process started. Look for obvious places of spiritual need (the low-hanging fruit) and begin addressing them.

Note: This process continues throughout the deliverance prayer session(s) as the Holy Spirit reveals truths to both the prayee and the pray-ers.

- Identify places where enemy rights/hooks are evident.
- Identify demonic strongholds and accumulations of "dirt."
- Deal with what's learned. As appropriate, have the prayee: confess, forgive, renounce, proclaim Scriptural truths, profess belief and trust in Jesus, etc.

---

[100]As best you can discern. If you don't perceive a specific "go-ahead," I suggest you evaluate the situation using your common sense, and if there is not a perceived "no-go," then carry on!

THE DEVIL IN THE BACK PEW

Audibly Speak Words of Heartfelt Worship and Praise

Proclaim the Lord's sovereignty and give thanks. I believe a special grace is extended when those present take a bit of time to actually *minister **to** the Lord* – just for Who He is.

Pray with an Ear Open to the Holy Spirit

- Audibly ask the Holy Spirit for guidance.
- *Important:* Deal with "inner healing" needs prior to commanding a demon out. The wound can be the point of attachment. As these are often misunderstood by the prayee, the Holy Spirit's leading is indispensable.

Note: "Inner healing" needs may not be obvious to the prayee. They are often deep and unrecognized. Hence, the probing should continue as prayer proceeds. (See Chapter 5.)

Minister in Love

- Lay hands on the person while you pray, but be sensitive.
  - ○ Victims of abuse may be uncomfortable and distracted by someone touching them. I always ask if it's okay.
- Be alert to the possibility of opposite-sex or same-sex attraction, and proceed with due caution.

Pray for Discernment

- Not every thought is spiritual revelation.
- Not every sin or weakness is tied to a demon.
- Not every display of emotion is a demonic manifestation.

Approach with Confident Humility

- Following Jesus and relying on His strength, you have nothing to fear.
- You, as pray-er, don't have to be perfect.
- A potential error on the prayee's part is thinking the demon is too powerful. Encourage the prayee:

238

The Confrontation

- º Continue to speak Scriptures ("Power Scriptures" below).
- º Remind the prayee that demons lie!
- Expelling demons taps the miraculous (*dunamis*) powers available to us. In Mark 9:38–39, Jesus referred to casting out a demon as working *"a miracle."*

Trust in Jesus and the Power You Have as a Believer

- Many spirits give little fight and are easily expelled, though often only after a right or source of attachment has been broken.
- Others are quite persistent and resistant.
- Don't relax the intensity of your focus.
  - º *Important:* Stay calm and relaxed, and remain gentle to the prayee.
- Don't let your guard down.
- Be alert to deception and distraction.
- Expect some dark spirits to be strong and aggressive.
  - º Expect Jesus to be stronger!
- If you find yourself becoming stirred up emotionally (angry, upset, frustrated, impatient, anxious), it is time to back off. Excuse yourself, take a break in the session, or shut the session down. That's okay. It is not about us; we are unworthy servants doing our duty. To take the burden of expelling a demon upon our own shoulders is simply wrong. And it won't work!

Engaging dark spirits

Begin by thanking God for the prayee's life and for the unique and special person they were created to be; speak blessings over all aspects of their life, work, and relationships. Continue as long as you feel it is appropriate, i.e., following the Holy Spirit as best you can. If I feel no specific prompting, I bless until it seems okay to stop.

THE DEVIL IN THE BACK PEW

Pray for healing of basic needs uncovered in the initial background interview. Command the enemy off and away from the person, and from physical, emotional, relational, etc. hurts.

As you proceed, ask the following, as appropriate:

- Are you "hearing" anything? Are you "sensing" anything?
- Is anything I am praying "stirring" in you or causing discomfort?
- Do you have a feeling of fearfulness, confusion, lack of control?
  - Or any other negative sensation or debilitating state of mind?
- Do bad/evil/unclean/frightful words or thoughts come to mind?
  - These thoughts can be related to virtually any sin – jealousy, anger, apathy, greed, lust, etc.
- Do you feel hostility toward me? Or to anyone else praying?
- Do you feel compelled to leave?

In our experience, these are common early indicators of a demonic presence.

As the prayee confirms a discomfort related to this initial prayer, we next typically pray more directly and aggressively at what has been indicated by the disturbance they sensed.

Sample Phrases

Listed below are sample phrases appropriate to the process. When dealing with demons, follow the Holy Spirit, your spiritual instincts, and your *common sense*. Don't use the examples as a formula.

It is important to speak by command, "In the name of Jesus ..." Don't "ask" or "request," and don't ever say "please." That would imply you are making a request, as if to a superior. You are in charge!

240

The Confrontation

"In the name of Jesus, I command you to …/order you to …/ you must …

- go
- leave
- begone
- come out/get out
- speak/speak in English
- be quiet/stop talking
- sit down/sit still/stop shaking
- stop complaining/whining

Additionally …

- You cannot stay.
- You must obey me.
- You must tell the truth.
- You may not be quiet.
- You may not hide.
- Don't close your eyes.
- Look at me.
- Do not change the subject.
- Stop talking about […] (if they try to engage you in super-fluous conversation).
- What is your name?
- What do you do?
- What kind of spirit are you?
- What right do you have to be here?
- Who told you [gave you permission] that you could be here?
- Is there someone inside who is higher than you? Who is it?
- I demand to talk to [spirit].
- Are you the boss here?
- Why do you think you can stay?

The prayee should be encouraged (helped, if necessary) to speak appropriate disarming commands. The pray-er should command likewise:

241

THE DEVIL IN THE BACK PEW

- I revoke/break any right you have to be here.
- I renounce any permission given to you in the past.
- I retract any vow or curse I have made which gives you any right or permission.
- I command you to go/I command the spirit of [...] to go.
- I break every curse, hex, or spell that has been spoken against me (be specific, if possible).
- I break the curse of [...] (alcoholism, anger, poverty, divorce, child abuse, etc.) which has been passed down through generations before me.
- I break every right that has been given to you.
- I do not want you here.
- I do not need you.
- You cannot stay.

Responses to arguments by demons

- This is a child of God.
- He/she belongs to Jesus.
- You have no authority here.

If the demons attempt to dodge your orders

- No, you must ...
- That's a lie, you are required to ...
- Yes, he/she *can* live without you.

Examples of blessings to speak over the prayee:

- Lord, pour your healing grace over [person].
- Fill [person] with your Holy Spirit now.
- Bless all facets of [person's] life and relationship with you, Lord.
- Lord, sanctify [person]; purify [person]; cleanse [person].
- Bring [person] closer to you, Lord.

The Confrontation

Power Scriptures

Though many relevant verses are quoted throughout this text, I restate here those I find myself most often citing or paraphrasing when demons are being confronted. Think of these as authoritative assertions of God's truth. They are written as I tend to speak them, some to comfort or instruct the prayee, others as enfeebling certainties spoken to the enemy:

- *"Every knee will bow and every tongue confess that Jesus is Lord – in heaven, on earth, and under the earth."* (from Philippians 2:10–11)
- *"Greater is He who is in you than he who is in the world."* (from 1 John 4:4)
- *"Jesus is the way and the truth and the life."* (from John 14:6)
- *"The Lord formed you in your mother's womb. You are fearfully and wonderfully made. All your days were fashioned by the Lord before you were born."* (from Psalm 139:13–16)
- *"satan comes to steal, kill, and destroy. Jesus comes that we might have life and have it more abundantly."* (from John 10:10)
- *"We have been given authority to trample on serpents and scorpions and authority over all the power of the enemy."* (from Luke 10:19)
- *"Death and life are in the power of the tongue."* (Proverbs 18:21)
- *"Take captive every thought to make it obedient to Christ."* (from 2 Corinthians 10:5 NIV)
- *"God did not give us a spirit of fear, but of power, love, and a sound mind."* (from 2 Timothy 1:7)
- *"Nothing can separate us from the love of God."* (from Romans 8:38–39)
- *"You will know the truth, and the truth will set you free."* (John 8:32 NIV)
- *"If we confess our sins, He is faithful and just to forgive us our sins and to cleanse us from all unrighteousness."* (1 John 1:9)

THE DEVIL IN THE BACK PEW

- *"As far as the east is from the west, So far has He removed our transgressions [sins] from us."* (Psalm 103:12)
- The Lord says: *"Your sins and lawless deeds I will remember no more."* (from Hebrews 10:17)
- *"There is no condemnation for those who are in Christ Jesus."* (from Romans 8:1)
- *"God is faithful, and will not allow you to be tempted beyond what you can withstand; but He will also make a way of escape, that you may be able to bear it."* (from 1 Corinthians 10:13)
- God spoke to Paul: *"My grace is sufficient for you, for My strength is made perfect in weakness."* Paul replied, *"When I am weak, then I am strong."* (from 2 Corinthians 12:9–10)
- *"Submit to God. Resist the devil, and he will flee."* (from James 4:7)
- *"The devil walks about like a roaring lion, seeking whom he may devour."* (1 Peter 5:8)
- *"The devil is a liar and the father of lies."* (John 8:44 NIV)
- *"satan is the accuser."* (from Revelation 12:10)
- *"If we cherish sin in our hearts, God will not hear our prayers."* (from Psalm 66:18 NIV)
- *"Trust in the LORD with all your heart, And lean not on your own understanding; In all your ways acknowledge Him, And He shall direct your paths."* (Proverbs 3:5-6)

I find it helpful to speak these encouraging truths to embattled prayees:

- The cross is good enough!
- The cross is big enough!

Also ...

Pray in tongues, if you are able.
After engaging and expelling a spirit, ask:

- Is that spirit gone?

The Confrontation

- You may wish to wait, to probe and to test. Audibly forbid spirits to hide.
- More under "Discerning Departure" in the next chapter.

As You Pray

Continue Speaking Blessings

- Pray for the Holy Spirit to fill the "empty space" once occupied by ejected dark spirits, curses, false beliefs, and false identities, with peace, joy, love, hope, grace, strength, abundance, spirit of adoption/sonship, and all the good things of God.
- Pray that the Kingdom of God would come into the situation. As explained in "Pray According to the Lord's Prayer" (Chapter 3, p. 60), when Jesus taught the Lord's prayer, He spoke *"kingdom come"* as a command, as if to proclaim, *"**Come**, Kingdom of God ..."* Accordingly, the Kingdom of God should be declared and commanded over the prayee and into the situation.

Use the Prayee's Feedback and Reactions to Guide You

- The prayee's responses are often helpful in assessing if a spirit is present.
  - The prayee's eyes can reveal the presence or departure of a spirit.
- To engage a spirit, sit opposite the prayee and look directly into their eyes. Forbid them to look away or close their eyelids. You may have to persist and repeat this. Often a demonic presence is obvious, but not always. If dark spirits have a right to be there, they are often able to hide. If a heavy oppression or demonization appears likely, look for root causes and resolve them.
- The prayee's countenance can reveal a demon's skill set or present attitude, such as fear, arrogance, anger, rejection,

245

THE DEVIL IN THE BACK PEW

and the like.

- o For example, a look of fear on a prayee's face could indicate the demon is a spirit of fear, which is attempting to make the prayee a fearful person. Alternatively, it could indicate the demon itself is afraid because it is being confronted.

- Deal with the prayee's barriers
  - o Resolve relevant issues. Look for unforgiveness, sin, disconnectedness from God, weak faith, etc.

- Probe life issues to identify "hooks" or "rights" a demon may have to remain with the prayee. Common grounds are instances of trauma, abuse, abandonment, loss, sin, or idolatry. Also look for involvement with "dark" TV, music, reading, movies, or video games.

- The prayee's feedback is mostly, though not 100%, reliable.

- Problems can be blamed on demons when they are personal issues.

Anoint the Prayee With Oil

The Bible speaks of anointing people with oil when healing is needed: *"And they cast out many demons, and **anointed with oil** many who were sick, and healed them"* (Mark 6:13, emphasis mine). We use olive oil, as in Biblical days, and pray something like, "Lord, following Your Word, we ask You to bless and sanctify this oil, a symbol of Your Holy Spirit, and (while using a moistened finger to lightly 'paint' a small cross on the prayee's forehead) we anoint you [person] in the name of the Father, and the Son, and the Holy Spirit. Lord, cleanse and heal." Often we may feel the Holy Spirit prompt us to pray further words of comfort and healing, but we avoid any inclination to make the effort appear like a ceremony or rite. (See Chapter 13, "More About Anointing With Oil," p. 260.)

When the Session Concludes

Always Pray a Cleansing Prayer after Praying for Anyone

Whenever we are involved in private prayer for an individual, for virtually any reason, we conclude by praying a "Cleansing Prayer." We know that, whenever we speak into the spiritual realm, whether directly confronting demons or not, dark spiritual powers can be "stirred." And folks who come for prayer often bring their own "dirt" with them. They may carry the residue of curses, past sin, trauma, and every kind of brokenness which results from mankind's fall. When the dark side is ruffled, whether or not a person is oppressed or demonized, those spirits want to find someone to rest on. Hence, a cleansing prayer is spoken to wash them all away.

Francis MacNutt, in a deliverance training video,[101] showed an actual deliverance of a man who was demonized as a result of many years of counseling suicidal people. Here was a good, noble, Christian man, whose career was helping folks in deep pain. Yet over the years, several dark spirits managed to attach, leaving him with persistent headaches and tormenting spirits. He did not know that, when concluding sessions with extremely broken people, he must command all tormenting spirits off the person, and off himself and the premises.

Occasionally, I come across folks who express concern about picking up demonic "stuff" when praying casually for others, like after a service or at a Bible study. I recall individuals being reluctant, even fearful, to pray because of what might get "on" them. My own perspective on this issue is that I could not care less. I have zero concern about it for the many reasons stated about understanding your rightful authority and protection in deliverance prayer (see Chapter 9, "Understand Your Authority," p. 188). The "Cleansing Prayer" is my protection of last resort, or failsafe.

At all events, the need to cleanse is real, and it's easy. A sample

---

[101]Video: Francis MacNutt, *Deliverance II* (Christian Healing Ministries, Jacksonville, FL).

THE DEVIL IN THE BACK PEW

outline is given below; personalize and adapt it as the Holy Spirit leads:

Cleansing Prayer

- Briefly praise and give thanks:
  - ○ Give thanks and praise for the Lord's presence and for His faithfulness.
  - ○ Thank Him for hearing the prayers, and ask Him to bring to completion that which was begun.
- Cleanse the prayee and prayee's environment; cleanse the pray-ers and venue:
  - ○ Command off the prayee and pray-ers all powers of darkness and unclean spirits – those spirits which have been loosed today, as well as any others attempting to cling or which are otherwise harassing.
  - ○ Command spirits out of the prayee's home, car, work-place, family, finances, relationships, etc.
  - ○ Command spirits out of the location and off the prop-erty where prayer has taken place.
  - ○ Forbid spirits to return, and if comfortable doing so, command them to go to Jesus.
- Request infilling and protection. Invite the Holy Spirit:
  - ○ to fill, renew, and strengthen all participants;
  - ○ to cleanse and protect all with the blood of Jesus; and
  - ○ to surround all with warring angels.

Chapter 12

After Praying

This chapter focuses on necessary follow-up to deliverance prayer – both when the session is deemed successful and when the outcome is uncertain.

After a spirit Has Been Ejected

It is a fact that the enemy will not give up just because he has been cast out once. He will continue sowing his seeds of doubt, lies, and temptations, hoping to find a way back in – and to bring some of his friends with him! Are his efforts difficult to overcome? No, not with the Holy Spirit's help and Scriptural guidance.

Much has been said in this book about *battling* the enemy and the related risks of re-entry, but I insert here the apostle Paul's encouragement to *stand* against the evil one: to *stand* as it were *firmly, resolutely, comfortably, and restfully,* relying on God's sovereignty and love, and *His* strength.

> *"Put on the full armor of God so that you can take your* **stand** *against the devil's schemes ... so that when the day of evil comes, you may be able to* **stand** *your ground, and after you have done everything, to* **stand**. **Stand** *firm then, with the belt of truth ..."* (Ephesians 6:11, 13, 14 NIV, emphasis mine)

249

THE DEVIL IN THE BACK PEW

And Paul continues with the remainder of the armor of God. Regarding this emphasis on the word *stand*, the image which comes to my mind is that of a tall, established oak tree. Encourage the prayee to be like that unshakable, unflappable, deeply rooted tree.

Encourage the prayee to live daily according to James 4:7: *"Therefore submit to God. Resist the devil and he will flee from you."*

Recall also the promise of 2 Corinthians 12:9–10, where Jesus said to Paul: *"My grace is sufficient for you, for My strength is made perfect in weakness."* And Paul's affirmation: *"[W]hen I am weak, then I am strong."*

If the enemy speaks of a prayee's sin, or of a prayee's victimization, or if bad memories otherwise come to mind:

- If a sin has not already been confessed, confess it;
- Renounce the desire, pleasure, and enticement related to memories of sinful activity; denounce and break the stronghold of the sin; then
- Command the enemy out/away.

If the thought or recollection persists:

- Repeat the 2nd and 3rd steps above.
- Resist (per James 4:7 and 2 Corinthians 12:9–10 above).

Again, I restate the core warfare strategies of this book:

- Take every thought captive.
- Reject all that is not Godly.
- Refuse the enemy's lies.
- Watch what you say.
- Immediately confess and renounce every slip of the tongue.
- Don't let your guard down.
- And do the foregoing without striving. Rest in your resistance.

In most cases, when an individual has been demonized, they have fallen short in their Christian walk in some manner. Whether the

After Praying

infestation resulted from self or externally caused open doors, the person must make a conscious decision to stand on the side of the Lord if they wish to remain free. It is of paramount importance that the individual's connection with the Lord grows in a healthy manner, that they seek God daily, attend church, are in Christian community (in active relationship with other believers), and feed themselves spiritually.

After a demon has been expelled, the "void" left by the dark spirit's absence must be filled with the Holy Spirit. The pray-ers and the prayee should pray accordingly.

Important: This praying and infilling step cannot be a one-time effort. It is a fact that we humans "leak," or slowly lose, our closeness (intimacy, intensity of commitment) to God if the connection is not kept active and alive. And if we permit such diminution, the enemy will begin to similarly "leak back in."

If a spirit Cannot Be Ejected

This section focuses on the frustrating situation where the prayer process seems ineffective. This could become evident immediately, at the first meeting, or an apparently insurmountable barrier may be encountered after several successful sessions. Keep in mind, a full "cleansing" is virtually never accomplished in one encounter.

A Legal Reason May Exist

An impediment may indicate there is a right or stronghold which must be broken first. The need to foil the enemy's rights is emphasized throughout this book. A few common examples:

- Unresolved inner healing needs (Chapter 5). These must be "prayed through." The enemy can hang on as long as these remain open wounds.
- Willful or habitual sin. When not addressed in good faith, the enemy's rights remain intact. Again, perfection is not necessary.

THE DEVIL IN THE BACK PEW

- Unconfessed sin. This is easily fixed.
- Unforgiveness. This must be dealt with (Chapter 6). The issue here concerns the *will* of the prayee. If the person sincerely chooses to forgive, the enemy cannot hang on, irrespective of whether hurt remains.
- Weak faith.

A prayee's sincere, righteous act, or overt step of faith, seems to have great spiritual power in overcoming an entrenched dark spirit. Think of this as putting a stake in the ground *for the Lord,* reminiscent of the Old Testament rock piles or altars commemorating a significant event. A prayee might proclaim, "As soon as I get home, I'm going to burn that [item] which has led me into sin so many times," and thereafter a demon can be expelled.

Note: A more severe re-entry could be expected if the prayee does not follow through! Pray with the person, seeking the Holy Spirit's direction for what might be done to take an explicit/overt stand for the Lord.

The bottom line about rights: if a person refuses to "let go" of the source of the attachment, the *demon does not have to leave!* People "holding on" fall into two broad categories: those who see the sin or problem clearly, but refuse to deal with it; and those who deny the problem. Each circumstance is frustrating for the prayer, and life-stealing for the prayee, but in our experience denial is more difficult to overcome.

Some years ago, I was called in to help a prayer team unable to gain ground with a thirtyish man who was demonized. This fellow was manifesting dark spirits in a wider variety of ways than I had ever seen in one individual. His history and situation were truly tragic, but he exhibited little willingness to make meaningful changes. His Christian "walk" was intermittent and shallow at best, and he remained deep in sexual sin, drugs, and illegal activity. After meeting a few times, much of which necessarily consisted of discipling and giving counsel, we had to give up. He would not, for example, stop selling illegal drugs, his primary source of

252

After Praying

income. This was tragic, but he was making his choices, and we cannot prevail over someone's free will.

Another example of the barrier of obvious sin was witnessed by a fellow church member. He and a friend were praying for a man who was demonized in connection with heavy usage of pornography. The men had aggressively prayed against the spirit of pornography for about an hour and a half, but were having no success in casting it out. As they paused and were in conversation with the prayee, it became apparent that he had no intention of stopping the porn or even trying to. The prayer session was abandoned. If someone willfully chooses sin, the enemy's rights remain intact.

Other challenging situations involve those who actively sin but refuse to admit it, and those who justify sin because they do not know a way out. From my experience, the most common example of refusing to acknowledge sin concerns unforgiveness, usually hidden behind the painful memories of the causal event. The focus on the hurt and revulsion masks the promise of freedom available from God (see Chapter 6). Others feel trapped by sin, finding themselves in a situation they don't know how to escape. Examples might be a waiter skimming tips every week to make his car payment, or a struggling single mother offering sex to her landlord in return for reduced rent. These practices may have begun in desperation, without expectation of recurrence, but the sin becomes embedded with the repetition, and the enemy persuades the victim there is no way out.

When dealing with a prayee who feels hopelessly stuck in sin, the evidence of demonic activity may be subdued, or even suppressed, at least until a demon-savvy pray-er attempts to confront it. I made the point earlier that, when a spirit speaks, this is normally its last desperate attempt to remain where it is. In this circumstance, the dark spirit is simply not threatened. It does not have to leave if the person hangs on to the sin. And it happily remains, saving the torment and harassment for a time when the victim has no prayer team to aid in their defense.

THE DEVIL IN THE BACK PEW

In summary, when there is a legal right, it must be identified and broken, whatever that may require: confess the sin, change the behavior, renounce the desire, and proceed in faith. Persistence is key.

Affirming this, well-known Catholic exorcist and author, Fr Gabriele Amorth, wisely states: "[C]onfession is stronger than exorcism!"[102]

The Prayee May Be "Hanging On"

At first consideration, this may sound absurd, but we have observed it many times. A wounded, or even actively sinning person, may "see" him/herself as defined by whatever it is the demon weighs them down with. For example, a victim of childhood abuse can carry the shame, low self-esteem, and victim mentality as part of their personhood, to the extent that they don't know who they would be without it. It is the only "self" they know. And this broken "self" is manageable, perhaps painfully and clumsily, but it is familiar, and they have learned how to cope. (See, "A Testimony," p. 269.)

Note: This is not a phenomenon peculiar to those who shun self-evaluation. It is just another type of demonic deception.

Is Prayer and Fasting Required?

When the disciples could not cast a demon out of a boy who had epilepsy, they asked Jesus why, and He replied: *"[T]his kind does not go out except by prayer and fasting"* (Matthew 17:21). In the context of the Scriptural account, it appears unlikely Jesus was telling them to stop, fast and pray for awhile, then go back and command the spirit out. Rather, the message appears to suggest that a lifestyle of regular prayer and fasting empowers us to overcome the tougher spirits.

Many authors, writing on the subject of deliverance, say little

---

[102]Amorth, *An Exorcist Tells His Story*, 86.

254

about prayer and fasting in conjunction with spiritual confrontation. Others speak of pray-ers doing so routinely, or of fasting only when specifically prompted by the Holy Spirit. One teacher explains he never does so unless progress stalls, whereupon he fasts prior to the next session.

I have been led to fast a few times in certain situations, even enlisting other pray-ers to join me. One man we prayed for volunteered to fast, and he recruited non-participating friends to fast on his behalf for the success of the deliverance sessions.

Can You Get Rid of a demon By Deliberately Ignoring It?

These examples cite situations of attacks on one's person, though they may reveal an effective strategy when praying for others as well. A few years ago, I heard a pastor who was very experienced with demonic confrontation tell of a harassing demon which, for weeks, was visiting him nightly in his bedroom. This pastor stated he prayed and commanded the spirit every way he knew, but this dark presence, which he could *actually see* next to his bed, would not leave. Finally, he decided to ignore it (stop resisting, stop commanding, even stop praying against it, and willfully rest in God's promises), and it went away.

I had a similar experience not long ago. Patti and I were on vacation and, while watching a television movie in our room one evening, I was suddenly overwhelmed by a very intense, heavy, dark presence. It literally caused my heart to pound. What its objective was or what triggered its appearance, I have no idea, but it was clearly demonic. And it was strong. I tried to sense what was going on in the spirit realm, and felt led to simply rest, that is, to give the presence no attention or regard whatsoever. I shifted my focus back to the TV movie, and it completely lifted not long after. I add that sensing a dark presence out of the blue is not at all a typical experience for me.

THE DEVIL IN THE BACK PEW

Discerning Departure

At times demonic spirits do not leave abruptly, but gradually fade as prayer continues. It is almost as if they deflate, like air escaping a leaking beach ball, before finally disappearing. Typically, both the prayee and the pray-ers notice the spirit becoming weaker and less combative.

On one occasion, we were praying for a spiritually sensitive young man who discerned a large, intimidating black-winged creature (a demon) widely arching its wings over him and covering him from the rear. We aggressively prayed against it, and after a time, he saw it scurrying away as a "disgusting little rat." We were confident that the spirit had departed, but it may not always be clear. The improvement experienced with a "deflating" demonic presence can be interpreted by the prayee as the spirit being gone, when actually it is not. It is suggested the pray-er continue probing until a release is felt by those present, all the while forbidding spirits to hide.

A complexity of managing these encounters is that, most often, demons are not alone. Typically, the confrontation unfolds like this: a demon is extricated, there are moments of peace and rest while prayer continues, then another demon begins to manifest. And the process repeats, sometimes quickly, sometimes slowly. We have, many times, prayed through this cycle and expelled a dozen or more dark spirits, stopping when the intensity slacks off. To be clear, a decrease in intensity is *not* an indicator that all the spirits are gone. We take it as a sign that enough has been accomplished for now. Obviously, we seek the Holy Spirit's peace about it. Notably, expelling demons is emotionally and physically draining on the prayee, and continuing on another day has never been a problem. It is recommended that pray-ers bind the remaining spirits and command them to "stand down" until they are dealt with at the next meeting.

Many teach, and we have observed on occasion, that demons leave through the prayee's mouth. A prayee may sense disturbance,

256

After Praying

distress, or pressure in the throat or upper chest area. Again, always command the demon to cease causing physical discomfort. Prayees have even complained they sensed a demon (or "something") stuck in their throat area prior to exiting. All this may result in a prayee burping, yawning, coughing, sighing, spitting, or huffing as spirits depart. If such responses occur, comfort the prayee, assuring them their reactions are typical, and there is no need to be embarrassed. In one unfortunate situation, a young lady we were praying for became so ashamed over her loud belching that she discontinued meeting with us. Despite our attempts, we could not assuage her humiliation.

The Timing May Not Be Right

Occasionally, in deliverance prayer, a barrier can be reached which prompts you to stop and continue the effort on another day. This is normal and common in the shorter term. Folks get weary. Also, I believe, delays are orchestrated by the Holy Spirit to permit heart-healing and restoration, or to prompt self-reflection, the resolution of stumbling blocks, or some other good. Then the process can continue, stepwise as it often does, to matters of increased complexity or gravity.

In addition to these briefer and perhaps understandable postponements, we have experienced curtailments of months, and even years, where a resumption yielded breakthrough when nothing obvious had changed. Surely it may be our lack of awareness, but nevertheless the long "break" did not impede success, and perhaps permitted it. In sum, when a prayee wishes to quit the deliverance process and we sense dark spirits yet remain, we are careful not to object excessively, subject to the Holy Spirit's prompting, of course. We trust God will do His business on His schedule.

The Holy Spirit Will Guide You

Keep your trust in, and dependence on, the Lord. Even the cleverest of spirits, when confronted and pressed, provide informa-

257

THE DEVIL IN THE BACK PEW

tion which is helpful to their ejection. Their obvious root of pride leads them, so often, to boast of their strength and their rights, by which they tip their hands and show you how to defeat them. As an oft-seen trait of the more combative demons, this is probably the most consistent vulnerability. Use what you learn to undermine them!

Chapter 13

Additional Information

This chapter discusses other topics pertinent to deliverance prayer.

Can You Pray Deliverance Prayers Over a Group of People?

Some people in ministry make a practice of praying deliverance over a group of people at one time. From my experience, not many take this approach, though I have been present for one such effort. On that occasion, there was a clear degree of anointing for confrontation of dark spirits with many evidences of demonic disturbance, but there was no opportunity for individual follow-up, only teaching on how to stay "clean." Significantly, prior to the prayer of deliverance, there was instruction on personal sanctification and tearing down strongholds.

Such an approach may be effective for those less severely demonized, or for those who are self-starters in their Christian walk, willing to do the necessary follow-up themselves. However, my experience is that, when a person deals with tougher spirits (occult involvement, entrenched sin, severe emotional trauma), individual coaching, discipling, and prayer are indispensable. To the degree there is a way to work with group prayer participants who need additional help, such a method could serve effectively.

Additionally, group deliverance may not address adequately an

259

THE DEVIL IN THE BACK PEW

issue the individual struggles with, thus leaving demonic "rights" unresolved, or the demon itself still holding on. Sin not confessed and renounced, unforgiveness matters not dealt with, spiritual debris ("dirt" from the past) not removed, all may give a spirit the right to stay or, if ejected, to re-enter more powerfully, perhaps with accomplices.

Notwithstanding these cautions, we know the Holy Spirit can empower things we cannot understand. Some of the testimonies I have heard of group deliverance sessions have been wonderful.

If You Feel Drawn to the Deliverance Ministry

For those interested in learning about deliverance prayer, it is suggested you start "small." Connect with believers who are involved in this ministry, and serve as a support pray-er or worshiper in a session.

Much has been said in prior chapters about resisting temptations to seek any "pride thrill" from casting out demons but, nevertheless, it is a wonderful experience to see God's people set free. Keeping the focus on God showing His love so tangibly and miraculously, deliverance is awesome and glorious!

More About Anointing with Oil

Not long ago, Patti and I had a remarkable revelation about the spiritual power of anointing with oil. I will explain it in the context of our related observations of our lives as Christians.

About thirty years ago, when Patti and I first started attending a church which pursued the 1 Corinthians 12 spiritual gifts, we commonly saw the pastors applying a bit of oil when they prayed with folks for healing. From that time until today, all churches we have belonged to often anointed prayees with oil – perhaps not every person seeking prayer, but it was a common practice. We also, in our prayer sessions, anointed prayees with oil when we felt prompted by the Holy Spirit. Candidly, we used oil in faith and

Additional Information

in obedience to Scripture, and didn't think more deeply about it. Then our eyes were opened.

I was contacted by a young man in his thirties who had been referred to us for deliverance prayer. At his request, I met him for coffee to discuss what such prayer entails. He shared details of how he had been emotionally victimized from toddler days through adulthood, and how he had turned to alcohol, drugs, and sex for distraction and comfort. Despite his battles, he was sincerely seeking the Lord, and finding intermittent peace. But the struggle against the demonic continued behind the scenes. Shortly thereafter, Patti and I began praying for him, and over the first two or three meetings, we were successful in confronting and expelling several demonic spirits. Though demons are often not particularly vocal, a few of those encountered with him were moderately so, making derogatory comments and expressing anger. The young man was very precise in describing the places in his life which the departed spirits had impacted, and likewise he expressed delight in the newfound freedom when they left. As we see so often, the improvement he experienced was palpable, and we all felt good about the progress, and praised God for it.

At some point during a subsequent prayer session, I felt led to say to Patti, "How about anointing him with oil …" and she pulled the small bottle from her purse. Patti always carries anointing oil with her. What happened next *really* surprised us both. As she quietly prayed and touched his forehead with her finger moistened with oil, he abruptly stiffened, jerked his head back, stretched his legs out rigidly, and exclaimed in a panicked voice, "Get that off me! Get that off me!" To be clear, this was the demon speaking, not the young man. It was as if Patti had touched his forehead with a red-hot poker! Of course Patti kept her finger against his forehead while he writhed in the chair, and both of us continued to command the spirit to leave. And it soon did.

The next time we met with him, Patti again reached for her bottle of oil. As she extended her hand to touch his forehead, the

THE DEVIL IN THE BACK PEW

young man again became rigid and tried to turn his head away, with another spirit mumbling, as if to himself, "I don't like oil." Again, Patti did not back off, and the demon was cast out shortly thereafter.

To us, these were "Wow!" moments. We had used anointing oil for years, and had done so in faith, but we never had any sense of the intensity of what was going on in the spiritual realm. I thank God for this revelation. For the record, we have never since observed a reaction quite so extreme, but now we have a better understanding of oil's supernatural power. As you might expect, we anoint with oil a lot more often than we used to.

Pleasantly scented anointing oils are available at many Christian bookstores and online.

Salt and Water

Somewhat similar to the usage of oil, there is an Old Testament account of the prophet Elisha using salt to miraculously "heal" the water in Jericho: *"[H]e went out to the source of the water, and cast in the salt there, and said, 'Thus says the LORD: "I have healed this water"'"* (2 Kings 2:21). I have heard anecdotally of a prayee exhibiting a physical reaction when unknowingly sprinkled with blessed salt, but I am not aware of this being a common practice outside the Catholic Church.

Also, the Catholic Church commonly anoints prayees with blessed water ("holy water") for similar purposes. Related, we regularly speak a blessing over drinking water given to prayees in active deliverance sessions.

Seals

In a secular context, we might think of a seal as an impression made in wax, formerly used to keep a letter closed and secure, or as the embossed emblem of a political authority which is pressed into a license or official document. *Merriam-Webster* defines a seal

Additional Information

as "something that confirms, ratifies, or makes secure: guarantee, assurance."[103] Seals are referenced dozens of times in the Bible.

One Biblical example of the authority of a seal is given in the narrative of Jesus' entombment. The chief priests and the Pharisees had requested that Pilate protect Jesus' burial place from tampering. Pilate responded: *"'You have a guard; go your way, make it as secure as you know how.' So they went and made the tomb secure, sealing the stone and setting the guard"* (Matthew 27:65-66, emphasis mine). In this context, a seal of Pilate or the priests would have been pressed into a small lump of wax or clay, proclaiming the authority behind that closure.

In other contexts, "seal" is used as an indication of dedication or assignment to God: *"And do not grieve the Holy Spirit of God, by whom you were **sealed** for the day of redemption"* (Ephesians 4:30, emphasis mine), and: *"Nevertheless the solid foundation of God stands, having this **seal**: 'The Lord knows those who are His'"* (2 Timothy 2:19, emphasis mine). These examples speak metaphorically, or perhaps in reference to a *spiritual* seal.

The relevance of seals to deliverance prayer assumes a similar spiritual authority or right, but in this case involving satan. In his book, *Deliverance from Evil Spirits*, Francis MacNutt explains the concept of seals and how they are established as connections to satan – by contract (agreement or promise), by dedication to satan, or before birth (generational carryover). Francis offers testimony of entrenched demons removed after a *seal* is renounced and broken three times. He states that, on several occasions, he witnessed a demon depart only after the third time the prayer breaking the seal was repeated.[104]

I am not aware of other authors or teachers mentioning a need to break satanic or demonic seals. Nevertheless, the concept is indirectly Biblical, or at least derivatively, and praying to *break a seal*, if not literally valid, is surely metaphorically so, like much of

---

[103]https://www.merriam-webster.com/dictionary/seal.
[104]MacNutt, *Deliverance from Evil Spirits*, 220–222.

THE DEVIL IN THE BACK PEW

our prayer language. I have the utmost respect for Francis Mac-Nutt and his ministry, and am quite comfortable with his teaching in this regard.

Chapter 14

Putting It All Together

This final chapter summarizes all we have said about deliverance prayer in Part III and concludes with a wonderful testimony.

Synopsis

The enemy is real, he is hard at work, and he gives up on no one. Too few people these days, even in the church, discern the extent of his intrusive attempts into their lives and the lives of others.

Clearly, satan and his followers are no match for Jesus. And He gave us the authority to cast demons out of believers and to take back that which has been stolen from their lives. Our authority is not unlimited, but it is real.

In his assault on the believer, satan's main strategy is to trick, to make people think he's not speaking, or influencing, or attacking. He's also quite skilled at tempting and accusing, as well as planting seeds of fear, hopelessness, and abandonment. And the list continues.

The enemy finds his best opportunities, and does the most damage, where circumstances are darkest: where the sin is the biggest, the abuse is the ugliest, the heartache is the deepest, the pain is the greatest. Sometimes his harassment is limited to beating one down, as in oppression, but at other times he "attaches" in some

265

THE DEVIL IN THE BACK PEW

way, as in demonization.

When seeking to expose dark spirits, it often takes time to break down their defenses. If there is suspicion of demonic harassment, be persistent.

Initiating the Process

To get a harassing spirit off, out of, or away from a person, it must be confronted and its permissions (rights) neutralized. Accordingly, the person's history must be probed:

- Personal sins must be confessed and renounced; "dirt" from the past must be removed.
- Emotional trauma and inner healing needs must be brought to the Lord.
- Unforgiveness issues must be resolved.
- Generational sins and curses must be renounced and broken, including:
  o Occult activities.
  o Dark affiliations – cults, Freemasonry, etc.
  o Carryover from emotional wounds – divorce, incest, violence, anger, alcoholism, sexual abuse, inherited vulnerabilities, behaviors, diseases, and so forth.
- Current life struggles must be surrendered to God.

Resolving these areas leaves the enemy with no right to remain. Discipling is an integral part of the process.

A private and peaceful venue suitable for ministry allows for a focused effort. Begin by acknowledging and worshiping God, giving thanks, and speaking blessings over the prayee. When you sense the Holy Spirit has released you to proceed, ask the Lord to send His angels to assist, and command all unclean spirits to submit. As led, sit face-to-face with the prayee, looking into the person's eyes:

- Forbid dark spirits to hide.
- Cancel all demonic assignments against the prayee.

266

Putting It All Together

- Bind interconnection between spirits, where they attempt to combine their power. Forbid them to communicate with each other.
- Bind the spirit of antichrist. Loose the Holy Spirit.
- Forbid demons to make the prayee ill, uncomfortable, agitated, violent, or physically disruptive.
- Confront the harassing spirit(s), per Chapter 11.

Dealing with a demon

A dark spirit may or may not reveal itself by speaking or via the physical reactions of the prayee. Many spirits leave having displayed no visible sign whatsoever, their departure perceived by the prayee only, or perhaps additionally by a discerning pray-er. When they do speak, demand to converse only with the demon in charge.

Commonly, the prayee's facial expression indicates the nature or underlying emotion of the spirit, and may give evidence helpful to the spirit's ejection. At other times, a spirit stubbornly hangs on until a right is discovered and broken. The effort to expose a demonic right is often the most time-consuming part of deliverance prayer. The prayee has to be completely open and cooperative, and both pray-er and prayee must be relentless.

When a demon manifests in a person, the situation can become noisy and/or emotional. Forbid behaviors which are distracting. If you want information from a demon, ask – commanding them to speak and to tell the truth, "in the name of Jesus." If you wish to stop them talking, order it. Respond to their questions or comments only if it serves you, which it occasionally does. As mentioned, if a demon is speaking, you may wish to command it to tell you how it gained entry, or what gave it its right to be present, or even what its name is. Regardless of the flow of communication, continually and expressly command the demon out.

Deliverance prayer is typically tiring for the prayee. Though prayees should be encouraged to remain relaxed and calm, they

THE DEVIL IN THE BACK PEW

often sweat and tense their bodies. Emotions most commonly displayed, reflecting the demon's demeanor, are fear, anger, arrogance, despair, and confusion. There will be crying at times, which could be the prayee struggling with a memory or the demon bemoaning its fate. Water, tissues, a lined wastebasket, and oil should be available.

Keep at it until the demon is gone. Incorporate "Power Scriptures" (Chapter 11, p. 243) in the dialogue, both those which affirm the prayee's and pray-ers' authority in Christ, as well as others which proclaim simple truths of God and His goodness. After a spirit departs, continue praying for the situation and speaking blessings over the prayee. Very often another demon will surface.

Continue until the process winds down or other constraints prevail.

Wrapping Up

When the session ends, if it is likely dark spirits remain, bind them, commanding them to stand down, and to do and say nothing until they are called on in the next prayer session. Encourage and comfort the prayee, being sensitive to possible confusion or embarrassment. Explain and debrief as necessary. Your goal is that the prayee leave the session feeling peaceful and better.

Important reminders for the prayee:

- Take every thought captive; eject all which are not of God.
- Watch what you say. If a word or statement is carelessly spoken, confess and renounce it, then proclaim Scriptural truth.
- Confess all sins immediately.
- Keep your focus on Jesus.
- Be actively connected to a Christian community.
- Don't let your guard down.
- Don't wait to get help if you begin to struggle.

The prayee must be *intentional* in heeding these important remind-

268

ers! Though they are good, everyday practices for the believer, they take on added significance where there has been successful deliverance prayer. Ground has been taken from the enemy, and he will certainly attempt to return. Reject his lies! There is nothing to fear with Jesus on your side.

Pray a cleansing prayer over all participants and the venue.

It is often helpful to follow up with the prayee a day or two after a deliverance session, especially after the initial encounter.

A Testimony

I begin with the statement below, shared by a gifted Christian woman who came to us for prayer, because it reveals specifics about the struggles and victories of someone in battle. It is a powerful and glorious story, and most would be flabbergasted to attach such a tale to a person so bright and gifted. She and her husband are in full-time ministry and are embarking upon even greater works.

Part 1 – in her words

Most mornings I wake early to pray, and on [one day in] April ... during my prayer time, it became evident to me that something was bubbling up inside of me – and it wasn't good. I used what I learned from [the deliverance class and other] ... training ... and called on the Lord's name for "it" to go to HIM and cease – and that I was covered in the blood of Jesus. It did retreat, but I was shaken, scared and frightened. I ran to ... my husband and confessed this experience, and he said, "There's nothing to be afraid of. The Lord is victorious – and I've been waiting and praying a long time for this to be made known to you, and am thankful it finally has." This experience made me feel like I had been violated in a whole new way, and I felt shame and panic. [My husband] ... suggested I get prayer, and so I did. The first time I received prayer ... I felt vulnerable and scared, but the prayer team made me feel at ease. ... They asked me to give them a snapshot of my

*life, and then they began to pray for me. I sat in the chair
and began to feel the "bubbling up" feeling again, and the
more they prayed the more this demon showed himself. He
showed himself by making me writhe in the chair and move
my arms in all directions and bend me over in the chair. It
was like I was not in control, but I was present. I think the
first creep was anger, and finally I felt something like a round
ball the size of an orange fly out of my chest, and I knew it
was gone. This didn't just happen once – it happened about
ten times that night with demons of shame, control, soul-
ties from my promiscuity, pride, pity, aloneness, resentment,
abandonment, rejection – and [I had to offer] forgiveness for
those that had abused me. If they were really pesky the prayer
team would have me denounce my wanting to hold on to
whatever it was. As an example, I never realized how much
I held onto my incidents of [being sexually abused] … it was
a huge part of my being, and if I had to let it go what would
be left? In the act of giving this abuse to Jesus I found I have
more space in my heart now to accept His love.*

*[The] … prayer team suggested we meet again. Sadly I
knew they were right. … We all knew that as miraculous as
the night had been, there was more work to do. That night I
… was shocked and amazed at what had happened to me.
We only had to meet once more and it was the exact same
sequence of events. There must have been six or seven more
creeps that left in the same rapid fashion. … A tough one was
the horror and thriller movies I watched and the creep that
had attached itself to me due to that. When we were finished
I remarked how light I felt – it is amazing the weight that
has lifted – emotional weight in my heart – gone. Just now
I am beginning to grasp the depth of His mercy and love for
me – and the power of His name. I sing about it during worship time and feel His presence, but knowing He died for all
of us on the cross, and overcame satan, makes my healing all*

the more sweet – knowing the price paid and the power of His blood. His great love has made me WHOLE. Whole in a way I didn't even know I was missing. My life is more joyful, and the problem I had with anger is at a two instead of a fifteen. I am happy, even joyful, and best of all my husband recognizes it. I feel it – he sees it. This was truly a ... gift. ... [A]nd now I'm sure the Lord did this for me to be a better servant to Him. I praise Him for setting this captive free."

Part 2

A few months later, this woman felt like further spirits were revealing themselves. One brief additional meeting quickly expelled another five or so.

Part 3

After another few months, I received a call from her that a powerful spirit was manifesting and significantly disrupting her life. She and her husband tried to expel it, but were unsuccessful. We happened to be out of state, and I was actually bicycling at the time of the call, so I told her that Patti and I would call back when I returned to the place we were staying. An hour or so later, after pondering what to do, I called her and suggested we bind the tormenting spirits and deal with them face to face in a few weeks when we returned. Patti was nearby praying while I was talking to her on the phone. I began by speaking "binding" and "stand down" commands to the spirit and gradually became more aggressive, ordering it out. I probably had prayed for a couple minutes at most, when this sweet woman exclaimed in a half-whispered, half-excited voice of astonishment, "It's gone!" This was a first for us – casting a demon out over the phone, Florida to Ohio. We serve a big God! She was once again freed.

THE DEVIL IN THE BACK PEW

Part 4

On at least two other occasions, a few years later, manifesting demons related to deeper, unaddressed issues were expelled.

I fervently believe every church should have testimonies like this one. It is a lie of the enemy that a special anointing is needed for simple deliverance prayer. The Lord is the One who provides the power, and of course He is available everywhere.

Freeing a prayee from demonization or from the less obvious demonic oppression differs little in objective: identify the area(s) of torment, and drive the enemy away. As a pray-er, I have many times seen a person freed of an actual demonic presence with the only evidence being the prayee's unmistakable description of the spirit's departure. (See Chapter 4, the first example under "Three Examples of demonic Manifestations," p. 113.)

I might wish for better discernment or understanding, but truly, it is not necessary. God is the authority in this effort, and all glory goes to Him! Frankly, if I knew more, I might get in the way. I am happy to serve and probably do better on a need-to-know basis. Still, most deliverances are not so subdued.

I must add, also, that in situations where demons have been encountered and ejected, very many of those confrontations were not expected by the prayee – and occasionally not even by the pray-ers. Those of us who have been doing this for a while, though, are seldom surprised when a demonic attachment is exposed. We pursue dark spirits whenever there is a hint of demonic activity.

I restate this to emphasize my motivation for writing this book: our world could well use many more believers who are equipped to deal with demonic spirits. I have seen far too many wonderful people of God miss opportunities to free the oppressed and demonized because they either did not discern the evidence of harassment, or did not know what to do with it when they did see it.

Afterword

This book was written to provide practical information and guidance for dealing with the very real enemy of our souls. Of course it cannot address all the issues, but I hope it has made you more sensitive to the means and methods of satan and his demons. Many titles listed in the Bibliography serve well to broaden this knowledge base, but a book or teaching can take you only so far.

Are You Needing More?

Spiritual Harassment in Your Own Life

Do you recognize evidence of debilitating spiritual harassment in your own life? If so, I strongly suggest you seek support from a pastor or Christian leader who is equipped to help. If your church leadership is reluctant, look for a leader who believes the Lord *still* heals and delivers, and who is willing to meet and pray with you.

Be aware that pastors commonly recommend counseling as the first step for people who struggle emotionally. Certainly, counseling can be God-directed and very beneficial, but if deliverance prayer is called for, counseling alone will likely be inadequate and, sometimes, unnecessary. Be persistent in your search for help capable of confronting the enemy. You may encounter people in Christian leadership, or with ministry credentials, who dismiss this subject matter as pure fantasy, though clearly the Bible states that Jesus does not! Rest assured, there are many who are ready to give you the support you need.

Spiritual Harassment of a Loved One

You may also suspect an acquaintance or loved one is being victimized by powers of darkness. I would recommend you be *very* careful in your approach. From my experience, not much fruit comes from coldly telling a person something like, "I think you have a problem with demons." It is much better that any related suspicion or awareness be, at least in part, a self-discovery, aided perhaps by a compassionate conversation, reading a suggested book, or attending a class on growing your spiritual gifts.

Inviting Jesus Into Your Life

Even more basically, you may feel you need help, but you are not a practicing Christian and don't know how to proceed. As hopefully was made clear in this book, you do not want to confront dark spirits without Jesus on your side. But, of greater importance, you do not want to live life, or face eternity at life's end, without Jesus. The solution is simple: invite Jesus Christ into your heart and life. Ask Him to take away your sins (He paid for them *all* on the cross). Ask Him to come live in you and to guide your life. He will … guaranteed! Then find a Christian church which believes the Bible is true for today, and that God saves and heals today.

Three relevant truths from the Bible:

- *"… for all have sinned and fall short of the glory of God."* (Romans 3:23)
- *"If we confess our sins, He is faithful and just to forgive us our sins and to cleanse us from all unrighteousness."* (1 John 1:9)
- *"… if you confess with your mouth, 'Jesus is [my] Lord,' and believe in your heart that God raised Him from the dead, you will be saved. For it is with your heart that you believe and are justified, and it is with your mouth that you confess and are saved."* (Romans 10:9–10 NIV)

Embrace the freedom that only Jesus offers. Then go back to "Spiritual Harassment in Your Own Life" above for suggestions on obtaining assistance.

Appendix I

The Poverty Mind-set

Prayerful completion of this form will highlight areas of personal need regarding Scripture's promise of abundance. Jesus said: *"The thief [satan] does not come except to steal, and to kill, and to destroy.* ***I have come that they may have life, and that they may have it more abundantly"*** (John 10:10, emphasis mine). I am calling this "lack" of promised abundance, this potential enemy stronghold, "The Poverty Mind-set."

THE DEVIL IN THE BACK PEW

The Poverty Mind-set
Abundance[105] v. Insufficiency in Your Life

Rate your present circumstances regarding …	Abundance (√)	Somewhere between (√)	Insufficiency (√)
Basics (food, housing, car, clothing, etc.)			
Church community			
Co-workers and incidental relationships			
Employment			
Family			
Finances			
Free-time activity			
Friends			
Health			
Personal growth/ improvement			
Relationship with God			

---

[105]Biblical abundance is peace of mind, contentment, satisfaction, happiness, adequacy, "rest" – a sufficiency rooted in the blessing of God. It is not a "Cadillac mentality."

The Poverty Mind-set

Questions

- Are you grateful for where you are in the above areas?
- Are there barriers[106] to your peace?

Resolution

Identify and deal *intentionally* with barriers by:

- overcoming sinful habits;
- confessing;
- renouncing;
- taking thoughts captive;
- praying;
- using your God-given talents;
- choosing "life;"
- refusing to believe satan's lies; and
- refusing satan's destiny for you.

> *"The abundant life can only be experienced when we do what we are created for."* —Danny Meyer

---

[106]That is, barriers which exist *in you*: unhealed hurts; unbiblical thinking (believing lies); enemy oppression; hopelessness; sin; etc.

Appendix II

Angelic Activity, Authority, and Power

Listed below are a number of Bible verses regarding angelic activity, authority, and power. *Strong's Concordance* defines "angel" variously as "messenger," "envoy," "guardian," "executioner of God's purposes," one with "charge over earthly elements," etc. The many references to "angel" in the book of Revelation show these heavenly beings to be messengers to the church as well as wielders of great power, both over dark forces as well as over nature. Formidable enforcers of God's will and judgment, they are certainly not the chubby little cherubs depicted in Renaissance art. Indeed, in several Biblical accounts they reveal their presence by first stating: "Do not be afraid," this being their necessary self-introduction.

Scripture also tells us *"we shall judge angels"* (1 Corinthians 6:3). In my opinion, it seems most likely that such judgment will pertain to their works on our behalf and their effectiveness as our guardians, all to be revealed after we enter the next life. What else could we be qualified to judge?

Occasions When Angels Appeared and Said: "Do not be afraid"

- To those seeking the body of Jesus after he was crucified (Matthew 28:5)
- To Zacharias, John the Baptist's father, when he was told he

would have a son (Luke 1:13)

- To Mary, when she was told she would bear Jesus (Luke 1:30)
- To the shepherds, when the birth of Jesus was announced (Luke 2:10)

Angels as Messengers

"... an angel of the Lord appeared to him in a dream, saying, 'Joseph, son of David, do not be afraid to take to you Mary your wife, for that which is conceived in her is of the Holy Spirit.'" (Matthew 1:20)

"Now an angel of the Lord spoke to Philip, saying, 'Arise and go toward the south ...'" (Acts 8:26)

"About the ninth hour of the day he saw clearly in a vision an angel of God coming in and saying to him, 'Cornelius!'" (Acts 10:3)

Angels as Servants of God

"So it will be at the end of the age. The angels will come forth, separate the wicked from among the just ..." (Matthew 13:49)

"And behold, there was a great earthquake; for an angel of the Lord descended from heaven, and came and rolled back the stone from the door, and sat on it." (Matthew 28:2)

"But at night an angel of the Lord opened the prison doors and brought them out ..." (Acts 5:19)

Angels as Spirits Ministering to God

"Then the devil left Him, and behold, angels came and ministered to Him." (Matthew 4:11)

"And He was there in the wilderness forty days, tempted by

THE DEVIL IN THE BACK PEW

*[s]atan, and was with the wild beasts; and the angels minis-
tered to Him."* (Mark 1:13)

*"Then an angel appeared to Him from heaven, strengthening
Him."* (Luke 22:43)

Angels as the Army of God

*"Or do you think that I cannot now pray to My Father, and
He will provide Me with more than twelve legions of angels?"*
(Matthew 26:53)

*"... and to give you who are troubled rest with us when the
Lord Jesus is revealed from heaven with His mighty angels."*
(2 Thessalonians 1:7)

*"But you have come to Mount Zion and to the city of the
living God, the heavenly Jerusalem, to an innumerable company of angels ... "* (Hebrews 12:22)

Angels as Ministers of God's Judgment

*"Then immediately an angel of the Lord struck him [the king,
Herod Agrippa], because he did not give glory to God. And he
was eaten by worms and died."* (Acts 12:23)

Angels as Guardians/Servants of Mankind

*"Take heed that you do not despise one of these little ones, for
I say to you that in heaven their angels always see the face of
My Father who is in heaven."* (Matthew 18:10)

*"So it was that the beggar died, and was carried by the angels
to Abraham's bosom. The rich man also died and was buried."* (Luke 16:22)

*"Are they not all ministering spirits sent forth to minister for
those who will inherit salvation?"* (Hebrews 1:14)

"Do not forget to entertain strangers, for by so doing some have unwittingly entertained angels." (Hebrews 13:2)

Angels as accomplices of satan

"Then He will also say to those on the left hand, 'Depart from Me, you cursed, into the everlasting fire prepared for the devil and his angels ...'" (Matthew 25:41)

"For if God did not spare the angels who sinned, but cast them down to hell and delivered them into chains of darkness, to be reserved for judgment ..." (2 Peter 2:4)

"And they had as king over them the angel of the bottomless pit, whose name in Hebrew is [a]baddon, but in Greek he has the name [a]pollyon." (Revelation 9:11)

Angels Compared to Man

"You have made him [man] a little lower than the angels; You have crowned him with glory and honor, And set him over the works of Your hands." (Hebrews 2:7)

"But we see Jesus [as man], who was made a little lower than the angels, for the suffering of death crowned with glory and honor, that He, by the grace of God, might taste death for everyone." (Hebrews 2:9)

"... nor can they [mankind resurrected in Christ] die anymore, for they are equal to the angels and are sons of God, being sons of the resurrection." (Luke 20:36)

Bibliography

Deliverance and Personal Spiritual Growth/Warfare

Anderson, Neil T., *The Steps to Freedom in Christ* [Booklet] (www.freedominchrist.com/thestepstofreedominchrist.aspx)

Bevere, John, *The Bait of Satan* (Charisma House, Lake Mary, FL, 2014)

Evans, Rick, *Healing an Orphan Heart* (Rick Evans, 2016) (www.orphanheartministry.org)

Frangipane, Francis, *The Three Battlegrounds* (Arrow Publications, Cedar Rapids, IA, 1989).

Jubilee Resources International, *Prayer of Release for Freemasons and Their Descendants* (http://jubileeresources.org/?page_id=650)

Kirkwood, Kerry, *The Power of Blessing* (Destiny Image Publishers, Inc., Shippensburg, PA, 2010)

Kraft, Charles H., *Defeating Dark Angels* (Regal Books from Gospel Light, Ventura, CA, 1992)

—*I Give You Authority* (Chosen, a division of Baker Publishing Group, Grand Rapids, MI, 1997)

Kylstra, Chester and Kylstra, Betsy, *Biblical Healing and Deliverance* (Chosen, a division of Baker Publishing Group, Grand Rapids, MI, 2005)

MacNutt, Francis, *Deliverance from Evil Spirits: A Practical Manual* (Chosen, a division of Baker Publishing Group, Grand Rapids, MI, 1995)

Bibliography

Maloney, James, *Living Above the Snake Line* (Westbow Press, a division of Thomas Nelson & Zondervan, Bloomington, IN, 2015)

Martin, Walter, *The Kingdom of the Cults* (Bethany House Publishers, a division of Baker Publishing Group, Grand Rapids, MI, 2003)

Meyer, Joyce, *Battlefield of the Mind* (Faith Words, Hachette Book Group, New York, NY, 1995)

—*Battlefield of the Mind Devotional* (Warner Faith, Time Warner Book Group, New York, NY, 2005)

Murphy, Edward F., *The Handbook for Spiritual Warfare – Revised and Updated* (Thomas Nelson, Inc., Nashville, TN, 2003)

Prince, Derek, *Blessing or Curse: You Can Choose* – 10th Anniversary Edition (Chosen, a division of Baker Publishing Group, Grand Rapids, MI, 2000)

—*They Shall Expel Demons* (Chosen, a division of Baker Publishing Group, Grand Rapids, MI, 1998)

Vallotton, Kris, *Spirit Wars* (Chosen, a division of Baker Publishing Group, Grand Rapids, MI, 2012)

Recommended Audio Teachings

Kylstra, Chester, *Dethroning Jezebel* (Restoring the Foundations, http://stores.rtfresources.org/audio/)

Kylstra, Chester and Kylstra, Betsy, *Shame-Fear-Control Stronghold* (Restoring the Foundations, http://stores.rtfresources.org/audio/)

Meyer, Danny, *Gospel of Wholeness* (Vineyard Church of Delaware County, OH, http://vineyardcdc.org/#/sermons-resources/gospel-of-wholeness)

Other Recommended Reading

Conner, Bobby, *Heaven's Host: The Assignments of Angels, Both Faithful and Fallen* (Eagles View Ministries, Bullard, TX, 2013)

THE DEVIL IN THE BACK PEW

—*Lineage-Line and Legacy* (Eagles View Ministries, Bullard, TX, 2012)

Johnson, Bill, *Face to Face with God* (Charisma House, A Strang Company, Lake Mary, FL, 2007)

Kasper, Dana Lynne, *Holding My Breath: Letters to the Father I Never Met* (Vineyard International Publishing, Ladysmith, KZN, South Africa, 2014)

Lewis, C.S., *The Screwtape Letters* (HarperCollins Publishers, New York, NY, 1942)

Liardon, Roberts, *God's Generals* (Whitaker House, New Kensington, PA, 1996)

Manning, Brennan, *The Furious Longing of God* (David C. Cook, Colorado Springs, CO, 2009)

Silk, Danny, *Culture of Honor* (Destiny Image Publishers, Inc., Shippensburg, PA, 2009)

Vallotton, Kris and Johnson, Bill, *The Supernatural Ways of Royalty* (Destiny Image Publishers, Inc., Shippensburg, PA, 2006)

Referenced Catholic Texts[107] and Online Catholic Resource

Amorth, Fr Gabriele, *An Exorcist Explains the Demonic* (Sophia Institute Press, Manchester, NH, 2016)

—*An Exorcist Tells His Story* (Ignatius Press, San Francisco, CA, 1999)

Baglio, Matt, *The Rite: The Making of a Modern Exorcist* (Doubleday Religion, an imprint of the Crown Publishing Group, a division of Random House Inc., New York, 2009)

Catholic Doors Ministry, *Rite of Exorcism* (http://www.catholicdoors.com/prayers/english/p01975b.htm)

---

[107]These books, pertaining to exorcism in the Catholic Church, cite many circumstances and experiences which mirror those of this author, as well as those described in other texts listed in this Bibliography. However, as explained in context, much of the methodology and recommendations described in *The Devil in the Back Pew* contradicts the teaching and practices of the Catholic Church, as detailed in these Referenced Catholic Texts.

Made in the USA
Middletown, DE
05 May 2020

93679972R10170